MEETINGHOUSE & CHURCH
IN EARLY NEW ENGLAND

MEETING
IN EARLY

HOUSE & CHURCH
NEW ENGLAND

BY EDMUND W. SINNOTT

JERAULD A. MANTER / PHOTOGRAPHIC COLLABORATOR

BONANZA BOOKS · NEW YORK

This edition publisehd by Bonanza Books,
a division of Crown Publishers, Inc.,
by arrangement with McGraw-Hill Book Company, Inc.
A B C D E F G H

Acknowledgments

For use of the illustrations indicated, the author makes grateful acknowledgment to these individuals and organizations:

E. H. Royce (Figure 77); the Canterbury Shakers (Figure 216); J. Gilbert Harrington (Figure 202); King's Chapel, Boston (Figure 185); Mrs. E. C. Leadbeater (Figure 154); Mary MacDonald (Figure 61); David Merrill (Figures 99, 100, 101, 141); Old Colony Historical Society, Taunton, Mass. (Figure 55); Park Street Church, Boston, and Lenscraft Photos (Figure 132); First Church of Portland, Me., and Christopher Miller (Figure 139); Josephine Pullen (Figure 161); Society for the Preservation of New England Antiquities (Figures 6, 50, 59, 116, 184, 187); C. Bronson Weed (Figure 136); Lawrence F. Willard (Figures 63, 112, 194, 195).

CONTENTS

Introduction

THE history and antiquities of New England are a source of continuing interest and delight to those who travel through the towns and countryside of these six states. Old houses, collections of early furniture and artifacts, burying grounds, battlefields, and historic sites of many other kinds attract their thousands of visitors each year.

Among these treasuries of the past stands the New England meetinghouse. Its history is the history of a community. As one gathers the records, stories, and traditions about the men who raised these buildings of oak and pine, the people who worshiped in them, and the events that took place within their walls, he learns much that is not in formal histories. Especially does one come to realize that the meetinghouse was the focus of New England life, not only ecclesiastically but socially and politically. In these old structures, imagination still can reconstruct more readily than elsewhere the vivid pattern of the Puritan community. Scores of such buildings, fortunately, still are standing, and although most of them are fallen from their former high estate, they are among the most eloquent of all the voices of the past. Within their walls was nourished the Puritan tradition. Today, when this tradition so often is disparaged and when we are searching for the secret of its nature and the sources of its power, where

can we turn with greater hope of success than to the ancient cradle in which it long was nurtured?

The present book, the outcome of an avocation pursued through many years, deals with the architectural and historical evolution of meetinghouse and church from the seventeenth century through about the first third of the nineteenth. Save for a few cases, there are mentioned in it only those buildings that still are standing and that were erected by the year 1830, a date that makes possible the inclusion of the Federal-period structures, together with early examples of the Greek Revival. Representative structures, about 200 in number, are discussed in some detail. The entire body, over 500 in all, are described briefly in the Appendix. This is a wider coverage than has been attempted before in any book on the subject. For the author and his collaborator to visit all of New England, village by village, has been impossible, and there may well be structures, particularly in smaller towns and away from the main highways, that have been overlooked. If any reader knows of such a case, I shall be glad to learn of it.

Many sources were used in gathering information about these buildings. In addition to the records and publications of the sort mentioned in Chapter 7, the following books were useful: J.

Frederick Kelly's *Early Connecticut Meetinghouses,* Columbia University Press, 1947, covers practically all of the old churches of that state. Mr. Kelly personally measured and photographed these buildings and delved deeply into their records, and no other book in the field approaches his in completeness. Eva Speare's *Colonial Meetinghouses of New Hampshire,* privately printed, Littleton, N. H., 1955, discusses, in most cases rather briefly, more than half of the pre-1830 churches in that state and includes the most important ones. Charles A. Wight's *Some Old-Time Meeting Houses of the Connecticut Valley,* privately printed, Chicopee Falls, Mass., 1911; George Francis Marlowe's *Churches of Old New England,* Macmillan, 1947, which describes about forty churches, and Aymar Embury II's *Early American Churches,* Doubleday, Page, 1914, were helpful. "From Meeting House to Church in New England," a series of four articles by Charles A. Place in *Old-Time New England* for 1922 and 1923, are authoritative and excellent. Early volumes of the *Congregational Yearbook* give the dates of erection of all the churches of this denomination. The *Guides* for each of the New England states, published by the Federal Writers' Project in the late 1930s, contain much information on old meetinghouses and churches. The two volumes of *Historical Collections* by John Warner Barber (that for Connecticut published in 1836, that for Massachusetts in 1839) are of special importance for their woodcuts of buildings as these appeared in the early years of the nineteenth century.

In addition to these sources, an extensive correspondence with ministers, church historians, town clerks, officers of local historical societies, and various other informed and interested persons has provided many facts not readily available otherwise. Conversations locally with many friendly people, usually eager to talk about their old meetinghouses, have been informative and delightful experiences. To this host of helpful collaborators the author expresses his sincere gratitude.

Almost every one of the buildings mentioned in the book has been visited either by my friend and photographic collaborator, Jerauld A. Manter, or myself, and many of them by both of us. Most of the photographs are the work of Mr. Manter. A few of the others are from a group of older negatives which, by good fortune, fell into my hands. A small number, duly credited, came from other sources.

It is our hope that this book may have some influence in awakening more interest in the preservation of these structures around which has centered so much of New England history. Many are now empty and some are suffering from neglect and decay. The growing number of examples of careful preservation and intelligent restoration show what can be done to take care of them. Fire and wind will continue to take their toll, but we should see to it that no more historic structures disappear through neglect or are despoiled by thoughtless "modernization." These old Puritan houses of worship are a vital part of our national heritage and, once gone, can never be replaced.

MEETINGHOUSE & CHURCH IN EARLY NEW ENGLAND

One   The Puritan in His Meetinghouse

BETWEEN an April midnight and dawn almost two centuries ago, there galloped up the Boston road to Lexington a rider who drew up his horse at the head of the green where

The meeting-house windows blank and bare
Gazed at him with a spectral stare.

Soon from its belfry the alarm bell sounded, not with the peaceful music of a Sabbath morning but summoning the people of the village to a more urgent and perilous convocation. Candles were lighted in the sconces of the meetinghouse. Across its threshold, one by one, hastily dressed and but half awakened, there came together the minutemen of Captain Parker's little company. The magazine door was thrown open. Each man equipped himself with powder and ball and soon all were fully armed and ready for what the dawn might bring. Shortly after, as the sun was rising, this little band drew up across the common almost in the shadow of the meetinghouse and, by offering there the first armed resistance to the British crown, made themselves immortal.

The story is familiar, but the point should be emphasized that the entire action revolves about the village meetinghouse. This was a structure which served not only for regular assemblies on the Sabbath and at town meetings, but as a gathering place of the inhabitants at all times of peril or emergency. This one building dominated and focused the entire life of the community. Here people met for every purpose and hence it came to be called, in all directness, the "meetinghouse." It was an edifice neither sacred nor purely secular, but appropriate for any honorable service.[1]

[1] The terms "meetinghouse" and "church" are often employed somewhat loosely. Technically, the first is a structure used for both secular and religious purposes, whereas the second is primarily a house for worship. Some old New England church buildings are still sometimes called meetinghouses, and going to church is "going to meeting."

Physically the meetinghouse was conspicuous both by its size and its commanding situation. It provided the only general gathering place, since outdoor assemblies were seldom practicable in the New England climate. It was the political forum where the voters came together to take corporate action on any matter of general importance, and these town meetings were the nucleus of the political life of New England and her chief contribution to democratic institutions. In many communities, especially in the early days, it was fortified as a place of refuge against Indian attack, and in quieter times it served as a storehouse for the common supply of the munitions of war. It was the center of public intelligence, where notices were posted and proclamations read, and in its shadow stood those implements of New England retribution, the whipping post and the stocks.

But in addition to all this, the meetinghouse served a purpose even more vital in the life of New England, for under its roof on every Sabbath there gathered the entire population of the community for the worship of God. Not only once on that day did they assemble, but twice; and in some towns, especially in the earlier years, there was a Thursday Lecture as well. Despite the attempts of some modern historians to belittle the influence of religion in the life of New England and to emphasize the role of secular motives among her people, the fact remains that the church was the dominant organization in these colonies for two centuries and that its affairs occupied a large share of the thought and energy of the people. Their re-

ligion was a vital matter to them. That among the population there was always an element who were little interested in ecclesiastical affairs is undeniable; but the strict control which the church and its ministers exercised over the lives of the people would never have been tolerated by such a stubborn and independent folk unless it had been emphatically supported by the great majority.

The weekly assembly of the whole parish at the meetinghouse, and the long sermons there delivered, were the most important events in the life of the Puritan. The building in which these convocations took place acquired for him a certain degree of sanctity, despite his abhorrence of the very thought of formal ecclesiasticism. The meetinghouse was not a church, nor was any part of it consecrated or set apart from secular uses; and yet on the lips of even the most rigorous Puritan divines it often became the "Sanctuary" or the "House of the Lord."

Artistry and ornamentation as accessories of worship were rigidly eschewed as suggesting too strongly the hated image-worship of the Papists; yet there finally began to appear, especially around the main doorway, the pulpit, and the belfry of the meetinghouse, a loveliness of design arising from the same reverent craftsmanship that had fashioned the splendid churches of earlier faiths.

The New England town meeting of early days was one of the best examples of practical democracy that man has ever contrived. With few exceptions, every citizen was privileged to attend. Everyone might make himself heard; everyone had a vote. The Puritan was no less an equalitarian in his church government, for every church was its own master and could do exactly as it wished. Counsel it would take from other churches in times of perplexity, but never coercion. No system of centralized ecclesiastical control was ever able to establish itself in Puritan New England. Congregationalists, Unitarians, and Baptists, who constituted the great majority of the population until well into the nineteenth century, were all agreed as to the independence of the individual church.

These Yankee Puritans, whose ideal was "a church without a bishop and a state without a king," evidently had a genius for democracy; and this must imply, we are accustomed to think, that the Puritan was a thorough democrat at heart, a man to whom distinction and privilege were abhorrent and who believed in the fundamental equality of every human being. A study of the Puritan in his meetinghouse, however, will convince even the most stubborn idealist that this conclusion is erroneous. All, to be sure—men, women, children, Indians, servants, and slaves—were admitted to the meetinghouse, and in early days were compelled to attend its services; but once inside, distinctions among them were rigidly enforced. In many of the earlier structures, especially the larger ones, there was a small upper gallery, close under the eaves, where it was the obligation of any man with a red skin or a black one to worship the Lord in safe isolation from the white saints below. Racial equality was an ideal to which the early Puritans had not yet attained.

But Indians and Negroes, after all, were not very numerous in the New England population, nor was their segregation anything more than naturally to be expected in the seventeenth and eighteenth centuries. A greater shock than this to our ideas of Puritan democracy comes when we examine the seating plan of a typical meetinghouse and understand what it was that determined the station that a particular individual should occupy therein. Just as some seats were evidently much better than others, so were some people considered superior to their fellows, and it was the essence of the Puritan's social philosophy to give the best men the "foreseats" and to reserve for lesser individuals those that were farther back or less desirable in other ways.

The theory of graded social distinctions was universally accepted, but its application in a given case often raised grave difficulties. Who *were* the "best"? So impossible was this problem of solution by general agreement or vote that it was invariably left in the hands of a committee whose duty it was to "dignify the meeting" by assigning every member of the congregation to his proper place. Sometimes this was done yearly, more commonly at longer intervals, but in the popular mind it was always regarded as involving one of the most momentous of questions, and as placing upon members of the committee a responsibility of the gravest sort.

Sometimes the church instructed the committee as to the basis of the distinctions to be made, but these were commonly understood to include age, wealth, birth, learning, and public service. On the highest eminence stood the minister himself. The parsonage pew, in which his wife and family sat, was always the best one, directly at the foot of the pulpit stairs; and the high elevation of the pulpit in the early meetinghouses was in part a tribute to the exalted station of the ministerial office itself. The stratification of a parish by a seating committee was a procedure remote from that democratic simplicity and equality which the famous phrase in the Declaration of Independence has led most of us to associate with the colonial mind. Politically, the early Puritan was a democrat; personally, he was still a good deal of an aristocrat; and nowhere is the contrast so clearly to be observed as in a comparison between the town meeting and the Sabbath service—both conducted under the meetinghouse roof.

Again, the Puritan is often presented to us as a man of intense religious convictions and an indomitable determination to act upon them, characteristics that sent him forth into the wilderness and caused him to stand like a rock for what he thought was right. This was unquestionably so, but we must remember that the Puritan's determination was by no means confined to moral and religious questions. He was an uncompromising individualist, and his most distinctive trait was a tremendous determination to have his own way. When directed toward proper ends, as it most commonly was, this trait brought out his finest qualities, but terrible indeed might be the consequences of its misdirected power.

Nowhere, perhaps, is this basic stubbornness so well displayed as in certain of the Puritan's relationships to the meetinghouse that he erected. Even before the plan was drawn or a stick of timber cut, the question of where the building was to be placed often brought forth such a storm of disagreement and bitterness that the "meetinghouse devil" seemed indeed to stalk abroad.

We must remember that this question touched more closely the life of every person than any other public matter. All were expected to attend Sabbath worship. At first the villages were compact but after the Indian menace had grown somewhat less, many people lived well outside the center. Roads were very bad and the hardships of this weekly journey often severe. It was thus important to every individual to live as close to the meetinghouse as possible. Since all could not be equally near, there inevitably arose, whenever a new meetinghouse was to be erected, a diversity of opinion about its location, much as there is today over the location of a new highway. The spirit of compromise and willingness to consider the general welfare seemed strangely absent in most such discussions. Everyone wanted his own choice, and though it might be hopeless, held out for it unwaveringly. Even when a majority decided on a site, the minority were sometimes so intractable that no decision could be enforced. Local autonomy broke down, and the town was only too glad to pass the decision to a higher authority, usually the county court or the legislature. One of these bodies would appoint an impartial committee, which visited the town, heard all the protagonists, and drove a stake at the point where, by its decision, the meetinghouse was to be erected. This committee would eventually require a formal report that the house actually *had* been built there.

Violence sometimes accompanied these disagreements, as when the minority at Lebanon, Connecticut, once forcibly prevented the demolition of the old house, and at Mendon, Massachusetts, where they attempted to destroy the frame of the new one. It is probably true that in all New England there were not a dozen meetinghouses built before the nineteenth century, save perhaps some of the very early ones, that did not precipitate a violent disagreement of this sort. So rare were the exceptions that they excited comment. Thus in the town of Stonington, Connecticut, where the location was amicably decided, the unusual event was celebrated by naming the site "Agreement Hill." Often these controversies lasted long after the houses were built, and they were a more frequent cause of schism and the formation of new churches than were theological disagreements. Legacies were sometimes left to a church on condition that it should or should not change the location of its meetinghouse.

Not only in its location, but in the plan of his meetinghouse did the Puritan show his uncompromising spirit. When he broke away from the Church of England, he determined to root out from his own mode of worship every vestige of what he regarded as idolatry and popish practice. No chancel formed a part of the meetinghouse design, and the communion table in early days was a simple drop leaf hinged to the deacons' seat. Even the orientation of the building was affected, consciously or not. The altar and pulpit of an English church were usually at the east end and the main entrance at the west, conforming to ancient Christian practice. The entrance of the meetinghouse, however, was commonly on the east or south and the pulpit opposite. There are few examples of meetinghouses which, in their original position, had the pulpit in the east.

In the conduct of his religious services, the Puritan further showed his determination to do things in his own way. During the early years, at least, the minister would never merely read the scriptures during the service, for this savored too much of formalism. When he read, he expounded, which removed the objection. Instead of kneeling to pray, the Puritan rose to his feet. This was a real hardship, considering the length of the prayers, but it was made somewhat easier by hinging the pew seats so that they might be tipped up, thus allowing the worshiper to lean against the rail. Even this was wearisome, and after a few generations, the Puritan prayed sitting down. To this day his descendants do not kneel.

Today the Puritan is often praised as a radical and an innovator. Such indeed he was in some matters, but he had a decided strain of conservatism in him, too. This showed itself in various ways. He had been daring enough to come across the sea to a new land with his fellow adventurers, but in some respects he was as much a slave of custom and fashion as the most parochial of men. In the design of his meetinghouse, for example, he rarely adopted new ideas, preferring to follow the lead of others. One of the facts that a study of meetinghouse evolution discloses is the remarkable uniformity with which its changing styles were adopted. The most frequent instruction of a society to its building committee when they were about to erect a new meetinghouse was to fashion it after the one in such and such a town. If one town acquired a bell, its neighbors had to do likewise; if one "colored" (painted) its meetinghouse, so did the rest; if one altered its old structure to conform to a new mode, others hastened to avoid the stigma of being old-fashioned. The Puritan was continually changing, remodeling, and modernizing his meetinghouses, not simply because these failed to serve their purposes, but because they were no longer in the mode. In marked contrast to the remodeled meetinghouses are most of the old Episcopal churches in New England, which, perhaps because they were consecrated buildings, have tended to remain closer to their original state.

The Puritan is frequently accused of being without eyes or ears so far as beauty was concerned, and it is true that music, poetry, drama, and the representative arts, save within narrow limits, were for generations almost nonexistent in New England. Much of this lack was due to the suspicion with which Puritanism looked upon any suggestion of image-making and every influence that might seduce the soul of man from the chief concern of its own salvation. Even in their appreciation of the presumably harmless beauties of nature, the Puritans seem to

have been deficient. Not for several generations do we find much indication that the flowers and birds and hills and sea of New England stirred the hearts of its inhabitants to joy or sympathetic awareness.

Yet the Puritan was far from being entirely without appreciation of beauty. One aspect of nature he clearly loved—a broad vista. His towns were often planted on hilltops, though doubtless there were practical as well as aesthetic reasons for such a choice. Whenever it was possible, he set his meetinghouse on a sightly spot, as witness the many "meetinghouse hills" in New England. At first this was for protection, but long after the danger of attack was over, the practice persisted. The worshipers willingly climbed the hill and endured the winter winds that blew more fiercely there; and often when the villagers had moved their homes to more sheltered locations, the meetinghouse stayed where it was. Perhaps a part of the reason was that a meetinghouse set on a hill cannot be hid and that the Puritan was proud of the work of his hands; but one cannot help believing that in large measure it was due to his delight in lifting up his eyes unto the hills— to his innate, though usually inarticulate, appreciation of this aspect of natural beauty.

But the meetinghouse offers us more definite evidence than this that the Puritan was not without his aesthetic side. Architecture and cabinet-making, among the few means of artistic expression upon which Calvinism did not frown, seem from the beginning to have had a particularly strong appeal for the New Englander. He was a natural craftsman in wood. Even in early years the dwelling houses and furniture that came from his hands bore the authentic marks of artistry. His first meetinghouses were very plain, but soon the Puritan builder could not resist the temptation to adorn the belfry, the porch, and especially the pulpit, with a gracefully turned column or a bit of pleasing ornament. As wealth and education increased and the rigors of the Puritan religion relaxed, the beautification of the meetinghouse became more and more the delight of builders, until during the first quarter of the nineteenth century there were erected some of the loveliest and most satisfying structures that have ever been seen in America. The men who could design the spire of the Farmington Church in Connecticut, or the pulpits in Rocky Hill and Cohasset, Massachusetts, certainly cannot be said to have lacked either the love of beauty or the ability to create it.

Finally, the meetinghouse demonstrates a trait of the Puritan character in its earlier years for which there is ample evidence from many other sources—his unwillingness to bind himself by the chains of the flesh. In the few examples of unaltered meetinghouse interiors that have come down to us from the eighteenth century many of the seats are simple benches, and in the earliest examples they were all thus. Even in the later pews, the seats were so narrow as hardly to afford a sufficient resting place for a person of normal size; and the vertical backs provided no comfort. No wonder that when the deeper, cushioned pews of the nineteenth century came into fashion, a generation which had been reared on these

wooden shelves decried the softness of modern days.

Nor were the eyes pampered. Whatever else it lacked, the Puritan meetinghouse was well-provided with windows. Here was no "dim religious light." The windows were on all sides, the pulpit wall equally with the rest, and there was an extra one immediately behind the pulpit itself. The glare, particularly during the afternoon service when the sun often shone almost into the faces of the congregation, must have been hard to endure. Before many years a heavy curtain was draped over the pulpit window, and the windows of the pulpit wall were often shuttered or closed up. They continued, nevertheless, as a feature of meetinghouse design until well into the nineteenth century.

The ability of the Puritans to withstand the winter cold of their meetinghouses has long been a matter of amazement among their descendants. Foot stoves were tolerated for the women, but the most that a man could do for his numbed extremities was to beat them together as quietly as he could. Water froze in the baptismal basin. The communion bread often froze on the plate. Ministers wore heavy coats and gloves. No wonder the shivering congregation could regard with some equanimity that dismal place where, in the words of the Reverend Mr. Wigglesworth's famous poem of 1662, *The Day of Doom,*

God's fierce ire kindleth the fire,
And vengeance feeds the flame
With piles of wood and brimstone
flood,
That none can quench the same.

Only as the fires of hell died down

with the coming of a more liberal theology in the nineteenth century did it seem necessary to heat the meetinghouse, and even then this was accomplished only over the opposition of the hardy oldsters who had been brought up on frigid Sabbaths. In half a dozen churches the story is told of how, on the first Sabbath after the stoves had been put in, some of the old-timers said they could not stand the heat, and walked out, not knowing that the fires had not yet been lighted.

Beyond all his other interests, however, the great concern of the Puritan was the salvation of his soul. To this end he regarded public worship and the "ordinances of the Gospel" as of prime importance. He listened eagerly and indefatigably to Biblical exposition and to exhortation from the pulpit. In Groton, Massachusetts, for example, a group in the congregation requested from the church society "that a sermon or other religious treatise be read by some suitable person during the noon hour on the Sabbath." Not only did these folk listen to a long sermon in the meetinghouse every Lord's Day morning, then listen to another in the afternoon; but they wished to devote their brief period of noontime relaxation and refreshment to the same purpose, so that no precious hour should be wasted that might be employed toward the salvation of their souls.

They were indeed remarkable men, these Yankee Puritans, as complex and contradictory as their own theology. They have puzzled the historians and slipped out of the molds in which biographers attempted to confine them. To their descendants they are amazing, often incomprehensible. Compelled to the harsh physical labor of the pioneer on a reluctant soil, they delighted in the things of the mind and kept brightly lighted the lamp of learning in their colleges. Intelligent above most men of their time, they could descend to depths of credulity and acts of superstitious infatuation that are entirely inconsistent with the brighter side of their character. Intolerant and bigoted to the degree that a dissenter from their beliefs in but minor matters of doctrine was often exiled or even put in peril of his life, they yet bore the seed that was to unfold into the most liberal religious thought of any age. So stubbornly individualistic that they brooked neither bishop nor king but maintained the town and the church as social units almost entirely free from outside control, they were yet willing on occasion to lay aside their differences and could then unite so effectively for common action through their representative assemblies that they were able to maintain a vigorous and independent state. Haters of mere external beauty, suspicious of every appeal to the senses, frowning at first on music, poetry and the arts, they yet displayed such a warmth of aesthetic feeling in those few channels where this could be expressed, notably in the construction of their furniture, their houses and their meetinghouses, that even the common artisan among them often plied his craft with the genuine touch of an artist.

Propounder and defender of a creed, logic-tight in theory, of predestination, foreordination, and an inescapable saving or damning of his soul, no one in practice has ever insisted more emphatically than the New England Puritan on the complete responsibility of every individual. Scorner of dishonesty but famous for sharp trading; grasping and acquisitive yet the first to give freely to a worthy cause; inhumanly cruel to the savages yet often laboring with patience to bring them to the light; making fortunes from rum yet the first to advocate temperance; slave trader and missionary; smuggler and saint; often lustful, drunken, avaricious, and bloodstained, but oftener self-denying, peaceable, and full of good works; human in his weakness, almost superhuman in his strength, the Yankee Puritan in his first two centuries was a man whose like has rarely moved between earth and heaven. Even today his influence lingers in the New England countryside, subtly investing with the flavor of his personality the houses where he dwelt, the village streets on which he walked, the stone walls that his hands put up, and, more than these, the houses where he worshiped. Although a creed was preached in them that most men have outgrown, and although many meetinghouses are abandoned and have no further active part in the communities they served so long, these structures that he raised on the hills and beside the highways of New England are lasting monuments to the character of the Puritan.

As did the Puritan himself, the meetinghouse changed with the years. His houses of worship faithfully mirrored the alterations in his social and religious life. As he became more and more the child of modern times, the meetinghouse changed accordingly, until in the urbane and intellectual atmosphere of New England in the early nineteenth century, it expressed the best of Puritan culture. The meetinghouse has always illuminated the character of the men who worshiped in it, and a study of its architectural evolution provides us with a vivid insight into the changes that took place in the Puritan himself.

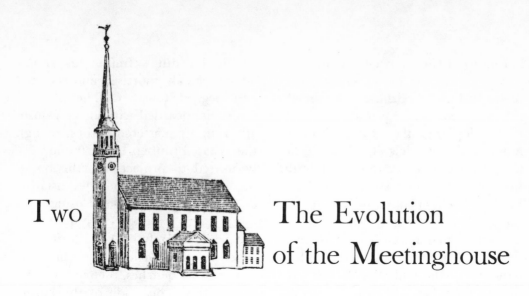

Two   The Evolution
of the Meetinghouse

ALTHOUGH we sometimes condemn the Puritan as a conservative who defended not only the faith of his fathers but their every custom, it must be admitted that he progressed amazingly in New England. The cultured Boston liberal of the nineteenth century had little in common with the witch-hanging bigot of the seventeenth save for a certain fundamental Puritanism, yet but a few generations separated the two. There seems to have been something germinative in the Puritan's character that urged him forward. The history of New England is the record of a persistent idea undergoing persistent improvements in expression.

This is well shown in the changes undergone by the design of the meetinghouse. In the progress from the primitive structures in which the first settlers assembled to the churches erected by their Victorian descendants, four rather sharply marked architectural periods can be distinguished. These mirror changes in New England life during its first two centuries. Sometimes they proclaimed the imminence of religious or political changes before these occurred, as when, about 1800, the meetinghouse design changed in a very few years to that of a typical church, anticipating the separation of church and state in New England by one or two decades.

During the early weeks or months of a new settlement the minister often preached to his congregation under the open sky, as the abundance of "pulpit rocks" and "bethels" in the New England countryside still attests. Soon, however, a temporary structure would be erected for more seemly worship. Of these makeshift meetinghouses we have almost no contemporary descriptions or illustrations. Sometimes, as in Plymouth, they were primarily stockaded forts, situated on an elevation from which the forest had been cleared to prevent a surprise Indian attack. These first meetinghouses cannot be said to have had a definite architectural style.

In a short time, however, craftsmen began to ply the broadax, saw, and plane and to erect those oak-framed, pine-finished dwellings that were soon to develop into the typical colonial homesteads of New England. The houses for public assembly were built in much the same style. The New England meetinghouse, unique in the dual purpose which it was to serve, showed at first no close resemblance to any communal or ecclesiastical structure of the Old World. The earliest framed and boarded meetinghouses seem to have varied considerably in plan and dimensions. Before the middle of the seventeenth century, however, a design evolved that was adopted almost universally and is distinctive of most of those built in the latter half of the seventeenth century and the early years of the eighteenth. It was of simple construction. Square or nearly square, it had entrances on three sides. The building rose high enough to accommodate a gallery on the sides where the entrances were found. Two rows of windows illuminated it, one for the ground floor and one for the gallery, all provided with small diamond-shaped panes set in lead. The roof sloped up steeply from each of the four sides to a central turret or cupola. In this, if the parish was fortunate enough to own one, the bell was hung. On the side of the house opposite the main or central door and connected therewith by a wide aisle or "broad alley" rose the high pulpit from which the minister could see his auditors in the gallery. Directly behind this was the pulpit window, intermediate in level between the two rows of windows and often differing from them in size and shape.

The building's frame was almost always of oak, mortised and tenoned and pegged together. The planked walls, clapboarded without, were usually roughly plastered within, though the uncased timbers of the frame were permitted to project into the building. A ceiling was sometimes installed at the level of the eaves, closing off a loft or attic, though this space was often left entirely open, at least for a time. In the earliest days the seats were simply benches, the men occupying those on one side of the house, the women those on the other. Later, the benches were given backs. Still later, square enclosures or "box" pews were installed. These were often limited to the space next to the walls, leaving the center of the main floor and all of the gallery occupied by benches. Though little in the way of ornament was present in this first type of meetinghouse, the general design, if we may judge from the only surviving example, was attractive in its symmetry and proportions.

Who first designed a meetinghouse of this sort we do not know, but by the middle of the seventeenth century it had appeared in Boston and the surrounding Bay towns. Soon afterward it was to be found in almost every part of New England. Of all these structures, unfortunately, there has come down to us only one, the stately "Old Ship" at Hingham, Massachusetts (Fig. 1), erected in 1681. Such was the typical meetinghouse of early Puritan New England, of those

1 "Old Ship," 1681,
Hingham, Massachusetts

years that saw the enthusiastic establishment of the new theocratic experiment, the pushing of frontiers up and down the coast and well inland, the grim extermination of the Pequots, the ravages of King Philip's War, the tyranny of Governor Andros, and the witchcraft delusion—the years of New England's first and stormiest century.

Early in the eighteenth century the tide of the first years of New England life had begun to ebb. The fathers were no more, and their sons and grandsons, reared in the rudeness of the new frontier, had lost much of the learning and culture of their sires. Economic distress was common and an almost constant dread of Indian incursions hovered over the land.

Worst of all, the faith of the early years had begun to falter. Formality was replacing enthusiasm. Drunkenness, licentiousness, and other breaches of the strict Puritan code were common. Many ministers were losing the spiritual leadership of their people. Even their own ranks, so solid before, were now broken by apostasy: in 1722 Timothy Cutler, rector of Yale College, and Samuel Johnson, minister of West Haven, in Connecticut, asked to be relieved of their charges, deserted the Puritan church, and went to England to take holy orders.

The times, many felt, were propitious for a revival of religion, a rebirth of the faith of the fathers. In Northampton, Massachusetts, in 1732, Jonathan Edwards began a series of sermons that gripped New England as no preaching had ever done before. Year by year the excitement mounted, stimulated by the arrival from England in 1740 of that incomparable

religious enthusiast, George Whitefield, and soon the whole region was in the midst of the ferment of new hopes and emotions and ideas that we know as the Great Awakening. The hysteria and excesses that sometimes characterized it were decried by many clergymen. The story is told that one of them, meeting Whitefield on the street in Boston, said to him: "Mr. Whitefield, I am sorry to see you here." Replied the doughty evangelist, "So is the devil."

The Great Awakening nevertheless served as a stimulus to independence of thought and action and to the rekindling of faith and courage. Thus fortified, New England boldly took her place at the head of the revolt against King George, and was able to sustain herself through the difficult years of the Revolution.

The Great Awakening was the climax of less conspicuous changes that had been taking place for some time in the religious life of New England. The so-called Saybrook Platform, for example, adopted by the churches of Connecticut in 1708, was the result of a desire for greater unity among the churches in their fight against their growing loss of spiritual power. Among the young people there were signs of revolt against the sterile formalism of the church services, especially the old-fashioned way of singing in which a deacon "lined out" a psalm and the congregation sang after him, line by line—certainly an uninspiring procedure. In the second decade of the eighteenth century this revolt burst into a violent contention between those who favored the "old way" and the advocates of a more melodious method of singing, by note and rule. The young people in time had their way, and from this movement came not only better church music but the New England "singing school."

There seemed to be no single event or particular time at which this growing restlessness in religious matters became particularly conspicuous, but it is perhaps significant that just at the end of the first decade of the century there came, rather suddenly, a radical change in the architecture of the meetinghouse. Whether there was any relation between this fact and the growing desire for reform in religious life itself is not clear; but the historian of New England might well give closer attention to what was happening about the year 1710 for evidence of the first stirrings of those changes, more than twenty years later, that brought about the Great Awakening.

Meetinghouses of the new type first appeared in Connecticut, Massachusetts, and New Hampshire early in the second decade of the century. These structures departed from the earlier design in being oblong rather than square. In place of a four-sided roof, the new house had a steep pitched roof ascending on two sides to a ridgepole. The cupola or bell turret no longer surmounted the building itself but was carried on a square tower that rose at one end of it. In most of the early meetinghouses of this type, however, the bell tower was not added until later. The main door was in the middle of one of the long sides and faced the road. Often it was entered through a porch. There was also a door in each of the narrow ends. These buildings at first had little external ornament, and those without a tower were almost barnlike in their simplicity.

The interior was not very different, save in its proportions, from that of the older plan. The pulpit, always the central point in the Puritan service, was not at one of the ends, as in a church, but opposite the front entrance, in the middle of the other long side, and thus as close as possible to the congregation. A gallery was built on three sides but not on the one where the pulpit stood. The pulpit itself was high so that the minister could see the people in the gallery and be seen by them. Over it invariably hung a sounding board. Below and in front of the pulpit was the deacons' seat, to which was usually attached a drop-leaf communion table. Most of the ornament of the interior was centered in the pulpit and its surroundings.

This second type of meetinghouse was characteristic of all parts of eighteenth-century New England. Many examples of it survive, although the interiors of most of them have been completely altered, often more than once. Externally, many of them look much as they did when they were built. The most notable example, equaled by none in beauty of design and richness of historical association, is the brick meetinghouse of the Old South Church in Boston (Fig. 2), built in 1729.

As to why this radical change in construction was adopted we cannot be sure, but it was probably related to the need for a larger building. The early square type could not readily

be increased to a size of much more than 50 by 50 feet, without involving difficulties in the roof framing, and the larger meetinghouses of the first type had already departed considerably from the square ground plan. Thus the "Old Brick" of Boston, the last of the earlier type, measured 72 by 54 feet, and the "Old Cedar" (the first meetinghouse of the Old South Church) was 75 by 51 feet. Regardless of their lengthening sides, both buildings had four-sided roofs and central turrets. The new building of the Old South, however, measured 95 by 68 feet, a gain of almost 70 per cent in floor area over its predecessor, and this could be achieved most simply by abandoning the four-sided hip roof for the pitched roof. This, of course, involved placing the belfry on a tower added at the end. In many meetinghouses of the new type the belfry was an entirely separate structure.

Another factor in the change, perhaps, may have been the more pleasing design of the new type and the greater possibilities for architectural embellishment offered by the tower and steeple. Certainly the designers often took advantage of this opportunity, for the steeples of some of these eighteenth century meetinghouses are among the finest examples of colonial architecture that we possess. In its interior ornamentation, also, the new house appears to have been aesthetically more attractive. It was usually ceiled from the first and the beams

were often cased. The almost medieval character of the earlier design was abandoned, and in its place appeared some of the characteristics of the English Renaissance under the influence of Sir Christopher Wren. Typical of the new style, as we see it developed throughout New England, is the greater emphasis upon more elaborate ornamentation, especially in the steeple, pulpit, and entrance porch.

The need for larger and more attractive buildings was especially important after the Great Awakening had attracted many new members into the churches, and widened the mental horizon of the population. It is therefore not suprising that the new type of meetinghouse should have been widely adopted; but the universality with which this occurred is remarkable. The rapid spread of the new design throughout New England testifies not only to the Puritan sensitiveness to changes in fashion, but to the close intercommunication that must have existed between widely separated places even in the days when travel was slow and difficult.

Such were the meetinghouses that echoed to the eloquence of Edwards and Whitefield. They saw the gathering of colonial soldiery before the siege of Louisburg, and their bells acclaimed the conquest of Canada. Within their walls were hotly discussed the momentous issues of the days before the Revolution, and from their pulpits more than anywhere else the stubborn resistance of New England to the British crown was nourished and maintained.

After the war came turbulent days of reaction and disillusionment. Yale

2 Old South Church, 1729,
Boston, Massachusetts

College, founded as a bulwark of orthodoxy, became a hotbed of infidelity. Harvard was moving away from Calvinism toward the more liberal Unitarian faith. Atheism and irreligion, stimulated by the French Revolution, were openly avowed by many. In addition, economic chaos threatened New England. The states were flooded with worthless paper money. Shays's Rebellion, a protest against the hardships of poor and heavily taxed farmers, shook the government of Massachusetts. For a time it seemed doubtful whether any of the New England states would ratify the proposed Federal Constitution. During this period many of the meetinghouses were almost abandoned by those who once had thronged to their doors. Thus the period of the second type of meetinghouse, like that of the first, coincided with a cycle of New England life, beginning with a rebirth of faith and ending with its decay.

Better times were in sight after the national government was organized. Prosperity began to revive in New England. Her shipping and trade flourished, agriculture throve, debts were paid. The New England spirit again felt itself renewed, but in a form more generous and tolerant than before. Massachusetts Puritanism, at least in Boston and the towns around the Bay, began to shake off Calvinistic theology and to develop the liberal attitude that in many churches was soon to lead to Unitarianism. Connecticut, always more conservative, moved toward no drastic break with tradition, but under the vigorous leadership of Lyman Beecher and of Timothy Dwight the life of her churches was

greatly stimulated. Everywhere religious toleration was more general, and although, in most of New England, Congregationalism was still the established order, and its meetinghouses were built and its ministers paid by taxation, other forms of worship came to be legally recognized.

There was still to be many a battle between the old order and the new, but the day of separation between church and state was not far distant. Literature and the arts, as well, gave promise of better days, not only because the beginnings of wealth and leisure had appeared, but because of a more lively appreciation of beauty by a people who were freeing themselves more and more from the prejudices of their fathers. All was in readiness for that remarkable period in New England history, lasting through the first third of the nineteenth century, in which her people, inspired by the promise of a new era but as yet undisturbed by the social and economic changes it was to bring, carried their life to such an abundant fulfillment that it may well be called her Golden Age.

This change might be expected to reflect itself in the meetinghouse, and it does so to a remarkable degree. Just as changes in its appearance marked the beginning of a new era in the years before the Great Awakening, so an even more profound alteration in character distinguishes the new meetinghouses erected by the men who stood at the opening of an even more auspicious century.

New England was still predominantly rural and agricultural, with her population distributed in more than three hundred towns that showed no very wide diversity in area or population. The town was still the unit of New England life as it had been for nearly two centuries. The meetinghouse continued to be the center of activity, serving both for worship and for secular assembly. It was still built and owned by the town, and its minister was supported by taxes levied upon the citizens. But a change in its character was beginning to be felt. In many places the building of the "prime society" was no longer the only house of worship. First Episcopalians, then Baptists, and later other dissenters were allowed to build their own churches and were generally exempted from the taxation that supported the established Congregational order. The larger towns, too, were often divided into two or more parishes, each with its own Congregational church organization.

The day was passing when one church could serve the whole population and when its affairs were decided in a general meeting of the entire town. Instead, each was an independent unit as far as its own ecclesiastical government was concerned, and matters pertaining to the houses of worship were settled by the vote of the parish or ecclesiastical society concerned. The town meetings and all the secular gatherings of the community were still held in the meetinghouse—or in one of them—but there was an increasing divergence between its two functions. The existence of numerous houses of worship which possessed no secular obligations, the growing feeling that these two concerns were not truly compatible, and

the active renewal of interest in religion that marked the last years of the eighteenth century, all combined to emphasize the religious function of the Puritan meetinghouse and to minimize its secular role.

How was this change reflected in the meetinghouse itself? The somewhat bare and barnlike structure of the Revolutionary period, with its main entrance on the side, entirely unrelated to the steeple, no longer seemed appropriate to the spirit of the times, and the new meetinghouse— our example is the Congregational Church at Avon, Connecticut (Fig. 3) —frankly adopted the design that had long been recognized as characteristic of strictly religious edifices. In general shape and dimensions the building was unchanged save for a gentler slope to the roof. The only entrances, however, were now at one of the narrow ends, and the pulpit was moved to the other. Over the entrance rose the steeple, no longer merely a projecting tower and belfry but a more elaborate structure which in most cases was set back, at least in part, over the main body of the house. Its design was more ornate than that of many of the older type, and the façade and entrance bay below it, often adorned with pilasters or columns, took on at once an elaboration exceeding anything before attempted. Within, there was a gallery on three sides, as in the older style, with the high pulpit and the pulpit window on the fourth. The woodwork, particularly of columns, doors, windows, and pulpit, was richly carved.

These lovely buildings, erected by the score in the villages of New England, came in time to be the most

typical expression of her sense of architectural beauty and religious dedication. They are still one of her chief glories. Not for the pleasure of muddy-booted, wrangling townsmen did the builders of these white temples design them, nor for the prosaic transaction of mundane affairs. A few stooped to this for a time, but it was a higher purpose which they chiefly served. The Puritan meetinghouse had become a church.

There seems to have been no one particular day or year when the New Englander consciously determined to build himself a church; but his slowly altering religious feeling came to a rather sudden architectural expression that coincided with the beginning of the new century. No meetinghouses of the older type were built after 1800, and hardly any of the new type previous to that year. Just before and after the close of the century, however, there were a few transitional forms, with a tower and entrance at one narrow end and the pulpit at the other.

The new type of meetinghouse did not find its expression in any single notable example that served as a general model. Its design was merely an adaptation of the style of the English Renaissance to local conditions, and although none of the New England meetinghouses were directly copied from Sir Christopher Wren's London churches—much less designed by him —his indirect influence, through various books written by his English and American disciples, was evidently great. Notable among these were the

3 Congregational Church, 1818, Avon, Connecticut

Book of Architecture, by James Gibbs, an English architect, and the *Country Builder's Assistant,* by Asher Benjamin, a carpenter-architect of Greenfield, Massachusetts. Benjamin's book found its way into the hands of builders all over New England, and powerfully influenced the design not only of meetinghouses but of other buildings, as well.

A few of the most notable of these churches in the larger towns were the work of professional architects who were acquainted with the masterpieces of the English Renaissance. It is significant, however, that for the rest, especially those in the smaller places, there is no evidence that any architect ever had a hand in their construction. They seem to have been designed by local craftsmen with the aid of a few books and drawings; and the fact that under these conditions their builders achieved such excellence of proportion and beauty of ornament, with so few examples of awkwardness or excess, is a tribute to the esthetic sense of men whose names today have often been forgotten.

There is no general agreement as to the name by which this climactic period in New England architecture should be known. Various writers have called it Late Georgian, Post-Colonial, Renaissance, and Federal. In this book the term Federal has been used. It should be remembered that the Church of England, particularly in the interiors of its edifices, was influenced by the English Renaissance much earlier than was the Puritan meetinghouse and the church that followed it. Domestic architecture in New England also adopted the new ideas earlier than did the ecclesiastical structures of the Yankee tradition. The Puritan meetinghouse held aloof for a long time from the rich ornament that came from Wren and his followers; but when this was finally adopted, New England builders showed that they could make as good use of it as anyone.

The War of 1812 dealt a serious blow to New England shipping, and in the ensuing years enterprising Yankees began to turn their attention more to manufacturing than to commerce. By the end of the third decade of the century, scores of little factory villages had sprung up along the rivers. Agriculture had begun to be reduced in importance, and emigration to the west was vigorously under way. These changes were marked by still another alteration in the architecture of New England's churches. The Greek Revival, as it was called, brought to America after the Revolution, and sweeping up from the Southern States, entered New England a little before 1830. For approximately the next twenty years most of the new churches endeavored to transform themselves into steepled temples, in the manner of the Unitarian Church in Quincy, Massachusetts (Fig. 4). Columns, especially slender ones of the Ionic order, had not been uncommon in the preceding period, but the temple-church of the Greek Revival showed an entire Doric façade, or at least a portico supported by Doric columns. The pitch of the roof was lower than before. The doors were heavy. The steeple was an attempt to treat in Greek fashion a structure that was foreign to the Greek style. Al-

though some Greek Revival churches were attractive, many were rather severe since they no longer showed the lightness of design and wealth of ornament that made the Federal buildings so charming.

In the late 1840s, temple-churches went out of fashion and there appeared in their stead the neo-Gothic buildings, often adorned with masterpieces of the jig-sawyer's art, that were the delight of our great-grandmothers. In this period, too, most of the churches of earlier years were "modernized" with a thoroughness that left them an unhappy mixture of two, or even three, architectural styles. After the middle of the century, no distinct tendency in New England ecclesiastical architecture can be traced. The Puritan himself was beginning to share his old home with men of other races, tongues, and faiths, who were soon to outnumber him in the land of his fathers. In such a diverse population the intimate relation between the house of worship and the men who worshiped in it is no longer apparent, and for a picture of the modern Puritan we must seek elsewhere than among the heterogeneous collection of churches with which he has supplanted the meetinghouses of his ancestors.

4 Unitarian Church, 1828, Quincy, Massachusetts

Three The Pioneer
Meetinghouse

THE few seventeenth-century buildings still standing in New England have the rather medieval character that once distinguished English architecture. They show little influence of the revival of classical ornament and design that in England had already begun to be felt. The older style went out of fashion there during the rebuilding of London after the great fire of 1666, when Sir Christopher Wren and his followers introduced classical forms from Italian models and ushered in the English Renaissance. In remote New England, this architectural revival made itself felt more slowly, and it was not until the eighteenth century that it had more than a minor influence.

The New England meetinghouse of early colonial days was therefore the work of craftsmen disciplined in the older mode but as yet uninstructed in classical art. Let us not conclude, however, that the meetinghouses they built bore any resemblance to Gothic churches. Such a likeness, indeed, was

an eventuality which the builders seemed most careful to avoid. There was nothing to suggest a religious atmosphere here; nothing but the simplest and most practical means of providing a shelter for gatherings that might be either secular or religious.

The general character of the mid-seventeenth-century meetinghouse was described in the preceding chapter. Many of these houses are known to us by nothing more than the date of their erection; of others, the dimensions alone have been recorded; of still others a few early descriptions reveal something of the character of the building; of only a very few do we possess reasonably reliable pictorial records contemporaneous with the building itself.

We know, for example, that the earliest meetinghouse in New Haven was "fifty foote square" and had a hip roof. Of the house that followed this in 1668 we fortunately have a picture, crude but presumably accurate, on the map of New Haven drawn in 1748 by

29

James Wadsworth. The building faced east in the center of the midmost of the nine squares that formed the original New Haven quadrangle, occupying approximately the site of the present Center Church. The map shows an elevation of a hip-roofed structure surmounted by a belfry. It had two rows of windows, implying the presence of a gallery, and also two dormer windows on the side. There were three front doors, an unusual feature.

As to the character of the first meetinghouse in Boston, little information has come down to us. When the Third Society (later known as the "Old South") was organized in 1669, however, we know that it built a substantial meetinghouse of cedar, surmounted by a belfry and with a large porch at each of its three doors, on the west, south, and east. The pulpit was on the north wall, and a gallery ran around the other three sides. This "Old Cedar" meetinghouse, almost as

5 *"Old Tunnel," 1682, Lynn, Massachusetts*

important historically as its famous successor, sheltered its congregation for more than sixty years. It was this house into which Governor Andros, unable to obtain lawful permission for its use, forced an entrance on Good Friday of 1687. Here on the next Sabbath—crowning indignity!—he caused the communion service of the Church of England to be celebrated for himself and his retinue while an exasperated congregation was kept waiting impatiently in the street outside.

Every Sunday for the next two years the owners of this meetinghouse were forced to share it with those whose forms of worship they detested. In this old house in 1697 Judge Samuel Sewall stood with bowed head and listened to the reading of his public confession of sin in having sent innocent people to their deaths for witchcraft, five years before. In a dwelling almost in the shadow of this meetinghouse, on a cold January Sabbath in 1706, there was born to a tallow chandler a sixth son. Before the morning service had ended, the sturdy young Puritan, bathed and swaddled, was carried into the house of God and borne to the foot of the pulpit stairs where the waiting minister, dipping his fingers into the icy water of the basin, baptized him Benjamin Franklin.

Other meetinghouses of the later years of the seventeenth century emerge but dimly from the records. In the village that was later to be Quincy, Massachusetts, the first meetinghouse, small and square, was built of granite about 1640. Malden had a hip-roofed meetinghouse, 33 feet square, in 1658. The second meeting-house of Northampton (1661) was 40 feet square; the first in Hadley, 45 by 36 feet; the second in Wethersfield, Connecticut (1685), 50 feet square, with dormer windows. In the eastern towns of Massachusetts there were similar meetinghouses, as in Dorchester (1677), Ipswich (1653), Concord (1667), Cambridge (1652), Sudbury (1688), Dedham (1673), Newbury (1700), Salem Village (1701), and Topsfield (1703).

Occasionally we have something more reliable than our imagination with which to reconstruct the appearance of these ancient buildings. The second meetinghouse of the church in Lynn, Massachusetts, erected in 1682, survived without major change until 1827, and an early picture of it (Fig. 5) has come down to us. Its steeply pitched hip roof, small-paned windows, and high, sharp gable have a medieval look. The peak of the cupola gave the name of "Old Tunnel" (i.e., funnel) to the house itself. The hitching rails near the door and the absence of the carriage sheds so characteristic of the meetinghouses of later years, are eloquent of the seventeenth-century roads over which the Puritan came to meeting on foot or on horseback, but rarely on wheels.

One of these old square meetinghouses was erected in West Springfield, Massachusetts, in 1702 by John Allys of Hatfield (Fig. 6). It was an awkward-looking structure, 42 feet square on the ground and 92 feet from sill to weathercock. There were three dormers.

Of the few surviving descriptions of the interiors of these early meeting-

6 *Meetinghouse, 1702,*
West Springfield, Massachusetts

houses, one of the best was written by the Reverend J. S. Popkins about the house in Newbury, Massachusetts, which was completed in 1700. "The body," he says, "was filled with long seats. Contiguous to the wall were twenty pews. The spaces for the pews were granted to particular persons who appear to have been principals. Before the pulpit and deacons' seat was a large pew containing a table where sat the chiefs of the fathers. The young people sat in the upper gallery, and the children on a seat in the alley fixed to the outside of the pews. The floor measured 60 feet by 50 feet. The roof was constructed with four gable ends or projections, one on each side, each containing a large window which gave light to the upper galleries. The turret was on the center. The space within was open to the roof, where was visible plenty of timber with great needles and little needles pointing downwards which served at once for strength and ornament. There were many ornaments of antique sculpture and wainscot. It was a stately building in the day of it." This house was evidently one of the finest of its type and more richly ornamented than most. The great and little "needles" must have been marvelous to see, and strongly suggest a Gothic character in the loft.

Few of the old square meetinghouses lasted into the nineteenth century, and, as we have seen, only a single survivor stands today, the Old Ship of Hingham, Massachusetts (p. 16). Built in 1681 of oak from the primeval forest, it has escaped conflagration, withstood decay, and avoided the more insidious hazard of intentional demolition, for at least once the town voted to tear it down. The source of its nickname is not known, but may be conjectured. The timbers in the loft, much admired, somewhat resemble a ship's frame and were probably put together by local ships' carpenters; and in the ceiling, under the cupola, is painted a compass.

Early in 1680 the first meetinghouse, built in 1645, had become outgrown, and the town "agreed to build a new meetinghouse with all convenient speed." As was usual in such an undertaking it appointed a committee of three men to "view" the meetinghouses of other towns and present recommendations as to the size and design of the proposed edifice. The

town then fixed its dimensions and adopted a plan. After the usual wrangling over location, in which the governor himself was finally forced to make the decision, the frame was raised in July, 1680. Aside from the material of the old house, the new house cost the town £430, a sum obtained by a special "rate" or tax on the inhabitants, levied according to their wealth. This tax list, which has been preserved, shows assessments ranging from the £15 12s. 6d. against Daniel Cushing to but five shillings against Joseph Jones, and nothing at all for John Beale, Senior, an ancient father in Israel.

The house as at first built was 55 feet long by 45 feet wide, with a height of 21 feet to the eaves, and it was covered by the typical four-sided steep hip roof surmounted by a cupola and probably provided with three dormers. The longer dimension was roughly east and west, and the main entrance occupied the center of the south side with the pulpit on the north wall. There were doubtless two other entrances, at the east and west ends, and the walls were provided with two tiers of small diamond-paned windows. Within, all was plainness and simplicity. On the floor stretched rows of oaken benches, and the gallery, similarly provided, occupied all sides but the north. No plaster was used in this original house, and the walls were clapboarded within as well as without. The brown tones of oak and pine and chestnut must have given the interior, severe though it was, a feeling of warmth. The entire framework was visible to the upturned eye—the great beams and the carved struts and braces, smoothly chamfered and firmly pinned together, rising into the high, unceiled loft.

On January 8, 1681, the people of Hingham first assembled here for the worship of God, and we can well imagine how on that day hearts were stirred not only by the noble work of their hands, so successfully brought to completion, but by a more intense personal concern as to the station therein allotted to each of them. The plan as drawn up by the seating committee has come down to us. Three hundred and thirty-five men and women, young men and "maydes," the entire population of Hingham, were there arranged in the order of their age, wealth, and dignity, the men on the west side of the house and the women on the east, and the young men and maids in the corresponding "gallaries." The seating was typical of the time. Below the pulpit and in front of it, at the end of the broad alley, were two seats. One, "the seate under ye pulpit," was for the "elders," not such in an ecclesiastical sense, but merely those old men who from their special dignity or hardness of hearing merited such a favored situation. Five of them were listed. Immediately in front of these and in the place of honor, facing the congregation, sat the deacons, John Leavitt and John Smith, and with them in this exalted station also sat one Matthew Hawke whose function it seems to have been to transcribe the weekly sermons that issued from the pulpit above his head. This arrangement of an elders' seat and a deacons' seat in front of the pulpit, often raised somewhat above the floor level and facing the main door, was not uncommon in New England meetinghouses for the next 100 years. More frequently there was just a single seat here, for the deacons only. A curved, shelflike table, hinged to the deacons' seat so that it could be dropped down out of the way when not in use, served as a communion table in these early churches.

On the main floor of the Hingham meetinghouse there were two rows of seven benches on each side of the alley, nine or ten persons being assigned to each bench, and nine shorter seats on the north side of the house, doubtless at right angles to the others. At the head of the women's benches, apparently adjacent to the pulpit, was the single pew, which was assigned to Mrs. Peter Hobart, widow of Hingham's first pastor, and to Mrs. John Norton, wife of the second.

Both on the floor and in the gallery the front benches or "foreseats" were especially esteemed, and it is therefore interesting to observe that wealth was not the only basis for their assignment. Thus, in the floor foreseat we find, to be sure, the heaviest tax payer, Daniel Cushing, and the next heaviest, William Hearsey, and two other men of means, Nathaniel Baker and Thomas Lincoln, "husbandman"; but here, too, sat Captain Joshua Hobart, Edmund Hobart, Thomas Hobart, and Doctor John Cutler, all of whom stood relatively low on the tax roll and were doubtless honored for other reasons, the last perhaps because of his profession.

Thus in the chill of that January Sabbath did the people of Hingham assemble themselves under this very roof,

Mistress first and goodwife after,
Clerkly squire before the clown,
From the brave coat, lace-embroidered,
To the gray frock, shading down.

After the confusion of the first seating had been quieted, the people turned to see their young minister as he gravely passed along the broad alley and ascended the stairs to the pulpit. The sermon that John Norton preached that day has long since been forgotten, but within the walls of the meetinghouse which then echoed for the first time to the name of Jehovah, men have never ceased to come together for His worship. This building has now been consecrated by the prayer and praise of more than fourteen thousand Sabbaths.

For nearly half a century the Old Ship served the needs of church and town, but as the population increased, it became too crowded. In 1730 the north or pulpit wall was pushed out 14 feet. The next year it was voted that the house be "sealed" overhead and a new belfry erected, and in 1734 the inside was plastered for the first time. More room still was needed in 1755 and the south wall was pushed out 14 feet, thus making the floor 73 by 55 feet, the long dimension now north and south instead of east and west. The extensions of 1731 and 1755 involved the building of a new roof on the north and south sides, necessarily at a somewhat gentler pitch than the original one; but the work was done without destroying the frame, and the meetinghouse thus assumed the external appearance it has today. Since the house was now oblong, the pulpit, newly built, was placed on the west wall, and a double pulpit window opened behind it. The main entrance now being at the east, the broad alley ran east and west.

For some years permission had been sought to "pew" a part of the house. This now being granted, two rows of square pews were built on all four sides. These were sold at public auction. The erection of these pews, with their smoothly paneled sides and gracefully turned spindles supporting the pew rail, must have added much to the appearance of the interior. The central body of the house kept its benches for those who could not afford the newer and more luxurious accommodations.

In 1791, critical days for the meetinghouse were at hand. It had now stood for over a century, and was both somewhat out of repair and—a more serious defect—out of fashion. By vote of the parish it was decided to alter the roof to the now universal pitch type. Subsequently it was decided to rebuild the old roof entirely. Then, a few months later occurs this ominous entry in the parish records: "Voted to take down the meeting house and build a new one similar to a plan exhibited in the meeting, which is on file, sixty in favor of it and twenty-eight against it." The twenty-eight must have been tenacious of their opinion and persuasive among their brethren, for a year later the parish voted "not to build a new one on any principles," but to "repair the meeting house in its present form."

The nineteenth century brought new ways of doing things. In 1818 it was voted that the Parish Committee make "such alterations in the Elderly seat as will make it convenient for the Moderator and other officers in publick meetings," indicating that the seat in front of the pulpit was the usual rostrum at town meetings. Although the town meetings had been held in this house from the beginning, the parish finally voted in 1827 that no more should be permitted, and the meetinghouse thus became in fact a church.

In 1822 stoves were placed in the building. After this there were no notable changes or additions until 1869, when the floor was found to be so badly out of repair that it had to be rebuilt. The pews were removed at this time. A few were kept as curiosities but the rest were not put back again. Instead, modern curved pews of oak were installed, conforming to the canons of Victorian taste, thus largely destroying the ancient character of the interior.

The latest chapter in the history of the Old Ship is a happier one, for its people were able to celebrate the two hundred and fiftieth anniversary of its erection by installing copies of the original square pews, by removing minor modernizations of the pulpit and gallery, and by taking out the ceiling which had covered the auditorium for almost two hundred years. Today the loft with the beauty of its original framework—king post, braces, beams, and famous "Hingham trusses"—is once more visible from below as in the day when the meetinghouse was new. The roof extensions of 1731 and 1755 are concealed from view, so that the upper portion of the building is thus essentially as it was in 1681, and the lower as it became after the altera-tions of 1755, a happy solution since it restores the best of each period.

Among all the meetinghouses still standing in New England the Old Ship is unique. Antedating by almost half a century its more famous neighbor, the Old South of Boston, it carries us back more vividly into the life of seventeenth-century New England than does any other meetinghouse. Seated in it were some of the men and women who had come over in the first settlement. The last of the Pilgrim fathers survived the Old Ship's completion and some of them may have worshiped under its roof. Those who raised its frame had just lived through the horrors of King Philip's War. Charles the Second was on the throne, and the tyranny of Andros not far away. More than ten years had still to pass before witches were executed in Salem. About the walls of the old house still cling the memories of those austerities, tribulations, and triumphs which made the first century of New England life a time both of light and darkness, of hope and despair. To every sympathetic student of our history and antiquities the wooden meet-inghouse in Hingham is indeed a shrine, and his feeling will be one of gratitude when he reads upon the parish seal the words that so well express the spirit of the house and its people, "Let the work of our Fathers stand."

For more than thirty years after the Old Ship was built, meetinghouses of the same type continued to be erected in New England. One of the last, a house of particular interest because of its size and design, survived until well into the nineteenth century. This was

7 "Old Brick," Boston, Massachusetts, 1712

the third, or Old Brick meetinghouse, of the First Church of Boston (Fig. 7). About the two earlier houses of this society almost nothing is known. The second was destroyed in the fire of 1711, and its congregation, the oldest and one of the largest and wealthiest in the town, at once began to rebuild. Perhaps with their recent experience in mind they decided to use brick instead of wood. This seems to have been the only case in which brick was used in a meetinghouse of the early type.

In other ways this building differed markedly from the typical design. For one thing, it was much bigger than most, being 72 feet by 54 and the larg-

est meetinghouse in New England at that time. The hip roof covering this oblong structure was markedly less steep than usual and it rose to an oblong platform, in the center of which was placed a graceful octagonal belfry with arched openings, surmounted by a spired lantern—altogether a more elaborate structure than customary. Three small dormers projected from the roof. The house itself was 34 feet in height, and was provided with three tiers of windows, indicating two galleries, one above the other. At its front door on the east side rose an elaborate two-storied porch the face of which was ornamented with pilasters and carved work. If this ornamentation was contemporary with the building, it constituted the earliest appearance of the classical treatment in a meetinghouse doorway.

The structure certainly had lost the medieval look of the earlier houses, and seems to be much more in the mode of those that were to follow it. The picture shows no door on the north end, although the plan of the interior indicates an entrance there as well as at the south end. Possibly these were later closed, for it is known that substantial alterations were made in the structure. Of the inside of the building we know little. The floor plan was of the ordinary type with the pulpit in the middle of the long (west) side, and the floor occupied with square pews. The pulpit, according to the boyhood recollection of an old man seventy years after the destruction of the building, was unusually large and elaborate, and was ascended by spiral stairways on each side. The cost of the new meetinghouse was £3,800, a large sum for those days, bespeaking a building of substantial construction and appointments, as befitted the society that built it.

The Old Brick marks the end of an era, for it seems to have been the last important meetinghouse built on the early plan. For almost one hundred years the Old Brick and the Old South, built not many years later, stood within sight of each other on opposite sides of Boston's main thoroughfare, one embodying the tradition of a century that had passed, and the other establishing a new tradition for the century that was to come.

Four Renaissance and Revolution

WHATEVER the underlying cause for the change in meetinghouse design from the early, square type to the oblong one, it took place with surprising suddenness. The Old Brick of Boston, apparently the last to be built on the old plan, was erected in 1711. In 1712, meetinghouses of the new type were put up at Guilford, Connecticut, Concord, Massachusetts, and Portsmouth and Newington, New Hampshire. The change was probably not quite as abrupt as these dates would indicate, for there may have been a few of the square structures built after 1711 and of the oblong type before 1712; but we can be sure that by early in the second decade of the century the new style had become well established.

The Guilford meetinghouse, 68 by 45 feet, with its long axis east and west, had two galleries, one above the other, and thus three rows of windows, and must have been a spacious building indeed. The main entrance was in the middle of the broad south side and there were others at the two ends. Against the north wall stood the pulpit. In 1726 a tower was added at the west end, surmounted by a belfry and a spire that rose 120 feet above the ground. A bell and a clock were installed, making this meetinghouse the first in the colony to have steeple, bell, and clock. It survived until 1830. During its existence more than 800 people first publicly professed their faith within its walls, and 1,600 children were baptised there.

Built on a similar plan, the second meetinghouse of Concord, Massachusetts, was of greater historical importance. It was also a "three decker." The outside, as shown in Doolittle's "View of the Town of Concord," published in 1775, was plain, and the building lacked a tower. There was a small porch over the main entrance on the broad east side. The meetinghouse at this time looked very much like the one at Lexington built two

8 Meetinghouse, Lexington, Massachusetts

years later (Fig. 8). The appearance of the interior is not known but it doubtless conformed to the usual fashion.

In the Concord meetinghouse, after General Gage had occupied Boston, the Provincial Congress of Massachusetts met, in October, 1774, and again in 1775, from March 22 until four days before the Battle of Lexington. Its windows looked upon the destruction of American stores by the British in their raid of April 19, and from it could be heard the sound of musketry at Concord bridge.

The house was given a tower at the north end in 1791, surmounted by an octagonal belfry and spire. In the same year the porch on the east side was enlarged to two stories, and a somewhat smaller one was built over the south door. A model of the meetinghouse as it appeared at this time is in the collection of the Concord Anti-

quarian Society. In 1841 during the height of the Greek Revival, the building was remodeled in the prevailing mode, its exterior and interior being completely changed. It burned in 1900. The present edifice, rebuilt on the same spot, is almost a replica of its remodeled form.

About the Old North meetinghouse at Portsmouth, New Hampshire, we know less. A likeness of it as it appeared before being remodeled in 1835 (Fig. 9) shows that it was a "three-decker" much like the one in Guilford. The tower, apparently at the east end, like those of the Guilford and Concord houses, was probably a later addition. The main door, in the middle of the broad south side, was entered through a two-storied porch. There were two tiers of galleries. The fact that all three of these early pitched-roof meetinghouses were thus

*9 Meetinghouse, Portsmouth,
New Hampshire*

provided with two galleries is further evidence that the demand for greater size was an important factor in causing the change to the new design.

The fourth of these earliest meetinghouses of the new type, at Newington, New Hampshire (Fig. 10) not far from Portsmouth, is still standing. It is the oldest building of the Congregational denomination in the United States. Still owned by the town, it has been in continuous use from the year of its erection. A smaller structure than the three just described, it is now much altered from its original state. On either side, at present, is a single row of long windows, and the belfry is set over the roof at its east end; under it is the present front door. The pulpit is at the west end. The records seem to indicate that originally there was a square tower at the west end, that the main entrance

was in the middle of the south side, that the pulpit was opposite, on the north wall, and that there were two rows of windows and a gallery on three sides. When built, the house was therefore of the new type, like those just mentioned.

In the early days of the Newington house, an English gentleman of the parish, John Downing, Jr., had a square pew near the east end and built himself a door from the outside directly into it. He requested in his will that he be buried under the meetinghouse, and there he lies today. On the green in front stands a large horse block made of a naturally cleaved boulder of gneiss, which was hauled from the woods by thirteen yoke of oxen soon after the house was built. The first minister at Newington, the Reverend Joseph Adams, was an uncle of President John Adams, and a vigorous patriot. It is said that some

*10 Congregational Church, 1712,
Newington, New Hampshire*

42

of the powder captured from the British in the raid on Fort William and Mary in December, 1774, was stored by Parson Adams under the pulpit of his meetinghouse.

Almost as old as the Newington meetinghouse, and originally of the same design, is the one built in 1717, and still standing, at West Barnstable, Massachusetts, on Cape Cod (Fig. 11). The church organization to which this belongs can claim to be the oldest one of the Congregational order in America. It was "gathered" in 1616 in Southwark, just across the Thames from London, from whence its members came over to Scituate, Massachusetts, in 1634. Five years later they moved to the "Great Marshes" on Cape Cod and founded the town of Barnstable, which soon divided into east and west parishes. The minister chose to go with the western one, and thus to the West Barnstable church went the records and the old communion silver. The meetinghouse this church built some seventy-five years

later is the one that stands today. It has been much altered. Originally, the building was a barnlike structure of the new type. The framing in the loft must once have been exposed, for the beams are chamfered at their corners, as though for public view.

In 1723, already too small, the house was sawn in two, the pieces drawn 18 feet apart, and a new section inserted. At this time the ceiling was added, a tower and steeple were built at the east end, and a weathercock—the Puritan symbol of repentance—placed above it. In 1834 the change from meetinghouse to church design was brought about in the usual way, and the main entrance put through the tower. The building was in such a bad state of repair by 1852 that there was talk of tearing it down. Instead, the society proceeded to "modernize" it. Both the exterior and the interior then became those of a typical church of the middle of the nineteenth century and quite undistinguished in appearance.

But the story ends happily. Beginning in 1955, the meetinghouse underwent a restoration, the purpose of which was to make it look, as nearly as possible, the way it did in 1723. The tower was rebuilt, a porch and main door were added on the south side, the ceiling was removed so that the beams could again be seen, and the old square pews and windows were replaced or rebuilt. Some of the old paneling, windows, and pew spindles were still in possession of families in the town, and these were either used or copied. Outside and inside, the building presents an excellent picture of an early eighteenth-century meetinghouse. It looks rather fresh in certain respects—for example, one might wish that a darker stain had been used inside to imitate old pine—but lovers of the past will be grateful for the vision, persistence, and skill of those who accomplished the restoration.

The church does not consider itself merely an antique. A spokesman puts it this way: "The West Parish Meetinghouse is not a museum. It is a memorial to the devotion of the fathers who built it, a testimony to the faithfulness of those who maintained it through the centuries, and a witness to the life of the active Church that worships in it today."

The "Old North Vestry" in Nantucket, another early example of the new type, was built, according to tradition, in 1711, although there is no documentary evidence for this date. Although the first settlers on the island were mostly Quakers (Friends), there were Congregationalists here early and this first meetinghouse of theirs is certainly very old. It began, apparently, as a quite typical eighteenth-century structure. In 1765 it was moved about a mile east to its present site. In 1795 a tower was added and in it hung the island's first bell. The house continued as the religious and social center of the parish until the erection of the present church in 1834. Connected with the new church, the old meetinghouse served as its vestry. The tower has disappeared and the interior is much changed from its original state, though it has been partly restored. It is now used for church services in the winter months.

The meetinghouses of the new type thus far described were all in comparatively small towns. Although their appearance within a few years in widely separated places indicates a general tendency to abandon the earlier design, the new one doubtless became more firmly entrenched in popular favor by reason of its embodiment in a notable meetinghouse in Boston itself. This was the second house of the Old South Society, technically the Third Church of Boston, a building so satisfying in its design and withal so intimately connected with the history of the colony, and of all New England, that it soon became well known everywhere (see p. 19). It is the most famous of all meetinghouses. Through the kindness of fate and the valiant efforts of those to whom it was dear, the Old South has been preserved to our day.

After about 1720, the Old Cedar meetinghouse, the first one of this parish, had become too small. The question as to whether to enlarge it or to build a new house was earnestly discussed at many a meeting. Finally, in April, 1728, a building committee was appointed with the Honorable Jonathan Belcher (the following year to be appointed Governor of the province) at its head. Tradition says that the man who supervised the work was Joshua Blanchard, a master builder of Boston. The choice of the pitched-roof type in place of the old square plan was doubtless made by the committee; but we may speculate on the possibility that the wife of Edward Winslow, one of its members, may have influenced the decision. She was a daughter of the Reverend Joshua Moodey of Portsmouth, New Hampshire, and must therefore have been familiar with the new-type meetinghouse erected there in 1712.

This Old South meetinghouse, built in 1729, was of brick, 94 feet long and 67 feet wide, exclusive of the tower. Probably it is the largest meetinghouse ever built in New England. Its long axis runs approximately east and west. The original main entrance (now closed) was in the middle of the south side, where there was a porch, and other entrances were at the east and west ends. The windows, in two rows, are exceptional in that they are round-topped and that those of the upper row are somewhat longer than those of the lower. At the west end rises the tower, steeple, and spire, ascending to a weather vane 180 feet above the street. The tower itself is about half this height, extending well above the peak of the roof. Unlike most such towers, it contains the bell. It is surmounted by an octagonal cupola with eight columns and arched openings (they were often square in later steeples), prolonged upward into an octagonal stage and spire.

The general plan of such a belfry was by no means new in 1729. The New Brick, of 1721, and the Old Brick, of 1712, each had an octagonal columned belfry surmounted by a second stage (the lantern) and a spire, although the spire element was rather short in the Old Brick. The bell turret in the old square meetinghouses was also often supported on columns, as in the Old Ship, where there are six, and in the Old Tunnel at Lynn,

where there were apparently nine or ten. The origin of the various elements in the steeple of the Old South may thus be traced readily enough, but their combination here stamps the unknown designer as a man with a sure sense of balance and harmony. The steeple fits the building perfectly. The tower is as severe and unadorned as the rest of the meetinghouse, and all variety of design and beauty of ornament are saved until the eyes have traveled far aloft, almost as though the Puritan builder were tempting us to look upward from the barrenness of earth to the beauty of heaven.

It has often been suggested that Christ Church, Boston, which was built in 1723, may have influenced the design of the Old South. The well-known aversion of the Puritan of that day, however, to anything related to the Church of England, would seem to indicate that the building committee adopted their design in spite of rather than because of its resemblance to a church of the older faith.

The interior of the Old South was almost completely destroyed by British troops during the siege of Boston. There are no reliable contemporary records of its original appearance, but we know that most of the floor was covered with square pews. There are now two tiers of galleries on the east, south, and west sides, and these may have been present from the first, a conclusion suggested by the greater length of the upper row of windows. The restoration after the siege of Boston, and other restorations in the nineteenth century, rendered the interior much more ornate than at the beginning, when it was doubtless relatively bare. The square pews are now gone and most of the floor has been transformed into a museum, so that its appearance as an eighteenth-century meetinghouse is left largely to the imagination.

Not only the beauty of the Old South but its place in our national history have made it for more than two centuries one of the country's most familiar and admired public buildings. The history of Boston during the critical years of the eighteenth century, and much of that of Revolutionary New England itself, could well have been written by a chronicler who never stepped outside the doors of the Old South. It had the largest auditorium in Boston, and often when Faneuil Hall was too small for a town meeting, it was held here.

The townsfolk were accustomed to gather at the Old South, too, for mass meetings in times of crisis. It was here in October, 1746, when the arrival of a hostile French fleet and army was hourly expected, and the militia were hastening in from the surrounding towns for the defense of Boston, that the minister, the Reverend Thomas Prince, besought the Almighty, before a crowded congregation, to avert the dreaded calamity. While he prayed, "A sudden gust of wind arose (the day had till now been perfectly clear and calm), so violent as to cause a clattering of the windows. The Reverend pastor paused in his prayer and looking around upon the congregation with a countenance full of hope, he again commenced, and with great devotional ardor, supplicated the Almighty to cause *that wind* to frustrate the object of our enemies

and save the country from conquest and papacy. A tempest ensued in which the greater part of the French fleet was wrecked on the coast of Nova Scotia."[1] Infidelity was struck a hard blow that day!

Here, too, within these old brick walls, occurred many of the events leading up to the Revolution. In 1770, on the day after the Boston Massacre, a public meeting, swelled by the people from the surrounding country who had been pouring into Boston all day, adjourned to the Old South from Faneuil Hall. A committee was appointed, consisting of Samuel Adams and others, to demand of the lieutenant governor that the troops be removed immediately from the town. All day the contest of wills was waged between the meetinghouse and the Province House; but the Old South was at last victorious, and before another day had gone, all the royal troops were removed to the "Castle" in the harbor.

On the day after the arrival of the first of the "tea ships" from England, another mass meeting voted that the tea should go back in the same vessels in which it had arrived. A little later, on December 16, 1773, after all lawful means to prevent the landing of the tea had been frustrated, a gathering of 7,000 persons, the largest ever seen in Boston, assembled in and around the Old South to await the governor's next move. When word of his refusal to send back the ships finally arrived, it was unanimously

[1] From *History of the Old South Church,* H. A. Hill, 1890, in which the story is attributed to a former minister of the church, Dr. B. B. Wisner.

46

voted that the tea should not be landed. "This meeting," then said Samuel Adams, "can do nothing more to save the country." But, quite informally, it could. A war whoop resounded from the meetinghouse tower, and a band of men disguised as Indians dashed by the door and down the road to Griffin's wharf, where they emptied every chest of tea from three ships into the waters of the Bay.

And here in the Old South, only a month before the battle of Lexington, Joseph Warren delivered to a huge congregation a commemorative address on the fifth anniversary of the Boston Massacre. About forty British officers were present, some in the front seats, some in the aisles, a few seated on the steps of the pulpit itself, which

was draped in black. The air was electric. Warren, fearing possible interference, climbed in through the pulpit window. This meeting, the last of the Revolutionary gatherings in the Old South, ended without violence but in a sense of impending crisis. A few weeks later the congregation had been dispersed, and the British began to take their vengeance on a building which had so long been at the heart of the patriot cause. They tore out and burned all the furniture, save for Deacon Hubbard's beautiful carved pew, which was taken away for a pigpen. They set up a bar in the gallery for the accommodation of the officers and their friends. They spread gravel on the floor, and upon this the dragoons of Burgoyne's light horse practiced their feats of equestrian skill.

After the Revolution the renovated meetinghouse had a more peaceful existence. Town meetings were still frequently held within its walls, and for many years the annual Election Sermon was preached here before the governor and legislature of Massachusetts. The church was used for worship until 1872. In the great fire that swept Boston in that year, only the most strenuous efforts saved the old meetinghouse. Its congregation now moved to a new church elsewhere. The destruction of the old one was seriously threatened, but through the efforts of many citizens it was purchased for the public as an historic shrine.

During the seventy years that followed the building of the Old South

13 Pulpit, Unitarian Church, Cohasset, Massachusetts

in 1729, meetinghouses of this type were erected all over New England. As the old square structures gradually disappeared, almost every town possessed a house of this newer design, until it became one of the most conspicuous and characteristic features of the New England landscape in the eighteenth century. Fire and decay have taken their toll and there are only about a hundred and fifty standing today. The majority of these have been greatly altered over the years. In a few cases, changes, especially of exteriors, have been relatively slight.

One such meetinghouse stands on the green in the center of the village of Cohasset, Masschusetts (Fig. 12), retaining its original appearance better than any other example in this state that is still in regular use. This is the church of the First Parish (Unitarian), built in 1747. It measures 58 by 48 feet, and the main entrance (now the only one) is in the middle of the long southwest side. Over the door rises a simple two-storied porch, built in 1768, the upper part of which was used as the minister's chamber. The tower, at the northerly end, was not added until 1799. The lateness of the addition is suggested by the character of the octagonal columned belfry surmounting it, since its openings are square-topped as in later examples elsewhere, instead of arched as in earlier ones. There is no door between the tower and the body of the church, an unusual condition. The original square pews in the auditorium have been replaced by ones of modern de-

47

sign; but the pulpit on the long northeasterly side, opposite the door, is original (Fig. 13). Behind it are two pulpit windows, now curtained, and above is a sounding board, all designed with a delicacy and a richness of ornament found nowhere else in the house.

The pulpit, sounding board, and double window closely resemble those of the Old Ship at nearby Hingham. The latter were constructed in 1755, suggesting that the Cohasset meetinghouse served as a model for the changes made in the one at Hingham in that year. The beams of the Cohasset frame project into the auditorium and are cased. Braces run out obliquely from the timbers of the long sides and end at the ceiling, recalling the similar appearance of the Old Ship before its ceiling was removed. In the Cohas-

14 Congregational Church, 1761,
Wethersfield, Connecticut

set house the loft and its framing may originally have been exposed.

Near the center of the village of Wethersfield, Connecticut, a few miles south of Hartford, stands a meetinghouse of 1761 (Fig. 14), externally much as it was before the Revolution. Aside from the Old South of Boston, it is the only brick meetinghouse of the eighteenth century that has survived, and one of the very few ever erected. When it was built it was said to be the finest in New England outside of Boston. The pitch of the roof is steep, as was commonly the case in the older houses. The long axis of the building runs east and west, with the main entrance still, as at first, on the long, south side. Regrettably, the interior was thoroughly modernized in the nineteenth century; but a part of the beautifully carved old pulpit, now

incorporated into the stair landing of the east porch, shows how richly ornamented the interior originally must have been. The changes are reflected externally in the alteration of the windows which, on the sides, were so lengthened that the two rows almost meet.

The chief architectural interest of the Wethersfield meetinghouse today is in its tower and spire, which seem to have survived just as they were built. They are almost a replica of those of Trinity Church at Newport, Rhode Island. How a Puritan congregation was persuaded to copy almost every detail of its meetinghouse steeple from an Episcopal church would doubtless make an interesting story, if we could learn it. The design of the Newport tower, in turn, was probably based on that of Christ Church, Boston. It is unlike anything we know on a Puritan meetinghouse of the time.

In the town of Farmington, Connecticut, stands a meetinghouse of this type, built in 1771, that has a spire regarded by many as the most beautiful in New England (Fig. 15). The house is of interest for other reasons. Its builder's name is known to us—Captain Judah Woodruff. He was one of the best builders of his time, though not a professional architect. At the centennial of the Farmington church, President Porter of Yale said of Woodruff: "He was a man of taste and ob-

15 Congregational Church, 1771,
Farmington, Connecticut

servation, and introduced a style of building which added to the respectability of the dwellings of this village. His carving on the front of the pulpit, representing vines of the English ivy, was greatly admired." The long axis is parallel to the street, and the main door, an exception to the general rule, is on the west side. The two rows of windows have been restored to their original complement of forty panes. Captain Woodruff's beautifully carved pulpit was taken out years ago, but one much like it has recently been installed. The porch over the main door, in the Greek style, is a later addition.

As usual in such a meetinghouse, the steeple is the most attractive feature. The tower is surmounted by an octagonal, columned belfry, and above this is another octagonal member from which rises the spire. There is nothing unique in this general design but the manner in which it is handled at Farmington is exquisite in its lightness and proportion. The delicate columns, the arched openings between, the carved wooden urns surmounting the corners above, the rich treatment of the woodwork, the upward sweep of line from cornice to vane, and the spire, flaring gracefully at its base like Gabriel's trump, together produce an effect unsurpassed by any other steeple. There are few things more delightful in New England architecture than this delicate structure soaring from the angularity of a Yankee meetinghouse.

Less fortunate than the meetinghouses of Cohasset, Wethersfield, and Farmington, in that they are no longer used for their original purpose, are two other houses of the period that externally, at least, are unaltered and remain notable examples of their type.

One, in Brooklyn, Connecticut (Fig. 16), was erected in 1771. It is a large house with its long axis east and west, its main door south, and its tower at the east end. Crowning the tower is an octagonal, columned belfry with arched openings and roof curved into a dome. The domed belfry was an early method of treatment, for we find it in the Old Ship and Old Brick meetinghouses. Indeed, the Brooklyn steeple is so like that of the Old Brick of Boston (p. 36) as to suggest that it

16 Old Meetinghouse, 1771, Brooklyn, Connecticut

was a direct copy. The original steeple blew off in the hurricane of 1938. The restoration is not an exact replica, and is less attractive in its proportions than the original. The interior of the house has been greatly changed.

Israel Putnam, who became a general in the Revolution, was at one time sexton of the Brooklyn meetinghouse. Across the road stood his tavern, and in a field adjoining it he heard the news of Lexington and Concord. The Brooklyn church went over to Unitarianism in 1819, the only one in Connecticut to do so. Religious services in this meetinghouse have been discontinued for many years. Happily, a program is now under way to restore the interior of the old house to its original condition.

At Jaffrey, New Hampshire, just over the Massachusetts line, is another of these externally unchanged meetinghouses (Fig. 17). The frame was being raised on June 17, 1775, the day of the Battle of Bunker Hill, and tradition has it that the sound of the distant cannonading was heard by the workmen. The long axis is east and west, with the main door in the middle of the south side. Originally there probably were porches at each end—at least the town so voted—but at some later time the porch at the north end was replaced by the present tower and steeple. The latter is unlike anything of eighteenth century construction and was apparently copied from that of the meetinghouse at Fitzwilliam, New Hampshire, about seven miles away, built in 1817. We thus have here a typical eighteenth-century meetinghouse surmounted by a nineteenth-century steeple. Services were

17 *Old Meetinghouse, 1775, Jaffrey, New Hampshire*

51

discontinued in 1844, and the interior was much altered in 1870. Externally the structure was restored to its original condition in 1922, and it is now adapted for use as a community house.

The six meetinghouses that have just been described—the Old South and those of Cohasset, Wethersfield, Farmington, Brooklyn, and Jaffrey, give us a good picture of the pitched-roof, square-towered meetinghouse as it looked from the outside, but their interiors are less helpful. Fortunately, a number of smaller, simpler houses survive that have retained their original character within as well as without. Most of these have not been in use for a hundred years or so, but have had friends to keep them in repair. Such buildings now serve as veritable museum pieces of the eighteenth century, telling us more about the meet-

18 Rocky Hill Meetinghouse, 1785, Amesbury, Massachusetts

inghouses and religious practices of that day than all the woodcuts and written descriptions we possess. Many of them, as it happens, stand in southeastern New Hampshire between the lower waters of the Merrimack and the Piscataqua, and on the nearby coast of Maine, a region that takes pride in preserving the atmosphere of the New England countryside as it was a century and a half ago.

On the north side of the Merrimack, just west of Newburyport, is the Rocky Hill meetinghouse (Fig. 18) of the former west parish of Salisbury (now in Amesbury), Massachusetts, built in 1785. The parish was separated from the older part of the town in 1716, when its first meetinghouse was built, and after this structure had stood for almost seventy years and had become seriously out of repair, the parish voted to erect a new one at Rocky Hill, nearer the river. The work was done by Timothy Palmer, one of the master builders of his day, who is said to have designed the magnificent meetinghouse of the First Re-

ligious Society in Newburyport. The Rocky Hill house, which is extremely simple, so closely resembles the one at Sandown, New Hampshire, as to suggest that Palmer also built the latter. It is a simple pitched-roof building of medium size with its long axis east and west, its front door in the middle of the long south side, and other entrances at the ends. It stands on a ledge of rock. The house has never possessed a tower or belfry. A two-storied porch for the stairs to the gallery is built over the front entrance. The cornices are simply but pleasingly ornamented, as are the lintels of the windows and doors. In front still stands a horse block, and the old parsonage is nearby.

On the outside nothing seems to distinguish this building, but as one turns the great key and throws open the door, he steps from the twentieth century into the eighteenth. Nothing has been changed. A visitor could well believe that the Puritan congregation had just departed. The first impression is of brightness. The light from

19 Pews, Rocky Hill Meetinghouse

more than two score windows, reflecting from white walls and ceiling, fills the ample room with radiance.

The floor, save for two benches in the front, is covered with square, unpainted pews (Fig. 19), with sides of paneled pine to which the sunlight of two centuries has given a deep, mellow, brown luster. Rich to the eye, like velvet to the touch; how much more loveliness there is in old wood like this than in any painted surface!

Opposite the central door at the end of the broad alley rises the lofty pulpit (Fig. 20), carved and paneled, with a pentagonal sounding board above. Behind it is the pulpit window, framed between fluted pilasters and covered with the folds of a heavy red curtain. Though the house itself is plain, on the pulpit was lavished all the richness of ornament that the builder knew how to achieve. The

contrast is significant. The pulpit, the focal point of the meetinghouse, the seat of authority, is the nearest approach to an altar that the image-hating Puritan allowed himself. In front of the pulpit and facing the congregation is the deacons' seat. The drop-leaf communion table can be lifted up and braced as it was in the days when the Lord's Supper was served upon it. In the center of the house, on either side of the alley, are two rows of plain benches. If these were for old people, age must have been something to dread, for the seats are but 12 inches wide and the backs rise vertically.

A gallery encircles the house on three sides. Next the wall in the gallery is a single row of square pews, the space toward the rail being filled with plain wooden benches. The benches for the choir were in the gallery oppo-

site the pulpit. The stairs to the gallery where, on either side, the "young men and maydes" had their seats, ascend through the porch and are well-worn, the knots in the treads smooth and protruding.

The timbers of the building's frame, unpainted and uncased, project into the room, but the turned pillars which uphold the gallery are painted a marbled gray-white. The pulpit and the face of the gallery are light gray. Aside from these surfaces, all the woodwork is unpainted, except that on the door of each of the fifty-five square pews is an oval spot of white on which the number of the pew appears. The one at the foot of the pulpit stairs, as was traditional, was for the "Parsonage," and in a humble corner stands one for the "Almshouse women."

The hardware throughout the building is noteworthy, the doors of the house being hung on heavy "L" hinges, and the pew doors on small "butterflies." In the pews the seats are hinged so that their occupants, standing through the long prayers, might be supported in their meditations by the sturdy wall of the pew. At the end of the prayer such seats were often dropped with a rattle as the congregation sank gratefully into them once more. The pillars of the Rocky Hill house often held up more than the galleries, for wherever they were accessible to a leaning worshiper, the paint at the level of a man's shoulder is worn away. The pew seats and backs —not to mention the benches—were

55

so ill-adapted to the human form that one marvels at the fortitude of the men and women—to say nothing of the children—who could occupy them without restlessness through the long periods of a Calvinistic sermon. But that despite this discomfort people listened critically is suggested by a device we find attached to the side of many pews in this meetinghouse—a simple arm rest, which tradition says was to aid the head of the household in taking notes on the minister's discourse.

The eye of imagination brings the whole Sabbath scene to life again: the elevated, dignified minister, the solemn deacons, the somnolent elderly folk, the population of the parish seated by families, the attentive adults, the restless children, the young men and maidens in opposite galleries.

The people are gone but their meetinghouse stands just as they left it. There is something moving about a structure like this, long outliving the community to which it was familiar and surviving lonesomely into a new age in the life of which it has no part.

How, we may ask, is it possible for such a structure to have escaped the altering hand of time? In this case it was a combination of circumstances. The parish began to decline soon after the new meetinghouse was built. Some members had been alienated by its location; others, still unsettled by the controversies engendered in the Great Awakening, left the old society to organize new ones. Soon the society found it difficult to support a settled minister, but it did so, with interruptions, and religious services were continued until the latter part of the nineteenth century. At no time were there the resources, or apparently the desire, to modernize the building. As the life of the church quietly flickered out, the meetinghouse was left undisturbed, a place of memory and pilgrimage. It is now the property of the Society for the Preservation of New England Antiquities.

There are a number of meetinghouses in this region that resemble the one at Rocky Hill in having no longer any active function. In most of them there is a memorial service in the summer. Notable among these is the one already mentioned, at Sandown, New Hampshire (Fig. 24), built in 1773–1774. Though a porch is lacking, this structure much resembles the Rocky Hill house, both outside and in (Fig. 25). The ornamental woodwork of the cornice and around the doors (Fig. 21) is more elaborate than in any other meetinghouse of this type, and bears the mark of skill in design and craftsmanship. In the gallery is the pew that was reserved for slaves (Fig. 23). The loft shows the typical heavy framing (Fig. 22). Religious services in this meetinghouse were discontinued in 1834 but town meetings still were held in it until 1929. The structure by then had suffered a good deal from neglect and vandalism, but in that year it was restored. It is now in the care of the Old Meetinghouse Association. Across the road is a stone-walled pound (for stray animals), often a neighbor of the meetinghouse.

A few miles away, at North Danville, New Hampshire, is another meetinghouse, somewhat older (1760) and much plainer than the one at Sandown. After the house was no longer used for religious purposes, but still served for town meetings, the pews were stored in the gallery and replaced by settees. The pulpit, said to be the oldest in the state, was lowered to floor level. The building was used occasionally as a dance hall. In 1936 the interior was restored as it was at first, and the house is now well taken care of.

21 through 25 Old Meetinghouse, 1773, Sandown, New Hampshire

22 Framing in loft

23 Slave pew in gallery

21

22

23

24

25

26 Walpole Meetinghouse, 1772, Bristol, Maine

The little village of Walpole in the town of Bristol, Maine, has a small but attractive meetinghouse (Fig. 26), built in 1772 and resembling the one at Sandown. The outside is covered with shingles, now painted white, instead of the more usual clapboards. Within, the spindle-top pews are gray. The pulpit (Fig. 27), although much like those just described, stands out in having an elaborately bannistered stairway. This meetinghouse was the home of a Presbyterian church until 1796, when it became Congregational. Regular religious services ceased in 1822, but some are occasionally held in the summer today. At its centennial in 1872 the house was repaired and restored.

A few miles north, in the same county of Lincoln, Maine, is the town of Alna, which went by other names until 1794. The meetinghouse was built in 1789, and is one of the larger and plainer structures of its type (Fig. 28). Unlike the others it has only one door. This leads into a porch whence the stairs ascend to the gallery. The front and back walls are clapboarded but the two ends are covered with

27 *Pulpit, Walpole Meetinghouse*

28 *Old Meetinghouse, 1789,*
Alna, Maine

29 *Old Meetinghouse, 1800,*
Fremont, New Hampshire

shingles. The interior is in excellent repair, with painted, spindle-top, square pews and a pulpit much like that at Walpole save for the stained centers of the panels (Fig. 31). It has an ingeniously designed stool on which the minister stands and which can be regulated to accommodate preachers of different heights. Joseph Carleton, of whom little else is known, was the builder of the house. The meetinghouse has been restored by the Pemaquid chapter of the Daughters of the American Revolution.

In the town of Fremont, in southeastern New Hampshire, is one of the youngest of these simple meetinghouses, built in 1800 (Fig. 29). It is unusual in having a porch for stairs at each end, thus saving room inside the house. The exterior has very little ornament. Within, there are box pews around the walls, but those that were in the center of the auditorium have been removed. The high pulpit is original, but the sounding board has been taken away. The wall behind the pulpit is unique among meetinghouses of this type in having no pulpit window.

The town of Webster, in central New Hampshire, originally a parish of Boscawen, was named for the illustrious Daniel. Its first meetinghouse (Fig. 30), built in 1791, a large, plain structure without a porch, stood at the foot of Corser Hill. After the

30 *Old Meetinghouse, 1791,*
Webster, New Hampshire

31 *Pulpit, Old Meetinghouse,*
Alna, Maine

building of the present Congregational church in 1823, near the top of the hill, the old house was used only for town purposes. When it served this end no longer and had begun to go to pieces, it was moved to a site not far from the present church and is now kept in repair. Much of the interior woodwork has been removed and the old house sits by itself, rather forlorn, as though waiting for some generous friend to restore it to its former state.

Farther west, just across the Connecticut River and a little above Bellows Falls, Vermont, stands the old meetinghouse of Rockingham, erected in 1787 (Fig. 32). Like the Rocky Hill house, it too was built in difficult times. When the center of population of the old town shifted to the newer villages in the valley, the house was gradually deserted. Religious services ceased here in 1839, and 1869 saw the last town meeting held within its walls. Thereafter the building fell prey to vandalism, but in 1906, through the action of the town and the generosity of many friends, it was restored to its original condition.

The Rockingham meetinghouse stands on a hilltop above the Williams River, surrounded by the town's old burying ground. Its long axis is east and west, the main door on the south side with porches at the two ends, and the pulpit on the north wall. The interior is essentially the same in construction and appearance as that of the Rocky Hill house, except that each pew has a row of delicately turned spindles, which makes the whole construction more open and attractive. It has been suggested that spindled pew tops in these old meetinghouses were not only for ornament but to allow small children to look out, and thus to prevent them from getting restless. The original pulpit was removed long ago, but the present one is a good reproduction.

The builder of the house was General John Fuller, a prominent resident of the town, and, as was often the custom with builders, he "rode the plate" (the main beam at the eaves) when it was lifted into place at the raising of the frame: "After he got everything ready the old General (Fuller) took his bottle of rum in one hand, a tumbler in the other, and stood on the bent of the plate on the south side, then gave the order to put it up in that position. He rode on the plate, and he was a man weighing 200 pounds. When they had got it up, he stood on the plate, drank his health to the crowd below, then threw his bottle and tumbler down and called for

32 Old Meetinghouse, 1787, Rockingham, Vermont

33 Chestnut Hill Meetinghouse, 1769,
Millville, Massachusetts

the ladder, coming down amid loud and long cheering." [1]

One reason for the dominance of New Englanders in the early life of the Republic is suggested by the statistics relating to Josiah White, a prominent member of this church, whose pew is marked with a memorial tablet. From it we learn that he was blessed in having 15 children, 160 grandchildren and 211 great-grand-children.

Most of the meetinghouses of this simple, "Rocky Hill," type that remain are in the three northern states of New England. There is one, however, on the southern edge of Massachusetts near the Rhode Island line. This is the Chestnut Hill meeting-house of Millville (Fig. 33). Built by the Friends but later turned Unitarian, it has long since been abandoned for regular services but is often opened in the summer. It was built in 1769 and has not been greatly changed. On three sides are doors, the front one southeast. The exterior is very plain, save for some ornament on the door frames. A single row of the original square pews, with their spindle tops, have been kept next the wall, in the auditorium, but those in the center were replaced in 1869 by modern pews. Pulpit, pulpit window and sounding board (Fig. 34) are much as in old meetinghouses of this type. Below the pulpit is the original

[1] From *The Old Meeting House and First Church in Rockingham, Vermont,* by L. S. Hayes, 1915.

34 Pulpit, Chestnut Hill Meetinghouse

35 *Gallery pews in*
Old Meetinghouse, 1796,
Foster Center, Rhode Island

36 *Old Meetinghouse, 1738,*
Salem, New Hampshire

deacons' pew and drop-leaf communion table. Plain wooden benches like those at Foster Center, Rhode Island (Fig. 35), have been retained in the gallery.

There are a number of other meetinghouses of the eighteenth-century, pitched-roof type, with exteriors relatively unchanged, though the interiors are radically altered, which are of interest for various reasons. Those to be mentioned here, unlike the ones just discussed, are all serving some useful purpose today. Most of them, as it happens, are in New Hampshire.

The oldest of these is the present town hall, originally the meetinghouse, of the town of Salem, New Hampshire, built in 1738. This is a plain building (Fig. 36) with a very steep roof and thus a large loft in which the roof timbers and their curved struts are visible. Since the clapboards are modern, no sign save the unequal spacing of the side windows indicates that the original door was in one of the long sides. In 1840, when a new Congregational church was built, the old house was moved to its present location nearby and turned around. The town took it over in 1846 and divided it into two floors, with the town hall downstairs, and what was called Salem Hall—a place for meetings and dances—upstairs. The frame and general form of this building are those of the old meetinghouse, but so many changes have been made in it that it now has little appearance of antiquity.

The town hall of Hampstead, New Hampshire, has changed very little, externally, over the years (Fig. 37). The main door is on the long side,

and at one end rises a tower surmounted by a graceful, columned belfry, dome, and spire, somewhat suggesting the domed steeples of southern
New England. Over all swings a handsome weathercock. The building was
actually begun in 1745, but although
the church services and town meetings were held in it from the first, it
remained in an unfinished state for almost fifty years. Finally, in 1792, the
interior was completed and the steeple
added. A Paul Revere bell was installed in 1809; on it appears a characteristic Puritan couplet:

The living to the church, I call
And to the grave I summon all.

When in 1837 the Congregationalists built a new church, the other denominations in town were given the
use of the old one. Finally, in 1852,
the town took over the meetinghouse,
removed pulpit and pews, and divided it into two stories. It is now
used for town business.

The hilltop town of Washington, in
central New Hampshire, has an attractive civic center—church, school,
and town hall—all painted white and
well maintained. Nearby is an old
tavern. The town was incorporated in
1776 and claims to be the first one
named for George Washington. What
chiefly interests us here is the town
hall, built as a meetinghouse in 1789
(Fig. 38). At one end is a tower and
steeple and at the other a porch; the
main entrance is on the long side between. The steeple, with belfry, lantern stage, and dome, suggests the
Asher Benjamin design (see p. 80),
and was added later. The windows,
with forty panes each, seem to be the

37 Old Meetinghouse, 1745,
Hampstead, New Hampshire

38 Old Meetinghouse, 1789,
Washington, New Hampshire

65

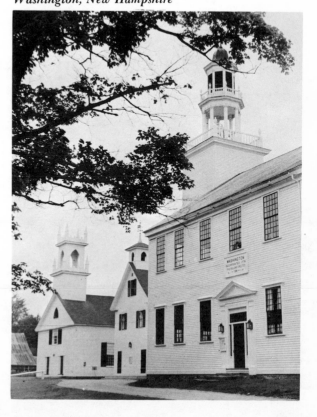

39 *Old Meetinghouse, 1794,*
Lempster, New Hampshire

40 *Old Meetinghouse, 1795,*
North Sutton, New Hampshire

original ones. Since the building of the church in 1840, the meetinghouse, now divided into two floors, has been used for town affairs. On the lower floor the columns that once supported the gallery can still be seen. When the house was built, it was stipulated that "all heavy timber should be cut in the old of the moon in Sept. and Oct." The man who put the frame together, one Cummings, claimed to be so expert at it that "Every joint he ever framed, he knew would pinch a hair."

The meetinghouse in Lempster, the next town to Washington, was built in 1794 (Fig. 39). The Second New Hampshire turnpike and the Croyden turnpike were put through a few years later, and Lempster, at the junction of the two, became a place of considerable importance. To take advantage of this, in 1822 the meetinghouse was taken down and re-erected at the center of the village, about a mile from its original location. After the church was built nearby, the house was no longer used for religious purposes. It was later divided into two stories and an academy was conducted in it for a time. Now called Union Hall, it serves as a grange hall and a place for gatherings of various sorts. There is a stage downstairs. The tower and steeple were added when the house was moved. The old main door, on the south side, is no longer used, but the original pulpit window, opposite, opens into the upstairs room. Across the street is a large tavern, built in turnpike days.

In this part of New England a meetinghouse was often built not by the town but by what was called a meetinghouse association, or society, which

41 Old Meetinghouse, 1758, Harpswell Center, Maine

then made the building available to several denominations. The money was raised by the sale of pews. The meetinghouse in North Sutton (Fig. 40) was erected by this means in 1795 and is still owned by the association that built it. Its builder was John Harvey, who was directed to copy the meetinghouse in nearby New London. It took three years to erect it. In 1816 more pews were added and in 1855 the building was divided into two floors, the upper for church purposes, the lower for a town hall. At this time the upper row of windows was replaced. The belfry and cupola were added in 1870. Despite these changes, the general plan is still that of an eighteenth-century meetinghouse. The town has a building of its

own today and the old meetinghouse is now used exclusively by the Baptist Church.

In the Casco Bay town of Harpswell there stands, at Harpswell Center, the oldest meetinghouse in the state of Maine still used for town purposes (Fig. 41). It was built in 1758. Near it stood the cemetery, horse block, pound, and training field for the militia. Church services were discontinued in this building in 1856 and it was taken over entirely for town purposes, though the house is not large enough now for town meetings. Outwardly it is a typical meetinghouse, with an entrance porch on one of the long sides. It has been considerably changed within, but the old pulpit and sounding board remain,

42 First Parish Church United, 1794, Westford, Massachusetts

43 Old Meetinghouse, 1743, Pelham, Massachusetts

as do some of the square pews and the gallery. Into one corner has been built a brick vault and the town office occupies another corner. In early days the town's supply of powder was stored in the loft.

In the town of Westford, Massachusetts, not far from Lowell, is a large, well-preserved old meetinghouse of the pitched-roof type (Fig. 42). At one end this has a tower on which is an attractive cupola belfry with arched openings and a gracefully flaring spire above. This meetinghouse, the third on the site, was built in 1794. The main door was originally on the long side, facing the road. In 1835 the present bell was given the church, and the clock dates from 1837. In 1847 the interior was divided, the lower room for the town and the upper for church services. The building was turned in 1868 so that the tower now faces the street, and the entrance is through a vestibule into it. The church organization became Unitarian, and in 1828 a group withdrew from it and formed a Congregational church. The two have now come together again under the name of the First Parish Church United.

The meetinghouse at Pelham, Massachusetts (Fig. 43), is of interest as the oldest town hall in continuous use in New England. It was built in 1743. When a new church was erected in 1839, the old house was moved back a little way and taken over by the town. The church is no longer active, but the old meetinghouse, after 220 years, still serves the town as faithfully as ever. Externally it is unchanged, but the interior is now divided into two stories. Pelham was the home of Daniel Shays, who mobilized a body of men rebelling against the injustices of the times, and tried to burn the courthouses in several Massachusetts counties. Part of his "army" encamped on the common in front of the meetinghouse for a cold week in January of 1786, and there is a tablet to him at the cemetery gate. The cemetery itself is picturesque, with many rough and primitive stones.

There are many other meetinghouses in New England that were built in the eighteenth century but they have suffered so much alteration, without as well as within, that they are of little value as examples of the pitched-roof type of design. Some of

them will be discussed in Chapter 7.

The meetinghouse of the Second Congregational Society of Preston, Connecticut, is an interesting reversion to the style of the eighteenth century. The first house was built about 1726 and was replaced, on almost the same spot, by the present one (Fig. 44) in 1817. The long dimension of the house is parallel to the road, with the single door in the middle. Over this is a modern vestibule. There is no steeple or belfry. Within, the house is very plain and probably has been little changed. The seats are plain pews with backs, and the simple pulpit is opposite the door. There is a gallery on three sides. This building seems to be the only one of the meetinghouse type built in the nineteenth

44 Second Congregational Church, 1817, Preston, Connecticut

*45 Old Meetinghouse, 1731,
Bridgewater, Massachusetts*

*46 Second Congregational Church, 1826,
Manomet, Massachusetts*

century and still standing. It was repaired in 1856. Although the Second Congregational Society of Preston is still in existence, no services have been held in this meetinghouse for many years.

Although most of the meetinghouses of this period are much alike in style, certain local differences do appear. In several cases in southeastern Massachusetts, for example, the belfry was a simple structure placed directly on the end of the roof and not carried on a tower. Such a one is shown in an engraving of the Bridgewater house of 1731 (Fig. 45). This arrangement persisted in some of the simpler houses built much later in this region. A good example is the church at Manomet, a village in the southern part of Plymouth (Fig. 46). This was built in 1826 and has a picturesque setting in the old cemetery. It houses the oldest Congregational church in Plymouth, since the one established by the Pilgrim fathers became Unitarian.

The general uniformity in the architecture of New England meetinghouses of the eighteenth century (after the first decade) is one of its distinctive features. This sameness of design came to a rather abrupt end about 1800, and was followed by the development of a wide variety of styles in the first quarter of the nineteenth century.

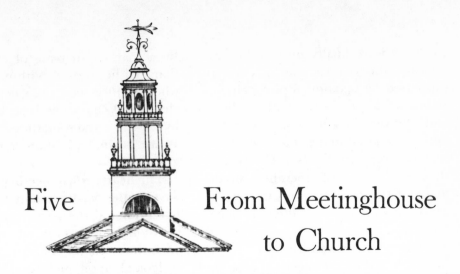

Five From Meetinghouse to Church

AS the nineteenth century began, the New England population was still extraordinarily homogeneous. Immigration continued into the still unsettled parts of the three northern states and some was moving westward, though the flood that would later pour across the Hudson was only beginning. Industrial development was in its infancy. The movement from the hills to the mills had hardly started, and the upland villages were still unweakened by the departure of their young people to stream-side factories.

After the end of the Puritan migration, about 1640, there had been only minor population additions from abroad, and the million people in these six states were almost all descended from the stock of the first settlers. Conditions were favorable as never before or since for the most complete expression of the matured genius of New England. Her history in the earlier years was more dramatic, and her wealth and power were certainly far greater in the decades to come; but it was from 1790 to 1830 that her indigenous culture attained its fullest development.

Increasing wealth and leisure, safety from the dread of Indian attack, wider contact with the rest of the world and a better educated population all had softened the harshness of frontier life and were converting the culture of New England, now more than a century and a half old, into a mellower pattern. Literature began to flourish. Emerson, Hawthorne, Thoreau, Longfellow, Bryant, Whittier, Melville and others of the New England galaxy were born and grew up in this era and absorbed its intellectual, moral and aesthetic atmosphere, to which they later gave such powerful expression. Architecture, always in good repute among the Puritans, now produced some of its finest achievements, not least in the design of meetinghouse and church.

The decline in religious faith that had followed the Revolution was ending, and the church and its affairs began to occupy their former dominant place in the thoughts of New Englanders. Soon after the turn of the century, however, the long established ascendency of the Congregational order and the union between church and state were finally broken, and as a result the church was no longer supported by taxation. Episcopalians, Baptists, Methodists, Universalists, and Quakers had little by little obtained equality under the law. As a reaction from the rigors of Calvinistic theology, a wave of liberalism swept many of the churches, and in eastern Massachusetts most of them became Unitarian.

These changes were to be reflected in the design of the meetinghouse itself. Town meetings were held there, but only part of the citizenry also worshiped in the house of the first church—the "Prime Society." Other denominations had built churches and these were all used as houses of worship. Among members of the established church itself a feeling began to grow that their meetinghouse, as well, should be less a secular building and more a House of the Lord; that both religious and secular functions could not be served adequately by the same structure.

A score or so of years before the legal separation of church and state actually took place, however, it was already foreshadowed by the changing character of the meetinghouse. Just before the turn of the century, the barnlike plan, with the door on one long side and the pulpit on the other, and with the bell tower, when present, at the end, was altered by placing the entrance at the tower end and the pulpit at the other, the typical arrangement for a church. Practically every meetinghouse built after 1800 was of this design, and most of the older ones were remodeled to conform to it. This change was accompanied

by a marked increase of ornamentation, without and within, and the whole edifice took on a definitely ecclesiastical character. It still was built by the town and sometimes still served as the town hall, though with poor grace.

The hearty town meetings of earlier days could hardly retain their vigor here, nor did the parish welcome the occasional intrusion of townsmen, with their secular concerns, into what it looked upon more and more as a house of worship. Sometimes there were regulations drawn up by the parish authorities to control these conditions, such as requiring everyone who attended town meeting to remove his hat in the house and to clean his boots before entering; and the church in Milford, Connecticut, directed the sexton "to put fresh sand in the spit boxes once a month." After the legal separation, when the society took title to the building, the town was often unceremoniously ejected from its former meeting place. For some time, however, the feeling of proprietorship in these old houses persisted, as in the almost vested right of young men in some villages to ring the church bell on the night before the Fourth of July.

For two or three decades the New England town meeting became a homeless institution. Sometimes the towns retained ownership of part of the meetinghouse, if it had been divided into two stories, and this arrangement persists in a few places to this day. Sometimes the society gave the town permission from time to time to meet in the old house. Sometimes these meetings rotated from one meet-

47 *"Old White Church," 1800,
West Springfield, Massachusetts*

inghouse to another. More often some other auditorium was hired. Not until the 1840s did most New England towns finally build halls exclusively for public purposes.

The change from the meetinghouse to the church plan of building took place within a few years, and provides another of those architectural turning points that coincide with other events. The legal separation between church and state occurred in Massachusetts in 1811, in Connecticut in 1818, in New Hampshire in 1819, and in Maine in 1820. In Rhode Island the two had never been united, nor had they actually been so in Vermont. In determining the approximate date when the decision to make this separation was reached in people's minds, we are helped by the fact that the change in meetinghouse design from the side-entrance type to the newer end-entrance type was made within the span of a few years just before and just after 1800. It was then that the people of New England seem to have made the decision to separate their political from their ecclesiastical affairs, although they did not give legal sanction to this decision until one or two decades later.

TRANSITIONAL CHURCHES

The first buildings to have the plan of a church, built near the turn of the century, merely changed the arrangement of the interior so as to put the entrance (or entrances) at the tower end, and the pulpit at the other. The

exterior of the building was left much as before, save for the closing of the entrance on the long side and the change in the position of the pulpit window. Gallery on three sides, square pews, high pulpit, sounding board— all these were retained. Such buildings, leading from the old type to the new, we shall call "Transitional."

The few surviving examples have all been radically altered within, and most of them without. A good example of one little changed outside is the old meetinghouse at West Springfield, Massachusetts (Fig. 47), built in 1800 on "Mount Orthodox." It looks like a typical square-towered meetinghouse save for its doors. The main one is through the base of the tower and there is another on each side of the front itself. Over the tower stands an octagonal belfry with a smaller octagonal stage above, the

73

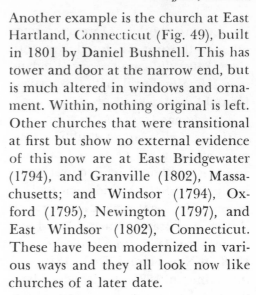

Another example is the church at East Hartland, Connecticut (Fig. 49), built in 1801 by Daniel Bushnell. This has tower and door at the narrow end, but is much altered in windows and ornament. Within, nothing original is left. Other churches that were transitional at first but show no external evidence of this now are at East Bridgewater (1794), and Granville (1802), Massachusetts; and Windsor (1794), Oxford (1795), Newington (1797), and East Windsor (1802), Connecticut. These have been modernized in various ways and they all look now like churches of a later date.

ORIGIN OF THE NEW TYPE

About 1800 the new churches of the Congregational order began to be built on a much more elaborate design. They show a number of similarities. Typically there is a two-storied entrance bay projecting slightly from the middle part of the façade, usually with three doors below and three windows above. In front of this in some churches is a portico of four columns. The pediment of this portico may sometimes be attached directly to the front of the church so that an entrance bay is lacking. Over bay or portico rises a square tower, partly set back on the roof. This carries the steeple, which may or may not have a spire, and shows much diversity of form. The designers of these new churches began to display their originality, particularly on the façade, bay, and steeple, which are often beautifully ornamented.

74

whole crowned by a spire. A new touch is the presence, just over the door, of a small Palladian window, an ornamental form much used in the next twenty-five years. This is really a group of three windows, a round-topped one between two that are shorter and square-topped. Of the builder, Captain Timothy Billings, we know little. The old house, now divided into two stories, is no longer used for religious purposes.

There are a few other relatively unchanged transitional churches. The best is the imposing structure at Strafford, Vermont (Fig. 48), built in 1799 for Congregationalists and Universalists, but for most of the time since then serving only as the town hall. Pulpit and downstairs pews are gone but the gallery and its old pews are unchanged. Externally the structure looks as it did when it was built.

49 *Congregational Church, 1801,*
East Hartland, Connecticut

Classical church models now had much influence, particularly examples from Wren and other architects of the English Renaissance. Wren's work, as we have pointed out, was not known at first hand by New England carpenters; but builders' books were available, most of them published in England, which contained many useful ideas derived from him. Almost all the New England churches were of wood and relatively small. The chief problem their builders faced was to translate the classical forms, developed in masonry construction, to the material with which they worked. The domestic architecture of the eighteenth century doubtless provided many suggestions, particularly as to ornament. Considering the difficulties, these builders did surprisingly well, and the countryside began to bloom with the lovely white churches that for so long have been one of the glories of New England. Some of these are true works of art. Others, less successful aesthetically, are sincere attempts of untrained artisans to master architectural problems with which they were unfamiliar.

The square-towered, pitched-roof meetinghouses of the eighteenth century were all so similar in design that they might have been turned out of a mold. There is no such uniformity in the churches built after 1800. Each was distinctive. Certain general groups can be recognized, but even in these there is an extraordinary diversity in façade, steeple, pulpit, and other details. Among the churches of this period there is no pre-eminent master-

piece that served as a model, as did the Old South in earlier years.

The greater originality of these buildings was doubtless the result of a new factor—the practicing architect. After the Revolution, a number of the more gifted builders turned their attention in a truly professional spirit to problems of design and construction. One or two became nationally famous. The history of New England church design during the first quarter of the nineteenth century is therefore in no small degree an account of the work of a few of these pioneer architects. Individually, they did not build many structures, but their examples exercised a great influence, since most building committees, unable to afford an architect's services, followed the easy, established custom of copying, more or less closely, some structure that they particularly admired.

A few buildings of the true "church" type, as opposed to the older meetinghouse and transitional structures, were erected in New England before 1800. The two earliest were the rather anomalous Brattle Street Church of Boston (built in 1772 and long gone) which, with its wide, deep porch, tall bell tower and absence of steeple, apparently had no imitators; and the First Baptist church of Providence (1775), with its steeple and apparently some other details taken directly from James Gibbs' *The Book of Architecture*. This church, which we will consider in Chapter 8, may have had some influence on later ones, but probably only in the larger cities.

There were a number of designers and builders who had a hand in the radical change; but it is hard to as-

sign the chief credit to any of them. Several contributed to the development of the new ideas and doubtless influenced one another. The change was "in the air." Many new churches were going up, and everyone concerned with the building of one doubtless gave thought to finding a design that would better express the expanding purposes of these structures than had the old Puritan meetinghouse. The contributions of each of the more important architects can best be discussed in connection with the churches they built.

CHARLES BULFINCH

Bulfinch (1763–1844) is best remembered for his design of the Massachusetts state capitol in Boston, and for his work on the national capitol. He was responsible for the plans of about a dozen churches, most of them of brick or stone and somewhat more

50 Bulfinch church, 1789, Pittsfield, Massachusetts

ambitious than a small country town could afford. Of these, only two now stand. For Pittsfield, Massachusetts, however, he built between 1789 and 1793 a wooden church (Fig. 50) that had a very important influence, directly or indirectly, on the design of most of the small, rural churches erected in the twenty-five years after 1800. It had a deep entrance bay at the gable end, with a single large door on the front and a smaller one on either side. Above this was a square tower sitting partly back on the roof and carrying a cupola belfry of eight columns and a dome. On the main building and porch were simple pilasters, and the corners of the tower were ornamented by quoins. Over the front door of the entrance bay was a Palladian window, and there were others on three sides of the square tower above. Such windows, rare before this, were soon to become common. The slope of the roof was much less steep than in the old-fashioned meetinghouses. The Pittsfield church is now gone, after a long period of misuse and neglect, and there are no good pictures of its original state.

The new ideas displayed in this structure evidently appealed to building committees from nearby parishes. The church at Salisbury, Connecticut (Fig. 51), built in 1800, is closer to the Pittsfield church in appearance than any other now standing. It has a cupola belfry and a deep entrance bay with doors on three sides. The church at South Canaan, not far away, was built in 1804 (Fig. 52) and is on the same general plan but with somewhat different proportions. A Greek Revival steeple replaced the original

51 Congregational Church, 1800, Salisbury, Connecticut

52 Congregational Church, 1804, South Canaan, Connecticut

77

in 1843. The 1801 church at Washington (Fig. 53), in the same region, also suggests the Pittsfield church, but the resemblance is masked by a markedly different steeple (a replacement) and by a columned portico across the whole front, built in recent years. At Otis, Massachusetts, is a church of 1813 (Fig. 54) that also resembles the Pittsfield original, especially in its cupola. In the balustrade around the tower it differs from the other churches of this group. The interiors of all these churches have been altered, that of Otis being divided into two stories. The church at South Canaan has suffered the least change.

The direct influence of Bulfinch's Pittsfield church, shown by the cupola belfry, the deep porch with doors on three sides, and the use of Palladian windows, was limited to a small area in western Massachusetts and northwestern Connecticut. Its indirect effect spread much farther, for it seems to have been largely responsible for Asher Benjamin's famous church design (p. 81), so widely used in the next three decades. Bulfinch's 1792 church at Taunton, Massachusetts (Fig. 55), no longer extant, may also have influenced later designs since, unlike the Pittsfield church, it had a shallow entrance porch with three doors across its front, as did most churches after 1800.

Two churches that are certainly by

78

54 *Congregational Church, 1813, Otis, Massachusetts*

55 Bulfinch church, 1792,
Taunton, Massachusetts

Bulfinch still stand. One is the present St. Stephen's Roman Catholic Church on Hanover Street, in the North End of Boston. Bulfinch built this in 1802 for the "New North" Congregational church, so-called to distinguish it from the "Old North" that the British had torn down. After most of the congregation had moved elsewhere, the church was sold to the Catholic diocese. It is a brick building with a tall, three-storied porch, suggesting those of the "Old West" and Charles Street churches in Boston, designed by Benjamin a few years later. Perhaps Benjamin got his idea for these from the Bulfinch church. The interior of the latter is now considerably altered.

Bulfinch's 1816 church at Lancaster, Massachusetts (Fig. 56), has been greatly admired. It is of brick, with a deep portico of equal arches, ornamented by wooden pilasters and carrying a wide frieze. Over the square tower is a round, open cupola of ten Ionic columns, crowned by a garlanded drum and dome. The interior has been little changed and has a columned pulpit of great beauty.

Another church that may have been designed by Bulfinch is the one at Peterborough, New Hampshire, built in 1825 (Fig. 57). Tradition has it that the building committee went to see him in Boston, found that he was out of the city, and bought a set of

56 Unitarian Church, 1816,
Lancaster, Massachusetts

79

57 *Unitarian Church, 1825, Peterborough, New Hampshire*

plans from his assistant. This church is also of brick, but has a wooden steeple. The wine-glass pulpit is modern. Oddly enough, the steeple is practically duplicated by that on the wooden church at Chester, Vermont (Fig. 58). The main road from Chester to Boston ran through Peterborough, and the builder, in passing, probably saw and admired the Peterborough church and resolved to copy its steeple.

ASHER BENJAMIN

Born in Greenfield, Massachusetts, in 1772, Asher Benjamin began his career as a country carpenter. As builder and architect, we find him at work in Nashua, New Hampshire; Windsor, Vermont; and in Boston. He seems to have been the first man to recognize the need felt by carpenters, untrained in the new church style, for help in planning buildings that would conform to it. His *The Country Builder's Assistant* was published in Greenfield, Massachusetts, in 1797, reprinted several times, and much used all over New England.

In this book there appeared a "Design for a Church" (Fig. 59) which had a great deal of influence throughout New England except in Connecticut and Rhode Island. It shows a structure with a rather shallow entrance porch that has three doors across it, the middle one the largest,

58 *Congregational Church, 1828, Chester, Vermont*

59 Asher Benjamin's "Design for a Church"

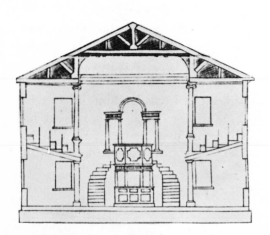

and three windows above, the middle one Palladian. Around the square tower is a railing with urns at the corners. Then comes an open belfry of eight columns with square-topped openings between them, over which are another railing and urns. Above this is a second octagonal stage with pilasters at the angles and (apparently) painted elliptical areas between them to simulate windows. Over all is a double dome. Within the building a high pulpit stands on columns and is reached by stairs on both sides. Behind it is a large Palladian window.

The origin of this design, which was widely copied in whole or part, is evidently of much importance for the student of New England church architecture. Bulfinch's Pittsfield church is generally credited with being the chief inspiration for it, and it does resemble this church in having a two-storied porch with a Palladian window over the door and an eight-columned belfry with a dome. Benjamin's design differs from Bulfinch's, however, in a number of important respects. The porch is shallower and it has no doors on its sides. There are three windows above the front doors instead of one. Over the belfry is an additional octagonal stage, so that the steeple is taller and of a more elaborate design. These last are all typical of the majority of the Puritan churches built during the next quarter of a century, and therefore we must give Benjamin credit for making significant additions to Bulfinch's design. Bulfinch's Taunton church also has three doors and three windows in a shallow entrance bay, and it may be that Benjamin knew about it. In this church, however, the belfry was crowned by a spire instead of the octagonal stage that was to become so common.

The evolution of the Benjamin design probably began in Berkshire County, Massachusetts, but the story is still by no means clear. At Lee, just south of Pittsfield, there was built in 1800 a church much like the Benjamin plan. Although the building is no longer standing, we have a picture of it (Fig. 60). In the three doors in front and especially in the details of the steeple, this resembles the Benjamin church. In the single Palladian window in the bay, the three in the tower, the relatively deep bay and the quoins on the corners, it suggests the Pittsfield church. Benjamin's book came out three years before the church

at Lee was built and probably had an important influence on its design. John Hulett, the builder of this church, is also credited with designing the one in nearby Richmond, built in 1795, *before* the appearance of Benjamin's book.

The Richmond church is said to have been much like the church at Lee. The question is complicated by the fact that the builder of the 1800 church at Salisbury, Connecticut, was directed by the committee there to model it after the church at Richmond. The Salisbury church, however, as we have already seen, is much like Bulfinch's Pittsfield church. It could not have closely resembled both the Pittsfield church and the one at Richmond, if the latter was like the Lee church. Unfortunately, the Richmond church is gone and we have no picture of it.

At Lenox, near Pittsfield, the "Old Church on the Hill," built in 1805 (Fig. 61), has a bay and pilasters like those of the Pittsfield church; but the steeple, save for the arched openings in the belfry, is like Benjamin's. It is not known who built it.

All this leaves us in a state of uncertainty. Three things we should like to know: (1) what the Richmond church was like, since Benjamin might have copied it for his book; (2) more about John Hulett, who perhaps designed this Richmond church; and (3) where Benjamin was working in the years just before 1797. Was he in Berkshire County getting ideas for

60 Congregational Church, 1800, Lee, Massachusetts

61 Community Church, 1805, Lenox, Massachusetts

62 *Congregational Church, 1805,*
Old Bennington, Vermont

63 *Baptist Church, 1805,*
East Poultney, Vermont

his book and perhaps conferring with Bulfinch?

A number of surviving churches resemble Benjamin's plan more or less closely. The best known is the 1805 structure at Old Bennington, Vermont (Fig. 62). In later years its interior underwent many changes, but thanks to the efforts of its friends it has now been essentially restored. The architect was Lavius Fillmore whose work is discussed in the next section. Fillmore introduced a few external differences from Benjamin's plan, especially the more graceful belfry, with its arched openings, and the round tops of the doors and of the upper row of windows. Within, the ceiling of the church is vaulted and groined and supported by six tall columns. During the restoration, several interesting discoveries were made. At the rear of the gallery two pews for Negroes were found with sides that were seven feet high, thus effectively segregating their occupants. In the south gallery, where the unmarried men sat, there were many initials carved in the panels of the pews, and even one Scriptural reference, Matthew 23:8–13, Christ's warning against hypocrites. On the women's side the pews were not defaced.

This is a historic spot, for across the road from the church stood the meetinghouse of 1763, the first one to be built in the New Hampshire Grants, and the one which became the capitol of the fiercely independent little Republic of Vermont from 1777 to 1791. In the cemetery are many old headstones, and here are buried soldiers, both Hessian and American, who fell in the Battle of Bennington, nearby.

Among other Benjamin-type churches is the one at East Poultney, Vermont (Fig. 63), built in 1805 by Elisha Scott, who came up from Connecticut and settled here. It was built a Baptist church and remains one. The window sash-bars and cornice carvings are outstanding. Many years ago the upper stage of the steeple was blown off, but it was restored in 1937 as a memorial to George Jones, a native of East Poultney and one of the founders of *The New York Times*. The house was divided into two stories in 1839.

At Bethel, not far away, is a brick church of 1816 (Fig. 64), formerly Universalist but now Federated, that has a Benjamin steeple. Five denominations united to build it—Universalists, Congregationalists, Episcopalians, Methodists and Baptists. It was divided into two stories in 1853, repaired in 1864, and had its steeple restored in 1953. The brick meetinghouse in Weathersfield Center, Vermont (Fig. 65), built in 1821, has a steeple resembling Benjamin's, set back on the roof. This building, at the old town center, is several miles uphill from Ascutneyville. Downstairs is the town hall, and upstairs, the church. Church and town seem to own and care for the house jointly. The pulpit is at the front, under the steeple.

Another steeple of the Benjamin design is to be seen on the church of the First Congregational Society (Unitarian) of Castine, Maine (Fig. 66), which was built as a typical meetinghouse in 1790 but much altered in 1831.

In Manchester, Massachusetts, on Boston's North Shore, is a Congregational church of 1809 (Fig. 67), which

64 Federated Church, 1816, Bethel, Vermont

85

65 Meetinghouse, 1821, Weathersfield Center, Vermont

66 *Congregational Church, 1829,*
Castine, Maine

67 *Congregational Church, 1809,*
Manchester, Massachusetts

shows Benjamin's influence, though it has a rather deep porch. Above it swings an old weathercock, bought by the town in 1754. The interior of the building was remodeled in 1845, and the square pews removed. This church organization has the distinction of being one of the few in the vicinity of Boston that did not become Unitarian.

Much like the church at Manchester and built in the same year is one in the hilltop town of Ashby, on the northern border of Massachusetts (Fig. 68). This is a large building, erected when the countryside was more populous. Its steeple is one of the best of the Benjamin type. In the tower is a semicircular window, as in Benjamin's design. Under the main cornice are small, downward-pointing brackets, and the square tops of the three doors are richly ornamented. There is the scar of a pulpit window in the clapboards at the rear.

The imposing church at Wayland, Massachusetts, built in 1814 (Fig. 69), stands on the old Boston Post Road. The steeple has a gilded dome, and in its arched belfry openings recalls the one at Old Bennington. Like the latter, too, its upper windows were apparently round-topped, as are the present ones on the porch. The others were altered when the building was divided into two floors. This church was built by Andrews Palmer of Newburyport.

The only church of the Benjamin

68 *Unitarian Church, 1809,*
Ashby, Massachusetts

type in Connecticut, and apparently the only one ever built there, is the 1816 church at North Woodbury (Fig. 70). Its belfry tower is beautifully proportioned. The interior is essentially unchanged, and the fanlights over the doors are noteworthy.

A quite different church in the Benjamin manner is the "Old South" of Windsor, Vermont, built in 1798 (Fig. 71). Benjamin was living there at the time and probably had something to do with it. The two upper stages of the steeple are much like his design. Below this, however, and above the square tower, is a square stage with pilasters, elaborate ornament, and louvered openings, apparently the belfry. This is unlike any other belfry in New England. At first this church had two rows of seven windows on either side instead of the present five. In 1844 the side galleries were taken out and the church was divided into two stories. The interior was modernized in 1879 and partly restored in 1922, when the columned portico was added. Despite many changes this remains a beautiful church, without and within.

The influence of the Benjamin design may be seen in many other churches, either in the original plan or as changes introduced when the buildings were altered. Benjamin himself became an architect in Boston in his later years, and built two churches there. For a time he worked with Ithiel Town, whom he helped with a plan for Center Church, in New Haven.

70 First Congregational Church, 1816, North Woodbury, Connecticut

89

71 Congregational Church, 1798, Windsor, Vermont

69 Unitarian Church, 1814, Wayland, Massachusetts

LAVIUS FILLMORE

Fillmore, a cousin of President Fillmore, was born in Norwich, Connecticut, in 1767. After finishing the church at Old Bennington, Vermont, he built in the next year (1806) the beautiful example at Middlebury (Fig. 72), also in the Green Mountain State. The details of its façade and the round-topped windows of the upper row are very much like those of his Old Bennington church. The steeple is unique, with two square stages, two octagonal stages, and a spire. This Middlebury church marks Fillmore as an architect of great skill. It is noteworthy that none of his churches have columns or pilasters.

But Fillmore's contribution was perhaps more than even these two notable churches, for he may have had a part in the development of the new church design itself. We know that in 1801 his firm of Terry and Fillmore built the church at Norwichtown, Connecticut (Fig. 73). The 1794 church at East Haddam (Figs. 75 and 74), not far away, is almost identical with this in the details of its façade—door design, quoined corners, shape of windows in bay and tower, and especially in the fact that the upper tier of windows are round-topped. The same man seems to have designed both buildings. That the East Haddam de-

signer was Fillmore is further suggested by the interesting fact that the interior of the East Haddam church much resembles the interior of his church at Old Bennington, especially in its arched and groined ceiling supported on long columns.

All this presents the possibility that Fillmore designed the East Haddam church, copied it (at least externally) at Norwichtown, developed it further at Old Bennington, with the aid of Benjamin's plan, and produced his masterpiece at Middlebury. All four buildings have round-topped upper windows, unusual in Puritan meetinghouses. The East Haddam church and Bulfinch's Taunton church of 1792 were the first to have the shallow bay, nearly universal later, and they

72 *Top left: Congregational Church, 1806,*
Middlebury, Vermont

73 *Top right: Congregational Church, 1801,*
Norwichtown, Connecticut

74, 75 *Congregational Church, 1794,*
East Haddam, Connecticut

76 Congregational Church, 1798,
Hinsdale, Massachusetts

77 Meetinghouse, 1800,
Georgia, Vermont

were built before Benjamin's book was published. Fillmore (who probably did not know Bulfinch's church) may therefore have developed a church design before Benjamin did and independently of him. Whether this had any influence on Benjamin we do not know, but it is an interesting possibility that he may have known Fillmore and admired the East Haddam church.

It seems clear that Bulfinch, Benjamin, and Fillmore each made important contributions to the new design. There are other architects and buildings, too, that should not be overlooked in this study of origins. The builder of the 1798 church at Hinsdale, Massachusetts (Fig. 76), very near to Pittsfield, was Nathan Warner. His contract referred him to the meetinghouse at nearby Chester (now gone) for exterior plan, and to Bulfinch's at Pittsfield for interior arrangements. Like most of the new type, the Hinsdale church has a shallow entrance bay with three doors. It resembles the one at Pittsfield in the quoins at the corners and a Palladian window in the tower. That this structure is not a remodeled meetinghouse is indicated by the fact that there is no evidence of the previous existence of a door or pulpit window on either long side. The bay, tower, and steeple seem to be integral parts of the original building. If they are, the Hinsdale church is one of the oldest surviving examples of the new design.

Another important meetinghouse was the one built by William Sprats at Georgia, Vermont, in 1800 (Fig. 77). This burned in 1952. It had a cupola much like that of the church at Pittsfield, but instead of an entrance bay, a shallow portico of four Ionic columns. This house, much like Sprats' courthouse at Litchfield, Connecticut, built shortly before it, embodies another and apparently independent attempt to develop a church design. Ebenezer Clifford, too, contrived a transition from meetinghouse to church quite different from any other, at Exeter, New Hampshire, in 1799 (see p. 111). And what of the magnificent church at Newburyport (1801), next to be discussed, which also seems to have been quite original? The transformation of the Puritan meetinghouse into a church evidently involved the ideas of a considerable number of men.

TIMOTHY PALMER AND SAMUEL MC INTIRE

The building of the First Religious Society of Newburyport, Massachusetts (Fig. 78), is another example of the new plan. This is one of the most beautiful of all New England churches, and it is a pity that its position, crowded by many other buildings, makes a good view of the exterior difficult to obtain. The entrance bay, somewhat reminiscent of Benjamin's design, is as deep as the tower. The octagonal lantern over the belfry and the windowed stage above it supplied the need of a seaport town for a lofty lookout. The whole steeple is treated with a richness of ornament rarely equaled. The most notable fea-

78 Church of the First Religious Society, 1801, Newburyport, Massachusetts

ture of the interior is the lovely pulpit resting on four columns (Fig. 79).
Back of this is a Palladian window set
in a frame where Corinthian pilasters
support an imposing pediment. The
architect of record is Timothy Palmer,
who built the much simpler Rocky
Hill meetinghouse. The designer evidently had become steeped in the
classical tradition, and we may question whether a country builder like
Palmer would have had the necessary
knowledge for this.

There is a tradition that Samuel
McIntire (1757–1811), famous for the
beautiful houses he built in Salem and
elsewhere, had something to do with
this Newburyport meetinghouse. The
South Church which he built at Salem
in 1803 (now gone) was very much
like it. Either he built the Newburyport church himself, or at Salem he
copied much of Palmer's church. Who-
ever did it, the source of its design
is unknown. Perhaps some English
builder's book will eventually give us
the answer.

Few country towns could afford a
meetinghouse as large and handsome
as this one. The imposing First Church
at Roxbury, Massachusetts, however,
built in 1803 (Fig. 80), was modeled
closely on the Newburyport church,
though there are a number of minor
differences. Its spire blew off in the
hurricane of 1815 and was never replaced. This large and handsome
church, a successor to the one of which
John Eliot so long was minister, seems
rather lonely in the crowded metro-
politan Boston of today.

79 Pulpit, First Religious Society,
Newburyport, Massachusetts

ELIAS CARTER

Many towns in central Massachusetts and New Hampshire owe the
beauty of their churches to Elias Carter, a country carpenter and builder.
He was born in Auburn, Massachusetts, in 1781, the son of an English
builder, from whom he is said to have
inherited many drawings and specifi-
cations that he used in his own work.
He himself was a skilled carver in
wood. Carter built many houses and
at least a dozen churches, two of them
widely copied. Particularly influential
was his church at Templeton, Massachusetts, built in 1811 (Fig. 81). Its
portico has four Ionic columns in two
pairs, and the three doors under it are
united by a common lintel. There is
no entrance bay. In the steeple, a

80 First Church, 1803,
Roxbury, Massachusetts

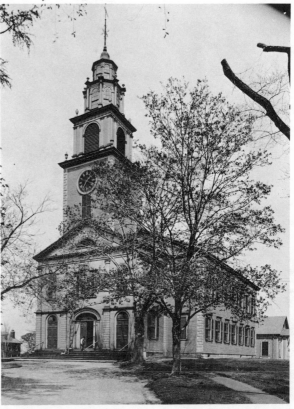

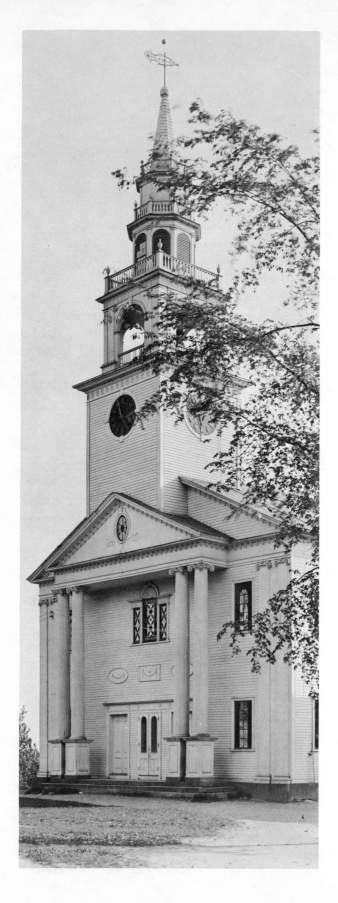

81 Federated Church, 1811,
Templeton, Massachusetts

square, open-arched belfry supports two octagonal stages and a spire. Churches derived from this one repeat two minor but typical features—the vertically elliptical window in the pediment, and the row of downward-pointing ornaments, or brackets, below the cornice. Said the preacher at the dedication of the Templeton church: "In this house we discover a just proportion; we see a majestic simplicity; we see a simplicity blended with elegance and beauty." These words remain true today.

The Templeton church was often copied, with minor modifications that increased with time and with distance from the model. The church at Fitzwilliam, New Hampshire (Fig. 82), not very far from Templeton, is an almost exact copy of Carter's original. Its predecessor was erected in 1816 but burned three months later. Undismayed, the people of the town at once built another just like it, finishing it in 1818. The ridgepole is a single pine timber 66 feet long, cradled in the tops of the foot-square, upright king posts. The bell survived the fire but was later cracked in ringing an alarm. When it was recast, three hundred silver dollars were added to its metal in the common belief—probably unjustified—that the tone would be improved. This church was at first used by several denominations jointly, but was finally turned over to the Unitarians as the others withdrew. Reli-

82 Town House, 1818,
Fitzwilliam, New Hampshire

83 Congregational Church, 1820,
Hancock, New Hampshire

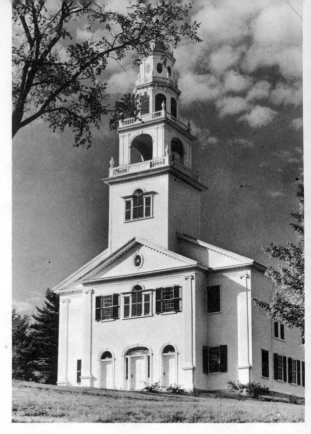

84 United Church, 1820,
Acworth, New Hampshire

gious services were discontinued about 1868, when the house was divided into two stories and taken over entirely for town purposes.

A little farther north is the church in Hancock, New Hampshire, built in 1820 (Fig. 83), in which the columns of Templeton have been replaced by pilasters, but where there is still a common lintel for the three doors. In 1851 the house was moved to its present site from the common across the road and divided into two stories. The upper one, with windows now lengthened, serves as the church auditorium, the lower one as the town hall. The church at Acworth (Fig. 84), also built in 1820, is still farther north. It stands on a hilltop, flanked by school and town hall, all facing on the common—the epitome of the New England village. It has Templeton's steeple, except that the spire is replaced by a dome. The three doors, too, are now quite separate. The two stories into which the house is divided are both used by the church. It was built in the pastorate of Phineas Cooke, sometimes called the "Apostle of New Hampshire," one of the early leaders in the temperance movement.

The farthest north of the "Templeton group" of New Hampshire churches is the one at Newport (Fig. 85), built in 1823. Its steeple repeats in almost every detail that of Acworth,

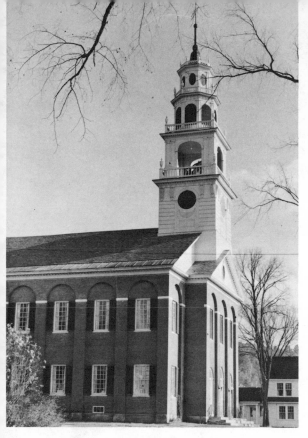

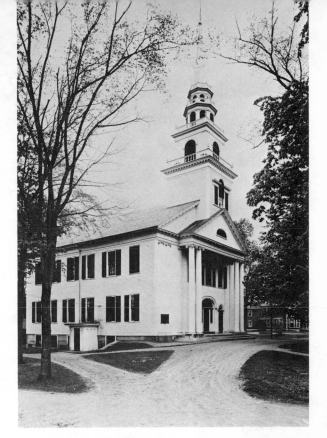

85 *Second Congregational Church, 1823,*
Newport, New Hampshire

86 *Baptist Church, 1825,*
Framingham Center, Massachusetts

fifteen miles to the south. But the main body of the church is of brick and, strangely enough, exactly like that of the brick church at Deerfield, Massachusetts, even to the course of light stone at the level of the window tops in the upper tier. The Deerfield church, however, was built a year later, so the architect at Newport could not have copied it. Probably the design for both came from the same builder's book or, more probably, from Isaac Damon's church at Greenfield, Massachusetts (now long gone), which they both resemble.

There used to be a church of the Templeton type in Dublin, New Hampshire, and—judging by a wood-cut in Barber's book—another in Leominster, Massachusetts. Perhaps there were more. The 1825 Baptist church at Framingham Center, Massachusetts (Fig. 86), closely resembles the one at Templeton. Its architect, Solomon Willard of Boston, must have studied with care the churches at Templeton and Fitzwilliam.

Carter's other much-imitated church, that at Mendon, Massachusetts, built in 1820 (Fig. 87), is a good deal plainer than the one at Templeton. It has a portico of four columns and a much simpler steeple. Within stands the original pulpit on four columns (Fig. 88), probably the work of Carter himself. The parish at

Granby, Massachusetts, evidently admired the Mendon church for they commissioned Carter to build one just like it for them.

The church at North Brookfield, Massachusetts, built in 1823 (Fig. 89), is also very much like the one in Mendon. Whether Carter himself built it we do not know. The one at Holliston, near Mendon, built in 1822, evidently had the same model, but it has been marred somewhat by being raised about four feet, thus changing its proportions. The old church at Milford, adjoining Mendon, was built in 1819. Its steeple is very much like Mendon's, but the rest of the church has been greatly changed. This may actually be the building in which Carter developed his Mendon design, since it is the oldest of the group. A number of other Carter churches have disappeared. The Milford congregation, in a vote of appreciation to Carter, called him "a skillful and faithful architect and an amiable and pious man." Carter does seem to have been a "pious" man in other ways, notably in his attitude toward liquor, one of the problems of his profession. Raising a meetinghouse required very hard physical labor and was usually the occasion for much drinking of rum. Some of Carter's raisings seem to have had a different tone, however. We read that in one of them, as the frame was going up, the workman who rode up on the plate to make it fast, instead of tossing off a tumbler of rum, led the company, from his lofty post, in singing the Doxology!

87 Unitarian Church, 1820,
Mendon, Massachusetts

88 Pulpit, Unitarian Church,
Mendon, Massachusetts

89 Congregational Church, 1823,
North Brookfield, Massachusetts

101

Another man who left his mark on the architecture of New England church buildings was David Hoadley (1774–1839). All his are in Connecticut, his masterpiece being the 1814 United Church on the New Haven Green. However, a less ambitious design by him, better suited to small towns, was adopted in more than a dozen places west of the Connecticut River, though it is not found outside this region. These churches, built by Hoadley or under his influence, have shallow entrance bays with either columns or pilasters. Palladian windows, so common in the Bulfinch, Benjamin and Carter churches, are absent. Their distinctive feature is the steeple, which has two octagonal stages. The lower is the belfry, set on a tower that rises over the porch. The upper is narrower. In both, the openings are arched and often closed by louvers. There are (or originally were) railings or balustrades around the tops of tower, belfry, and upper stage, with urns at the corners. The steeple is crowned by a spire.

There are some variations in this "double octagon" plan, but it forms a very distinct type. Not all such churches were built by Hoadley himself, but four almost certainly were. In most, the pulpit was originally placed at the entrance end of the church, but before many years all had reversed this arrangement. It would be interesting to know what Hoadley had in mind in connection with this feature. Perhaps the idea was to discourage late comers. It was found in a few other New England churches, par-

ticularly in the northern states, but has seldom been retained.

The Hoadley steeple looks much like that of Carter's Templeton church with the square belfry stage removed —a tower, a double octagon and a spire. Carter's steeple was built three years before Hoadley's earliest, but it is too far away to have been a probable model. I would like to suggest another possible source for his design. In the records of St. Paul's Episcopal church in Woodbury, Connecticut, there is a sketch of the steeple, labeled "1785," the year when the church was built. This sketch much resembles the steeples of the Hoadley churches. The church long remained in its original state, as shown by a picture of it on the Woodbury map of 1853. Hoadley was probably familiar with it, for he was brought up in Waterbury, only ten miles away. My suggestion is that he used the St. Paul's steeple as a model for the spires of the churches he built between 1813 and 1830. Tradition has it that this steeple was built or rebuilt in 1812. If so, Hoadley may perhaps have had a hand in the work, since he was then a practicing architect.

Of the churches built certainly, or probably, by Hoadley himself, the earliest is the 1813 structure in Norfolk (Fig. 90). It originally had pilasters on the front, the present portico of four columns having been added in 1927, when the three doors were also redesigned. The interior was renovated in 1846, when the remaining box pews were removed and the windows at the pulpit end closed. The pulpit and lectern are modern, as is the large stained-glass window behind

90 *Congregational Church, 1813,*
Norfolk, Connecticut

them and the elaborately ornamented frame around it. The ceiling has a barrel vault. The Avon church of 1818 (p. 23), built where canal and turnpike once crossed, is particularly lovely in its proportions and its setting. Its bell was cracked in 1865, while celebrating Lee's surrender at Appomattox. The building suffered from a bad fire in 1876, and the top of the steeple was blown off in the hurricane of 1938. It has now been restored.

The church at Milford, Connecticut (Fig. 91), built in 1823, is much like the previous two, but a little larger. It is the first of Hoadley's churches to have columns rather than pilasters on the front. The fanlights over the three doors have been much admired. Within, the ceiling is almost filled with a large dome, found in several other Hoadley churches. In 1868, an addition of 15 feet was made at the rear where the pulpit now stands, having been moved from its original position just inside the doors. The church in Cheshire (Fig. 92), built in 1826, is much like the one in Milford save that the spire is conical instead of eight-sided. The floor of the auditorium, originally sloping down toward the pulpit and doors, has now been leveled. This church has a pleasing situation at the end of the small village green.

These four churches—Norfolk,

91 *Congregational Church, 1823,*
Milford, Connecticut

92 *Congregational Church, 1826, Cheshire, Connecticut*

93 *Congregational Church, 1829, Litchfield, Connecticut*

Avon, Milford, and Cheshire—were certainly, or almost certainly, built by Hoadley. Others are so similar in design that his influence on them seems preponderant. The old church at Southington, adjoining Cheshire, was built in 1830 and is so close to the Cheshire plan that it is evidently a direct copy, though there seems to be no evidence that Hoadley was its architect. Like the churches in Milford and Cheshire, its interior has been reversed.

The Litchfield church (Fig. 93), much like the last five, has had a very unusual history. Built in 1829 to replace the meetinghouse where Lyman Beecher preached for many years, it was moved from its location in the 1870s to make way for a Victorian Gothic structure. Without its steeple and long known as "Colonial Hall," it served various purposes, including the showing of motion pictures. In 1929 something very unusual occurred in Litchfield, for the Victorian church was taken down and the old one brought back to its former place. With the aid of an early photograph and other records, it was restored to its original loveliness, without and within, and there it stands today, facing the green as it did for so many years.

There are several other Connecticut churches which, though not built by Hoadley himself, are in his style. One of these is the First Church of Woodbury, built in 1817 (Fig. 94). When the town decided to erect a new meetinghouse, early in the century, a dispute of even greater vehemence than usual broke out. This finally resulted in the splitting of the congregation and the erection of two buildings, the First Church and the North Church. For those who like old churches the break perhaps was fortunate, for the two buildings, with St. Paul's, built in 1785, give Woodbury the distinction of having three early churches of high architectural merit. The plans for the First Church seem to have been made by one Harman Stoddard. He, like Hoadley, may have used the steeple of nearby St. Paul's for a model. In the vestibule of the church is preserved the gravestone of his ancestor, the Reverend Anthony Stoddard, a true father of his flock, who served not only as minister but as physician, lawyer, and clerk of the probate court.

At Warren is another Hoadley-type church, built in 1818. Its steeple, after being destroyed by lightning in 1891, was replaced. It has now been restored more closely to its original design. South Britain, a village of Southbury, has a Hoadley-type church of 1825 similar to that in nearby Woodbury, though somewhat smaller. The 1826 church in North Cornwall conforms to the general type, but the railings on the steeple are rather heavy in proportion to the whole. Its wrought-iron lighting fixtures, designed for candles and made by a local blacksmith, were installed when the church was restored in 1926. The Hoadley-type church of 1822 in East Canaan today lacks railings on any of the steeple stages, though they probably once were present. The 1824 Congregational church at Sharon (Fig. 95) is the only one of the Hoadley type to be built of brick. There are no pilasters or columns on the porch, but the steeple conforms to type. In 1863,

94 First Congregational Church, 1817, Woodbury, Connecticut

95 Congregational Church, 1824, Sharon, Connecticut

105

the interior of the house was much altered, but some of the early design has now been restored. There is also a Hoadley-type church at Derby (1820).

The church in Guilford, of 1829 (Fig. 96), has a steeple of the Hoadley form but shows the early influence of the Greek Revival in the three front doors. The top of the steeple was blown off in the hurricane of 1938 but promptly restored. The portico has four Ionic columns, with well proportioned capitals. Within, there has been considerable change. The raising of this house was less convivial than in most cases, but somewhat safer, for the sweating workmen were served no

rum. Instead, as the old record has it, "The ladies furnished a good supply of cake which was carried daily onto the grounds, and no accident occurred."

The earliest Congregational church built by Hoadley is the one at Orange, erected in 1810 (Fig. 97). Its appearance is quite different from the churches just described. In its tower and steeple it somewhat resembles the Episcopal church at Bethany, built by Hoadley in 1809. The upper tier of side windows has been lowered a little and two on the front and on each side have been closed. Many changes were made in the interior of this church after 1830.

96 Congregational Church, 1829, Guilford, Connecticut

97 Congregational Church, 1810, Orange, Connecticut

98 Congregational Church, 1812, Northampton, Massachusetts

ISAAC DAMON

Another builder of importance was Issac Damon (1781–1862), who at different times was associated with Ithiel Town and Asher Benjamin. One of his early churches, built in collaboration with Benjamin in 1812, was the large, elaborate structure in Northampton, Massachusetts (Fig. 98). Its high, three-storied porch somewhat resembled those of two Boston churches by Benjamin. This church burned in 1878.

Damon is best known today for the surviving group of churches he built in the Connecticut Valley region of Massachusetts between 1818 and 1830. These have several features in common. The belfry, unlike that of most other Puritan meetinghouses and churches in New England, is in the top of the tower instead of in the first steeple stage above it. As a result, there is a louvered opening on each side of the tower, round-topped and often in a recess. The second feature, a corollary of this, is that the upper steeple stages are "blind," with no openings. Balustrades are small or absent, and none of the Damon churches has a spire.

The first and largest of the group is the 1819 church at Springfield (Fig. 99), facing Court Square. The frieze

99 First Congregational Church, 1818, Springfield, Massachusetts

100 *Congregational Church, 1823,*
Blandford, Massachusetts

101 *Congregational Church, 1824,*
Southwick, Massachusetts

above the four-columned portico, carried around the whole building, is beautifully ornamented. Unlike that of most churches, the front of the tower goes down through the portico to the ground and thus projects part way from the building. Above the whole is a weathercock, four feet from tail to beak, that has swung over this church and its predecessors for two centuries, one of three brought over from London in 1752. In his capacious breast repose some church records. Within, the auditorium has a dome that once was encircled by a band of "ginger-cooky" ornaments—groups of wooden disks alternating with other carvings. Children used to count these when their interest in the sermon lagged. In this church Jenny Lind sang in 1851, and a few years later Louis Kossuth spoke for the freedom of Hungary.

A few miles to the west is the Blandford church, built in 1823 on a hilltop a little distance up from the village (Fig. 100). The Puritans loved sightly spots for their meetinghouses, and when this house was built, before there were so many trees, twelve meetinghouses could be seen from Blandford hill. The upper windows have been lengthened, but this is a typical Damon church. Near the old pulpit recess at the front of the church (the pulpit was later moved to the rear), stands a massive "church viol" with strings a quarter of an inch thick, once the only musical instrument tolerated in a meetinghouse. The township of Southwick makes the small "jog" where Massachusetts projects into Connecticut, as a result of the long-contested boundary dispute, which was finally settled in 1804. Here is a Damon church of 1824 very much like that in Springfield, even to the gilded dome, though the whole is on a smaller scale (Fig. 101).

In the historic village of Old Deerfield is the Unitarian church of 1824 (Fig. 102). This is of brick, with a steeple that shows the traits characteristic of Damon, for it has the belfry in the square tower, blind octagonal stages above, and a dome. It was not built by Damon, however, but by Winthrop Clapp, a student of his. The close resemblance of the body of this church to that of the Second Congregational church of Newport, New Hampshire, has already been mentioned. At Deerfield, the pulpit is still at the vestibule end of the church. Old Deerfield Street is a New England shrine and it is fitting that there should be on it a meetinghouse of this quality. Near the church is the post office, a modern structure built on the general design of the third meetinghouse, that of 1696–1728, which stood near this spot.

The only Damon church in Connecticut that resembles those in Massachusetts is in Simsbury. It was built in 1830 (Fig. 103). As in all his churches, the square tower contains the belfry. Above this are two other square stages, without openings but ornamented on their faces with elaborate carving and thus unlike his other steeples. This church, particularly in its doorways, suggests the style of the Greek Revival, soon to become dominant. Damon's other Connecticut church, also built in 1830, is at East Granby (Fig. 104), and is of a very different design. It is built of stone, and the front has a single door and

*102 Unitarian Church, 1824,
Deerfield, Massachusetts*

*103 Congregational Church, 1830,
Simsbury, Connecticut*

109

104 Congregational Church, 1830,
East Granby, Connecticut

four stone pilasters. The square wooden belfry, set back on the roof, lacks a steeple. In 1856 the galleries were removed, windows changed, and pews and pulpit replaced.

Damon's influence is shown in the design of several other churches in Massachusetts. Notable among these is the one in the little hill town of Shutesbury, built in 1828 (Fig. 105). This has a typical Damon belfry and steeple. The single, heavily paneled door, however, and the four Doric pilasters are of the Greek Revival in character. The steeples on the churches at Chicopee (1826) and East Longmeadow (1828) have some Damon characteristics.

RICHNESS AND VARIETY

Almost every town in New England, in the first quarter of the nineteenth century, either built a church of the new type or achieved the same end by modernizing an earlier meetinghouse. The seven groups that have just been described include only a small number of the churches that were erected. In most cases no architect was employed, and for many even the builder is unknown. These structures show a wide variety of design and often combine features taken from the work of the architects just discussed, or from books. Despite their lack of professional training, the gifted amateurs who built them often produced structures of pleasing individuality and great beauty. Here we shall single out a few that are of particular architectural or historical importance.

The church that is regarded by many as the loveliest of these early

105 Federated Church, 1828,
Shutesbury, Massachusetts

nineteenth-century examples stands on the elm-shaded main street of Old Lyme, Connecticut (Fig. 106). It excels in beauty of design and proportion, and has been photographed and painted innumerable times. Unfortunately, this is not the original building, erected in 1817, for that burned in 1907, but it is an accurate—and fireproof—reproduction. Instead of an entrance bay it has a portico of four Ionic columns, with a square clock-tower above. Over this is a square belfry, an octagonal stage, and a spire, richly ornamented with pilasters and columns. The church was built by Samuel Belcher of Ellington and in some respects suggests the much larger Center Church of New Haven, built three years before.

The 1799 church at Exeter, New Hampshire (Fig. 107), is of interest for several reasons. It was built just at the time of the change from meeting-house to church, but it is not at all the type that we have called Transitional. The long axis is parallel to the street, as in a typical meeting-house, but the entrance, on the middle of the long side, is a more elaborate one than any simple meeting-house ever had. It is in a projecting two-story bay with three doors below and three windows above. Over this rises the tower, with a belfry, lantern and dome.

This church has a hip roof, another unusual feature. Running around the front and sides, between the upper and lower tiers of windows, is a heavy cornice like that at the eaves. In the porch and at the corners, pilasters extend from the ground to this cornice, and from this to the upper one. There

106 Congregational Church, 1817, Old Lyme, Connecticut

107 Congregational Church, 1798, Exeter, New Hampshire

111

are no Palladian windows, save for the pulpit window on the rear wall opposite the entrance. The interior has been much changed and is now in two stories. This church, built by Ebenezer Clifford, bears only a distant resemblance to the work of any other architect and may be an attempt, independent of the ones we have described, to alter the meetinghouse design into that of a church.

Another notable building of the period is the Congregational Church of Dover, New Hampshire (Fig. 108), built in 1829. This is of brick and has windows in round-topped recesses, as did many of Bulfinch's churches. The wooden steeple is beautifully ornamented, with octagonal belfry, octagonal lantern with large windows, tall spire, and strutting weathercock. The whole reminds one somewhat of

the Newburyport steeple, for here are the columns at the angles, each with its little cornice above. George Pendexter and Samuel Drew, the artisans who did the woodwork on the steeple, may have taken some of their ideas from Bulfinch. In the previous church on this spot preached that versatile Yankee patriot and historian, Jeremy Belknap.

Smaller and simpler than the Dover church, but worth mentioning, are three in the western part of New Hampshire. The Congregational church at Lebanon (Fig. 109) is in the general style of the time when it was built (1828), but shows a number of traits that bespeak the work of an architect with original ideas. He was a local man, Ammi Young, who later gained a considerable reputation for his work on public buildings else-

108 Steeple of Congregational Church, 1829, Dover, New Hampshire

109 Congregational Church, 1828, Lebanon, New Hampshire

where. His treatment of the front of the building is unusual in that the portico and the stage above it are narrow, covering only the central of the three doors. The church seems never to have had side galleries, or more than a single row of side windows.

The 1810 Congregational church at Lyme (Fig. 110) is interesting for its steeple—a series of square stages and a dome. The doors are especially well designed. In 1847 the building was divided into two stories. For many years the town used the lower as a town hall, and in the upper, in which the windows were lengthened a little, the church held its services. Beside the church is a row of twenty-seven numbered horse-sheds, well cared for and among the best examples of this vanishing type of New England architecture.

Still farther north stands the delightful little church of Wentworth (Fig. 111), erected by a meetinghouse association in 1828. The square-staged steeple is particularly attractive. The structure is now divided into two stories. For many years the church organization was rather feeble, and in the words of its pastor in 1856, "The state of this community calls loudly for the prayers of God's people in behalf of Zion." It is now thriving as a Community Church, affiliated with the Congregational denomination, and maintains the old meetinghouse well.

The towns in Vermont near the Connecticut River were largely settled by people from the valley farther south who were rather conservative in their politics and their religion. But west of the Green Mountains, where

110 *Congregational Church, 1810,*
Lyme, New Hampshire

111 *Community Church, 1828,*
Wentworth, New Hampshire

the immigrants came from the western counties of Connecticut and Massachusetts, there were many less conservative folk, and even some free-thinkers, rationalists and deists, like Ethan Allen. It is therefore not surprising that the first Unitarian church in the state should have been gathered west of the mountains, in Burlington. Its building, the brick church of 1816 (Fig. 112), is remarkably large and ambitious for a town that then had only 2,000 inhabitants. It has a projecting tower with porches on either side. The commanding steeple has an open belfry, a lantern with eight large windows, and a tall spire. Weakened with the years and damaged by lightning, the original steeple was replaced by a replica in 1945. Peter Banner, the architect of the Park Street Church in Boston, is said to have designed the building and Bulfinch may also have had a hand in it, but it is less of a church and more of a Yankee meetinghouse than anything else these men ever built. The resemblance to Banner's Park Street Church is especially evident in the two porches. The interior is much changed.

The church in Norwich, Vermont (Fig. 113), built in 1817, looks much like one of Hoadley's transplanted far up the Connecticut Valley. Many of the early settlers in this region came from Connecticut. The church has no entrance bay, but a shallow portico of four slender Ionic columns in two pairs projects from the front. The pulpit and pews are not original, but the

112 Unitarian Church, 1816, Burlington, Vermont

original Palladian window back of the pulpit still remains. The church first stood on the common across the road, and was moved to its present site in 1852. Two years later it was lengthened enough for twenty new pews. The school that later became Norwich University (now in Northfield) was a near neighbor for a time, and held its commencements in the church.

In Hartford, Vermont, is an interesting church built in 1828 (Fig. 114). The outside has been little changed. Its tower looks much like those on some of Damon's churches in Massachusetts, in its ornament and its round-topped recesses. The church is also unusual in having only two doors in its entrance bay and a single row of windows. These are very large ones, however. The interior was altered in 1872 and again in 1885.

One of the most unusual of the new churches of this period is the 1816 Unitarian church at Bedford, Massachusetts (Fig. 115). Here the entrance bay is carried up for an extra two stories on either side of what would normally be the free portion of the tower. A high-shouldered, four-storied porch results. The idea for this probably came from two churches designed in Boston by Asher Benjamin when he was a practicing architect there. One was the Old West Church of 1806 (Fig. 116), which is today a library. The other was the Charles Street Church, of 1807. Both these structures are of brick. The West Church has four stories in its porch, the Charles Street Church three. Except for the Bedford meetinghouse this design seems to have had few imitators.

113 Congregational Church, 1817, Norwich, Vermont

114 Second Congregational Church, 1828, Hartford, Vermont

115

117 *Town Hall, 1812,*
Ashfield, Massachusetts

118 *Congregational Church, 1808,*
Hadley, Massachusetts

Much admired for its steeple is the present-day town hall of Ashfield, Massachusetts, built in 1812 (Fig. 117). At first a Congregational church, this was moved to its present location in 1858, and was bought by the town in 1870. It has a Benjamin-like entrance bay, deeper than was common, and an unusually wide and slender-columned octagonal belfry. Colonel John Ames of Marlboro is said to have designed the Ashfield church. The belfry suggests the one at Townsend, Massachusetts, which was added in 1804 to the earlier meetinghouse of 1771 in that town.

A notable church in the Connecticut valley is the one at Hadley, Massachusetts (Fig. 118), built in 1808. The deep entrance bay, with a door in front and one on either side, somewhat suggests that of the Bulfinch church at Pittsfield, but the slender, soaring steeple, with its clock tower, belfry, lantern, and tall spire, is very different. In 1841, after the "Battle of the Streets," when the village had moved some distance eastward from its original site, the church moved also. At this time the interior was divided into two stories and greatly changed. Over the steeple stands the gilded weathercock that came to Hadley from England in 1753. After it was set up on the previous meetinghouse, a young Negro slave, Zeb Prutt, climbed up to the top of the spire, bestrode the rooster, and crowed for all to hear. When in 1786 General Lincoln was pursuing Daniel Shays and his army and came to Hadley on a winter Sabbath, he assembled his three thousand men so that the local minister, standing on a high pulpit of snow, could preach a sermon to them.

At North Amherst, adjoining Hadley, a church was erected in 1826 (Fig. 119) by Winthrop Clapp, who had built the one at Deerfield two years before. There are a number of similarities between the two, especially in the doors and cornice. The usual dissension arose as to location, but this was solved by a strong-minded and well-to-do member, Oliver Dickinson, who put up the money to build the church, chose the site for it, and approved the design. He further stipulated that no Negro should buy a pew or occupy the pulpit. He deeded the pulpit to the minister of the church on condition that it should be used only for the worship of God, and that the preaching should conform to the doctrines set forth in the Westminster Assembly's Briefer Catechism! These provisos were later nullified by Dickinson's son. In 1842 the interior was remodeled and the pulpit moved from the entrance end to the one opposite.

The lovely church in Northboro, Massachusetts, built in 1820, burned in 1945, but the people of Berlin, a few miles to the north, had made it the model for their church, built in 1826. The Berlin church (Fig. 120) has a deep entrance bay and over the steeple is a conspicuous gilded dome. The building was divided into two stories in 1859. The original church organization became Unitarian in 1829, and the orthodox minority withdrew to found their own church. The two united in 1843, separated again in 1871, and finally came together as the Federated Church in 1947.

The organization of what is now the Allin Congregational Church of Dedham, Massachusetts, was the occa-

119 Congregational Church, 1826, North Amherst, Massachusetts

119

120 Federated Church, 1826, Berlin, Massachusetts

sion of a bitter controversy and a historic lawsuit, a knowledge of which is important if we are to understand the break between the Congregational and the Unitarian churches which resulted in the erection of so many new church buildings of the former denomination in the early nineteenth century. In 1818 the majority of the *parish* of this church were Unitarians, but the majority of the *church members* were Congregationalists. They disagreed on the choice of a new minister. As the result of a suit brought by the church, the court, interpreting the Massachusetts constitution of 1780, decided that the parish rather than the church members owned the church building and all other property. The Congregational (Trinitarian) members then withdrew and founded the present Congregational church, later named the Allin church after the first minister in Dedham. This decision served as a precedent, so that in most of the old churches in eastern Massachusetts the Unitarian majority took over the church property and the Trinitarians were forced to build new structures for their worship. In a few cases (such as West Bridgewater, Westford and Berlin, Massachusetts, and Belfast, Maine) the two churches, after many years, united.

The Allin church (Fig. 121), built in 1819, is notable for its deep entrance bay with doors on the three sides, the side doors each having a

*122 New North Church, 1807,
Hingham, Massachusetts*

121

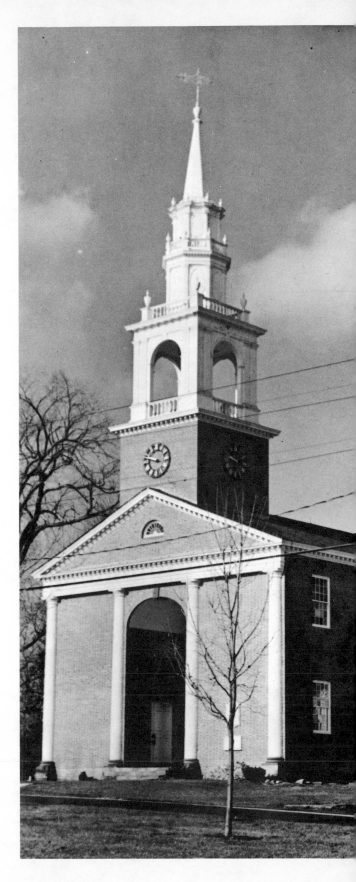

123 *Congregational Church, 1824,*
Marblehead, Massachusetts

small portico. The interior has been much changed.

The members of the New North church of Hingham, Massachusetts, withdrew from the Old Ship in 1807 after a disagreement over the choice of a minister, and erected a new church (Fig. 122) close to the old one. It is an impressive building. The eight-columned cupola with rounded dome suggests Bulfinch's work, and he may have had a hand in the design, though the architect is not certainly known.

The ivy-covered Congregational church at Marblehead, Massachusetts (Fig. 123), is different from most others in this state in being built of stone and in having no side galleries. Above the three-doored front the tower carries a belfry and windowed lantern, as do so many seaport steeples. Over this is a dome with a vane in the shape of a fish, as becomes a fishermen's town. The pulpit and pews were eventually removed but the pulpit has now been restored. After it had become unsafe, the front wall was taken down, in 1886, and completely rebuilt.

The brick church in the historic town of Lebanon, Connecticut (Fig. 124), was built in 1807 from plans drawn by Colonel John Trumbull, after an unusually bitter controversy as to where to put it. It is unusual in that the single front door is set in a deep, vaulted recess. The interior had square pews and a pulpit on columns. In 1875 the building was divided into

124 *Congregational Church, 1807,*
Lebanon, Connecticut

123

two stories by a floor at the gallery level. After almost total destruction in the 1938 hurricane, the church was restored to its original state, thanks to the efforts of a multitude of friends.

The Congregational church at Truro (Fig. 125), near the tip of Cape Cod, was built in 1827. It is unusually long, and one end of it is used as a vestry. On the front is a deep bay, and the two doors entering the church are on either side of this, in the main building. In the early days there was always an unusually large congregation on the Sunday in spring before the "bankers" left for their long and perilous season of fishing on the Grand Banks. The church is on a hill, to serve as a landmark for ships. Until about 1860 the town was allowed to use the galleries of the church for town meetings. In 1955 the church was thoroughly repaired, and at that time a reproduction of the old wallpaper, that had been on the walls for over a century, was hung.

In Stonington, Connecticut, the "Road Church" of 1829 (Fig. 126) is on the old Pequot Path, later the Post Road. It stands on Agreement Hill, near the original town center, facing *away* from the road. This is one of the simplest churches of its period, and somewhat suggests the one at Chaplin, Connecticut, with its perfectly plain front, single door, and small belfry. Below is a basement, built by the town and long used as the town hall. The pulpit is next the entrance, and the floor slopes up from it to the rear.

North Guilford, Connecticut, is a quiet hilltop hamlet, the most conspic-

uous features of which are its two old churches and large cemetery. The Congregational church of 1813 (Fig. 128) was built by Captain Abraham Coan, who designed several others in this part of the state. Unusual features are the presence of the belfry in the tower, and the open, domed cupola above it. The interior was much altered in 1855. A commentary on the times is the vote of the society, shortly after the church was finished, "that those who chaw tobacco be requested to furnish themselves with a spitting box provided they chaw in the new meeting house."

Stone churches are relatively few in New England, but Plainfield, Connecticut, has a handsome one (Fig. 129), built in 1816 by Ithiel Town. On the front and tower the stones are in regular courses; elsewhere they are laid at random. Around the three front doors is a line of raised blocks. The church was divided into two stories in 1849.

Another stone church, built on a hilltop in New Preston Hill, Connecticut, in 1824 (Fig. 127), has masonry of great beauty. The fanlights over the front doors have interlaced sash-bars. Inside the church there has been little change, and the pulpit is still at the

125 Congregational Church, 1827,
Truro, Massachusetts

126 Congregational Church, 1829
Stonington, Connecticut

127 Old Congregational Church, 1824,
New Preston Hill, Connecticut

128 Congregational Church, 1813,
North Guilford, Connecticut

129 Congregational Church, 1816,
Plainfield, Connecticut

125

127

129

128

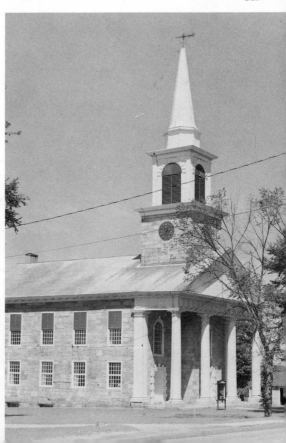

130 *Congregational Church, 1820,*
Kingston, Rhode Island

131 *"Round Church," 1812,*
Richmond, Vermont

entrance end. In 1962 the church was repaired and rededicated.

The meetinghouse of 1805 built for the Congregational church in Rocky Hill, Connecticut, is an excellent example of artistic craftsmanship, though we may regret the replacement of the original spire by a Greek Revival belfry in 1843. The architect is unknown. Within, the auditorium is also of unusual charm, especially the columns, gallery face, and Palladian window behind the pulpit. The original box pews were replaced in 1842 and a new pulpit installed, but otherwise there have been few changes in the interior.

In a few churches of this period, notably those at Bridgewater and Orange, Connecticut, and at Kingston, Rhode Island, the tower projects for its full height from the front, much as in many Episcopal churches. The Kingston church of 1820 (Fig. 130) is also unusual in having its belfry in the tower.

One of the most remarkable of the early nineteenth-century churches is the "Round Church" of Richmond, Vermont, built in 1812 (Fig. 131). It is sixteen-sided. The building has three doors and two rows of windows, a window to each side. The interior is almost unchanged. A gallery extends almost three-fourths of the way around the auditorium. The pews are square. Everything is now painted white except the excellent pulpit, which is supported on four columns. Five denominations—Congregationalists, Baptists, Methodists, Universalists, and Christians—erected this church jointly. William Rhodes was the builder, and apparently the design was his, though where he got it we do not know. Religious services were discontinued in 1880 and the town has since owned the building and used it for town meetings and other purposes.

THE CITY CHURCHES

Most of the nineteenth-century churches that have been discussed so far were built in towns and villages, and the majority were relatively simple in design and ornament. In the *cities* of New England, however, where wealth was greater, there were built soon after 1800 a number of large and impressive Congregational and Unitarian churches. They are to be found in Boston, Hartford, New Haven, Providence and Portland.

Boston's Park Street Church, built in 1809 (Fig. 132), is an outstanding example. Henry James once called it "the most impressive mass of brick and mortar in America." The occasion for its erection was a vigorous attempt by orthodox Congregationalism to meet the Unitarian challenge on its own grounds. The church is built of brick on a slope at what was then the north end of the Common, and its tall, slim steeple still dominates the area. The architect was Peter Banner, whose only other church in New England, the one at Burlington, Vermont, we have already discussed. At some time the roof was raised several feet, as can be seen by the brickwork, and the side walls were probably extended forward, making the present rather awkward angle with the tower. The interior has also been much changed,

132 Park Street Church, 1809, Boston, Massachusetts

but the church is still a beautiful structure. "Brimstone Corner," as its site is called, derives not from the preaching of hell-fire here but from the storing of a large quantity of sulphur under the church during the war of 1812. It was in this church that "America," was first sung publicly, on July 4, 1832. William Lloyd Garrison delivered a famous antislavery address here in 1839.

Hartford was the first town settled in Connecticut (1636), and its First Church is therefore the oldest ecclesiastical organization in the state. The present brick house (Fig. 133), its fourth home, was begun in 1806 and dedicated the next year. David Wadsworth, a prominent and wealthy member of the society, is generally believed to have been the designer. Over the square tower with its double cornice is a square belfry with columns at each corner, then an octagonal stage with sixteen columns, another with eight, and an octagonal drum with a short, conical peak. The effect of the whole is somewhat heavy and "over-columned." Inside, the pulpit and galleries have twice been lowered, the pews have been replaced, and the ceiling changed. The interior is imposing, and the gallery columns, extending from floor to ceiling, are particularly handsome. In the quiet "burying lott" behind the church, dating from 1640, lie many of the notable early citizens of the town, among them the Reverend Thomas Hooker, its first minister, whom many regard

133 First Congregational Church, 1806, Hartford, Connecticut

as the father of American democracy. His were the ideas in the "Fundamental Orders" of Connecticut, the first written constitution in the world.

The Second Church of Hartford (Fig. 134) was organized in 1670 as the result of doctrinal differences. The present building, its third home, was finished in 1827. Built of brick by General William Hayden, it is a structure not greatly different from the First Church. Corinthian columns support the portico and the sides are ornamented by brick pilasters. This church is unusual in having a single row of windows on each side instead of two. Much of the interior was changed after a serious fire in 1884, but the Corinthian columns supporting the gallery and ceiling remain.

The three old churches on the New Haven Green, (the two mentioned here, and Trinity, p. 188), form a group that has long been admired. All were built within approximately two years of one another, and in the midst of the War of 1812. Most of the oak timbers for their frames were floated down the Connecticut River and had to be brought through the British blockade. Permission was readily given for the first two shipments since Commodore Hardy, who commanded the blockade, when assured that they were for the construction of churches, said he made no war on religion. When the third lot appeared, however, he is said to have exclaimed, "Don't these damned Yankees do anything but build churches?"

134 Second Congregational Church, 1827, Hartford, Connecticut

Center Church, the middle one of the three, goes back to the first days of the settlement in 1638, when New Haven was a theocracy, and town and church were the same organization. Not until 1664, when New Haven joined the Connecticut colony, were citizens allowed to vote without regard to their membership in this church. The present brick structure (Fig. 135) was built in 1814 by Ithiel Town (1784–1844), one of the foremost architects and engineers of his day. He was an associate of Isaac Damon, but Damon had no part in designing this building. A plan purchased from Asher Benjamin, with whom Town had worked in Boston, seems to have formed the basis of the church design, though Town probably modified it somewhat. This building has often been compared to St. Martins-in-the-Fields in Trafalgar Square, London, built by Wren's student James Gibbs. Both churches are distinctive in having a balustrade above the roof cornice.

The wide portico of Center Church is supported by Doric columns and its frieze ornamented in part with bucrania, or conventionalized bulls' skulls, architectural ornaments that go back to the days of animal sacrifices. The face of the pediment has an elaborate carved ornament. Careful measurement shows that the columns of the steeple are inclined inward slightly to produce an illusion of greater height. There is a tradition

135 Center Church, 1814, New Haven, Connecticut

that the spire was built on the ground and lifted up through the tower to its final position—a remarkable feat of engineering, if it was so done. The pulpit and gallery have been lowered and the original pews removed. In the recent restoration the modern stained glass windows, save for the fine one behind the pulpit, were replaced by clear glass.

Until 1895 the Yale Commencements were held in this building, and it was the scene of many other public gatherings. On the Green behind it is the town's first burying ground where are interred the four or five thousand townspeople who died before the opening of the Grove Street Cemetery in 1797. The present church, erected a little behind its predecessor, was built over a part of this old burying ground, and in its crypt stand the 135 head-stones that were in this portion of the ground. The others were removed to the Grove Street Cemetery in 1821.

Beside Center Church stands David Hoadley's masterpiece, the brick United Church of 1815 (Fig. 136). This organization left the First Church during the time of the Great Awakening, in 1742, and later divided into two churches. However, in 1796 these came together again, hence the present name of the church. The design of the building, and especially of the steeple, have been much admired. It is quite different from Center Church and somewhat lower, so that the two

136 United Church, 1815, New Haven, Connecticut

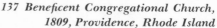

do not compete but complement each other. The domed interior was considerably altered in 1849, when the gallery was lowered and the pulpit recess added. In this church, Henry Ward Beecher preached in 1855 to eighty men who were about to set out for Kansas to join the antislavery forces of John Brown. The congregation presented each man with a Sharps rifle and a Bible.

In Providence, Rhode Island, stands the Beneficent Congregational Church, or "Paddy Wilson's Meeting House," built in 1809 (Fig. 137). Its dome makes it unique among New England churches. James Wilson came to Providence from Ireland in 1791 as a young minister and a disciple of John Wesley. In time he became the pastor of this church, then called the Second Congregational. When it was necessary, in 1809, to build a new home for his church, Wilson, recalling the features of the Dublin customhouse of his youth, determined that his new meetinghouse should also be of stone and have a large dome and a portico of four columns. Beneath its veneer of brick, the building *is* of stone. Most of the bricks were English, brought over as ship's ballast, but there were not quite enough of these and the brickwork had to be pieced out with lighter-colored local bricks. On the west side of the church can be seen the line that separates the two. The portico is a Greek Revival reconstruction of the original.

The First Unitarian Church of Providence (Fig. 138), designed by

139 First Parish Church, 1825, Portland, Maine

John Holden Greene, is of stone and was built in 1816. Its rather elaborate design somewhat resembles that of Bulfinch's New South Church of Boston, no longer standing. In its belfry hangs the largest bell ever cast in Paul Revere's foundry.

The First Parish Church in downtown Portland, Maine, built in 1825 (Fig. 139), is unusual not only because it is built of granite but because no professional architect had a hand in planning it. The tower projects fully from the front, and on each side of this, below the roof line, is a small porch so that the effect is of an entrance bay with three doors. The wide octagonal belfry holds a bell of more than two tons. Over the auditorium is a broadly arched ceiling from which hangs a large crystal chandelier. Part of the chain supporting this is a British cannon ball fired into the predecessor of this church, "Old Jerusalem," during the bombardment of the town in 1775. The interior of the present building was much altered in 1853 but partly restored later.

These city churches represent the highest expression of the possibilities that became available to builders when the simpler, more standardized meetinghouse design of the eighteenth century was abandoned and the wider architectural resources of the English Renaissance, expressed in the new Federal style, found popular support. Even today the influence of these admirable buildings on American church design is still evident.

133

Six   Greeks, Goths, and Vandals

IN the third decade of the nineteenth century the people of New England began to move down from their hills to their valleys. Sea-borne commerce had been ruined by "Mr. Madison's war," fishing was confined to the sea-coast, and agriculture did not present opportunities enough for her energetic population. So began New England's long career as the manufacturing center of the early Republic, a career that was to make her wealthy and powerful, but which was in time to alter profoundly not only her traditions and mode of life but the very character of her population.

Water power was the only driving force known in those days, hence on almost every stream were built the little factories to which flocked men and women from the surrounding upland farms to exchange the drudgery of agriculture for the affluence of wages. The downward migration began not long before Lafayette made his triumphal tour through the land in 1824 and 1825, and when French clothing, cooking, customs, and consequently names had become popular everywhere. The new villages commonly took the name of their chief mill owner plus the French suffix *ville*: Collinsville, Whitinsville, Fitchville, etc.

Again a decisive change in church architecture coincides with the onset of a change in New England life. In the four or five years after 1825 there were built the last of those Federal churches in which appeared the lightness and grace of the English Renaissance, inspired by Wren and Gibbs and their followers, and coming to its late development in New England. Perhaps if life had remained as it used to be, the craftsman-architects of New England would not have ceased to build these churches. The fashion had changed, however. Beginning in the southern and central Atlantic states there appeared a growing enthusiasm for the styles of classical antiquity. This soon captured the imagination of architects throughout the young

136

now set back entirely on the roof and is often somewhat anomalous in character. The columned portico, usually present, is the dominant feature of the design, and commonly extends entirely across the building's front. The doors are square, heavy, and deeply paneled. The capitals of column and pilaster are usually of the Doric order. Wherever there is a frieze, on sides or front, it is much wider than in the earlier type.

As in the previous evolutionary changes in church design, there are transitional structures which combine the new style with the old. A notable example is the Center Church of Meriden, Connecticut (Fig. 140), built in 1830 by Sidney Stone, a New Haven architect. Its truly lovely steeple is reminiscent of that over the United Church of New Haven. Projecting well out in front of it, however, is a portico under which any Greek would have felt at home, upheld by six sturdy Doric columns and leading to three heavy doors.

Other churches attempted, as did this one, to combine the new style with the old; but most later ones frankly adopted the Greek Revival design. In some cases the effect is one of strength and simple dignity. This is true of the "Stone Temple" of the First Church of Quincy, Massachusetts (p. 26), beneath which Presidents John Adams and John Quincy Adams are buried. It was erected in 1828 with Alexander Parris as its architect. The granite of which the church was built, presented to the parish by John Adams,

nation. Public buildings and many private houses took on the character of pillared Greek temples. In church design, architects had a problem that they did not face in most public buildings, that of putting a steeple on a temple. Sometimes this was satisfactorily solved and the result was an attractive church. Often, however, the combination of the two different elements produced an incongruous effect.

The style of this Greek Revival did not begin to influence church architecture greatly in New England until about 1825. The churches of the next two decades are plain, and devoid of much of the wealth of ornament lavished on their predecessors, a natural result of imitating, in wood, the severity of stone. As becomes temple covering, the roof is flatter. The steeple is

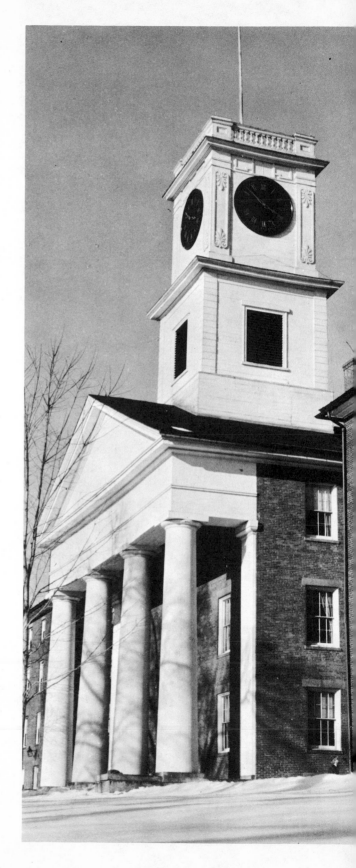

makes its resemblance to a temple less
artificial than if wood had been used.

Another example is the three-storied
Johnson Chapel at Amherst College,
built, in 1826, of brick (Fig. 141).
The builder was Isaac Damon. The
wooden steeple, set far back on the
roof, bears his characteristic features
—belfry in the lower stage, and above
this a stage without openings. The old
chapel occupied the two upper stories,
at the rear. Many smaller churches
were built or rebuilt in the Greek
Revival style. Typical is the Congregational Church at Burlington, Connecticut (Fig. 142). This was first built
in 1804, but in 1836 it was taken
down, moved, and rebuilt in the
Greek Revival style. The steeple with
its two square stages is typical of such
structures. Some small churches of this
period lack the portico. In them, the
influence of the Greek Revival appears chiefly in the use of Doric pilasters somewhere in façade or steeple,
and in the square steeple stages.

The Greek Revival church architecture is associated with the breaking
up of the old village life which had
been the heart of the New England
tradition. The white temple-churches
heralded the end of the Puritan culture. In the period since 1830, there
has been no other turning point comparable to this beginning of industrialism in New England. The changes that
occurred were in one direction—
toward more mills, greater production,
wider markets, bigger bank accounts.
As for the children of the Puritans,
they never took enthusiastically to

sance, but longed for a return to the gloomy splendor of the middle ages. Especially in the design of the church was their influence felt. For what other style, they asked, could ever be so inherently conducive to prayer and meditation as that long consecrated to religion in the ancient churches of Europe? And so lightness and grace, the well-turned molding and the ornament so loved by Federal designers, gave way to narrow windows, dark interiors, and the omnipresence in door, window, and vaulted roof of the pointed Gothic arch.

The Gothic has been consistently and skillfully applied to the design of Episcopal churches in New England almost from the beginning, and no one can question the beauty and appropriateness of this style in such exemplary structures as Trinity Church, New Haven. It cannot be harmonized, however, with the traditional design of the Puritan meetinghouse. One's quarrel with the Victorian Goths is that they often endeavored to force their fashion into incongruous molds. Pointed windows on a little wooden church do not make it Gothic, nor does an application of burnt umber to unpainted pine recapture the mysterious gloom of the Middle Ages. Worse still, some zealots, seduced by the vogue for fretwork and "gingerbread" —so easy to achieve in wood—incorporated in some of the worst of their buildings the products of the Victorian jigsaw.

After the Gothic invasion gradually spent itself in the seventies and eighties of the last century, no single ec-

factory life, and were soon replaced there by labor from other lands. Today even the farms of New England are gradually being redeemed by land-hungry folk of other racial stocks. These changes have made New England life, especially in its three southern states, more complex and cosmopolitan. No longer can we look to church design for an interpretation of the character and thought of the people.

With the onward sweep of industrialism, the beginning of the alien immigration, and the influx of new ideas and modes of life, even the slender hold on past tradition which the Greek Revival maintained was broken, and temple-churches gradually ceased to be built. Instead, soon after the beginning of the Victorian era, New England was invaded by architectural Goths who would have none of the classicism of the Renais-

clesiastical style distinguised New England. In recent years there have been hopeful signs of a return to the best examples of early work, and new churches may be seen here and there which embody the true spirit of the Golden Age. Better still, a few brave souls, like the people of Litchfield, Connecticut, have actually removed a Victorian building and restored the beauty of an earlier meetinghouse that still was standing; but the opportunities for such a happy consummation are more abundant than the will or the means to bring them to pass.

For Goths we may have respect but not for Vandals. It is one thing to succumb to a prevailing fashion in the design and erection of a new building; it is quite another to destroy a thing of beauty that already exists in an attempt to wrench it into a style that is foreign to its entire spirit. Such, alas, has been the fate of many a New England church. First the old square-towered meetinghouses were converted into churches; then Federal churches were altered into steepled temples. These changes one may tolerate, if they were sympathetically accom-

plished. But when an enthusiastic committee, fortified by a little money and a mandate from the parish to "modernize the church," laid desecrating hands on a lovely old meeting-house, stripped off its columns, lengthened its windows and gave to them false pointed tops; then stained its interior, put in curving slips of golden oak, a jigsaw pulpit and sharp-backed chairs; finally frescoing the plastered walls in curlicues and painting on them Scriptural texts in Old English lettering . . . this was desecration.

The sins of the fathers have indeed been visited upon the children; but after about the second or third generation these children, if they possess the means and opportunity, have usually shown a commendable desire to restore the glories of Israel. It is perhaps too much to say that every old church is now safe from the spoiler; but certainly any attempt to lay hands upon one for purposes other than genuine restoration is likely to raise such a clamor that sagacious committees with their eyes on contributions are no longer likely to make this mistake.

Seven   Modernizing the Meetinghouse

MUCH as we may regret the alterations that have changed the appearance of many of the old meetinghouses and churches, perhaps we should be thankful that so many of them have survived at all. The Puritan was no conservative. "Change and decay in all around" he saw. A permanent spiritual order in the midst of a transient and mutable world was his conception of things. The past of New England was neither as long nor as venerable to him as it has become to us; and we must forgive the ruthless way in which he laid hands upon his places of worship, tearing them down or building them over to conform to need or fashion. The taste of the early modernizers was often good, as may be seen in many of its results; but as the years went by, successive attempts to "improve" the meetinghouse were less happy.

In addition to the changes obviously resulting from the appearance of new fashions, and less obviously from the need to keep a building in repair, we discover others reflecting the modification in religious practices that began to be felt after the first quarter of the nineteenth century. In the early days, religious education was not a formal matter but the natural result of a religious atmosphere and family devotions at home, and the constant attendance of young people at church. In time, this proved to be insufficient, and Sunday Schools were established. The American Sunday School Union was organized in 1824, and before the middle of the century practically every church in New England had such a school. The church building itself was hardly suited to the informality of a Sunday School. Other activities upon which the church now embarked— "sociables," suppers, sales, and so on— also required accommodations that could not be provided in the sanctuary itself. Despite the austere Puritan

tradition, the sanctuary was beginning to be regarded with a feeling of some reverence.

These needs were met in two ways. The more affluent churches erected parish houses or vestries nearby and usually connected with the church building. A few lifted the original structure and built a new story beneath it. More commonly, and more unfortunately from an architectural point of view, the auditorium was cut into two stories of which the upper one, with windows usually lengthened and gallery removed, became the church proper, while the lower one gave space for Sunday School, social hall, and kitchen.

To trace the history of such changes in a building can be a fascinating pursuit. The devotee will find some meetinghouse that has escaped fire and decay, but upon which one committee after another has laid its hands until the original character is all but extinguished. Equipped with camera and flashlight, tape and compass, he

will effect an entrance wherever he can, and clamber through lofts and up creaking belfry stairs to examine frame and truss and boarding. He will measure window spacing, note the places where clapboards have been patched (Fig. 143) that indicate former window or door openings, and discover extensions of plate, sill, or cornice. Old window frames and pews stored in the attic will tell him much, and occasionally he may discover somewhere a picture of the meetinghouse in its earlier days. Such a reconstruction of the past will usually mean far more than an exercise in puzzle solving, for these alterations were not the result of perversity or caprice but were determined by changes in community life which the evolving meetinghouse faithfully portrayed.

In his search for the architectural history of a given house, the student will use every source of information that may provide a clue. Most important, of course, are the church records themselves. If well kept, they will at least provide for him the dates when various structural changes were made. But these records have often been destroyed, and even when extant, may be difficult to find. The policy pursued by the Connecticut State Library and other centers in gathering and preserving the records of individual towns and churches is to be commended. The records, however, often prove disappointing. There was an astonishing diversity among parish clerks, not only in the legibility of their handwriting—often an important factor—but in the zeal and thoroughness with which they performed their duties. The name of the builder is sometimes given, but rarely that of the man who drew the plans. In the case of alterations made from time to time, the records usually describe the changes only in a most general way, if at all. However, the total material of this sort is enormous, and most of it has not yet been adequately studied.

Second to church records as a source of information are the numerous church and town histories and memorial volumes published during the last hundred years or more. There is hardly a town in New England which at some time or other has not had an anniversary celebration, some account of which found its way into print. Such volumes are treasure troves for students of meetinghouse history, for in them the gist of the old records is often given, together with a wealth of information from other sources. They must be used with some caution, however, for their authors were rarely competent historians, and often accepted tradition as fact. Contemporary sketches or plans of the meetinghouses themselves may be given in these publications, as well as reproductions of the few early pictures that have been preserved. Local historical and antiquarian societies often have pictures and particular information with regard to the early meetinghouses in their towns, or as to the original condition of those still standing. For more recent changes the memories of elderly townspeople may often prove valuable.

The most useful source of information, and final arbiter in every case, is the old building itself, for the mute evidence it provides, if read aright, will usually tell the main points in the story of the successive changes to which it has been subjected. Certain similarities are found in most of these changes. For example, when a meetinghouse of the eighteenth century was altered to the church form it was usually turned 90 degrees so that the new door or doors, now at the gable end, faced the road as once did the old entrance on the long side. Where a tower was present, the front of the building was usually built out around both sides of it, flush with the tower front. To this, in most cases, a shallow entrance bay was added. Within, the gallery was changed to conform to the new positions of door and pulpit. In most cases the pulpit was lowered, in turn requiring the lowering of the gallery, so that the minister could be seen from it. This often made it necessary to lower the upper tier of windows, or at least to drop them down a little at the bottom. If the building was divided into two stories these windows almost always were lengthened. Alterations to the Greek Revival type were usually not so radical, and most frequently included the addition of columns, either in a portico or in front of a recess, together with a widening of the frieze, a reduction in ornament, and a plainer design for the steeple.

With these basic facts in mind, let us consider some specific cases.

On the west side of the highway as it passes through the village of South Hingham, Massachusetts, stands a

144

is also unusual. On the south side, as pictured, the two windows nearest the rear are close together. Then comes one which is well separated from its neighbors, then a pair close together, and finally a single one set well apart. On either side of the window between the two closely spaced pairs, and above it, the clapboards are evidently newer than the rest, and we find that the patch-marks outline the position of a large opening, now closed. We have now found the location of the original front door on the broad south side. Since the door was here, there should have been a pulpit window in the middle of the other side. We walk around the building and discover the "scar" in the clapboards exactly where it should be.

The credibility of the date over the door has thus been enhanced. But what about the entrance bay? Here, again, the side windows help us. The ones nearest the front are well-separated from the rest and in line with the tower over the roof. The windows on the front of the church are also noteworthy, for the upper ones are set well below those on the side. Our conclusion is that the porch and the whole front of the meetinghouse were built out around the base of a square tower. This deduction is supported by an examination of the main cornice, for on both sides of the building this is clearly pieced out by an addition at the front, and the joining place can readily be seen as a break in the boards just in line with the rear face of the square tower. Everything in

church which seems typical of the first quarter of the nineteenth century (Fig. 144). Its tower, set well back over the roof, surmounts a simple pilastered bay into which lead three doors, and over all rises a Benjamin-type belfry. However, the legend over the front door reads, "Erected 1742."

Which tells us the correct age of the church, its appearance or the legend? Looking at the roof, we observe that its pitch is steeper than it should be in a meetinghouse of the Golden Age. This does not prove an early date but certainly points strongly to it. Better evidence is to be found in the windows. The upper tier at the sides extends close up under the eaves, an almost infallible sign of eighteenth century construction. Their spacing

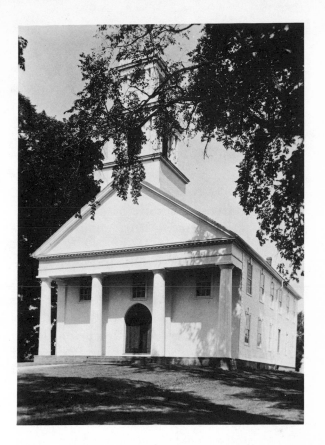

145 *Congregational Church, 1794, Windsor, Connecticut*

front of that, including the bay itself, is thus doubtless of more recent construction than the main part of the building.

The interior of the church bears out this interpretation of its history, for the gallery, which must have been completely changed by the new position of the front door, is evidently relatively modern, as is the pulpit. The framing of the roof in front clearly agrees with the evidence of the external markings, for the timbers of the tower can readily be distinguished from the more recent work on either side of it. The frame of the tower, too, evidently continued down through the porch. There is a suggestion that the tower was built at a later date than the rest of the frame.

We now conclude that there was at first a small, simple meetinghouse with an entrance on the broad south side; that a square belfry tower was added at the east end, built sometime before such towers went out of fashion about 1800; and finally that sometime before 1830, there occurred the construction of the new front, bay, and belfry, the closing of the door on the broad side, and the transfer of the pulpit to the west end. In the case of this South Hingham church we can put our conclusions to the test against its recorded history. The church records show that the meetinghouse was indeed built in 1742 as a simple towerless structure; that in 1792 a tower was added; and that in 1829 there were made the precise alterations in the door, pulpit, gallery, and other re-

145

spects that our direct examination has indicated.

As one goes up the river road from Hartford, Connecticut, toward Windsor he sees on a terrace just above the bridge a white Congregational church (Fig. 145). A Greek Revival building, the observer will say at first, looking at the heavy Doric columns that support its portico. The square belfry, and square, columned stage above are identical with those of a dozen Greek steeples in towns nearby.

But as one strolls back through the old burying ground and looks more closely at this church, the suspicion begins to grow that here, once more, is an old meetinghouse in disguise. The roof is high and steep, not like the low temple coverings that the churches of the 1830s sought to copy. The wide frieze that should be found below a Greek cornice encircles the portico but is absent on the rest of the building. The front of the church is of board sheathing but the sides are covered with clapboards, and the quoin blocks on the corners do not extend around to the front. The character of the interior seems to correspond to the age of portico and steeple.

Hopefully, we climb the stairs from gallery to loft. Here, as in the South Hingham church, the framing tells the story. The heavy timbers end with the front wall of the main church showing that the portico is a later addition. In the middle of the front are traces of a tower, now gone. This looks like an eighteenth century meetinghouse to which a Greek portico and a steeple have been added. But in an old meetinghouse there should have been a door on one long side and a pulpit window opposite. Here we are baffled. There are two tiers of six windows on either side, an even number, whereas in the eighteenth-century meetinghouses almost invariably there was an odd number in the upper tier, the middle one being over the door. Our perplexity increases when we find not the slightest indication of the former existence of a door or pulpit window on either of the sides. Window scars there are at the rear, but the old side clapboards are evidently quite undisturbed.

Does Barber's *Historical Collections* by any chance show this meetinghouse in its description of Windsor? We open the book and find a woodcut (Fig. 146) of the meetinghouse as it looked in 1835. No Grecian pillars

then but a square tower capped by a simple belfry. Thus far our suspicions are justified, but what of the side entrance? Not a sign of it. Here are the two rows of six windows just as they exist today. The only door in the picture is at the front, through the tower. Only one answer is now possible. This must have been a Transitional church, built in those few years just before or just after 1800 when the door on the side of the meetinghouse had been abandoned but the square-towered design still persisted. The records confirm this, for our church was built in 1794. The tower was removed and the Greek Revival portico and steeple were added in 1844.

When an old meetinghouse was patched up, altered, or all but rebuilt in response to the demands of necessity or fashion, the results were sometimes unfortunate, but sometimes

147

reasonably happy, as in the two churches just described. Only when the structure was completely reconstructed, and when this was done by a builder of taste and judgment, did a wholly satisfying result usually ensue. Two such cases deserve mention here.

On the Connecticut River about fifteen miles north of the Massachusetts line is the quiet town of Westmoreland, New Hampshire, once a place of considerable importance when the river carried traffic through the heart of New England. In 1767 the town hopefully built a meetinghouse some distance up from the valley, in the northern part of the township; but "meetinghouse politics" persisted, and twelve years later, even in the midst of the war, the citizens voted to move the house two or three miles to the south. Accordingly, it began its arduous journey uphill and down.

Perhaps the building was taken down and moved in pieces. Tradition has it that when the movers had brought their freight up the particularly steep and crooked bit of road entering the village of Westmoreland Hill (now Park Hill), they were tired and thirsty and a bit discouraged, for their destination was still some distance to the south. Grasping the possibilities in the situation, the village tavern-keepers offered the moving crew a barrel of rum if they would place the meetinghouse permanently on the knoll above the green. The bargain was struck and there the house remains, though the taverns vanished

long ago and the busy village has dwindled to a few old houses under the trees around the common.

But the white-columned meetinghouse (Fig. 147) that now dominates the ancient village is hardly the structure that found its way to this site in 1779. It was doubtless a simple pitched-roof house then. The records speak of its "porches"; probably these were at the doors on three sides. The original frame exists in the present church, but in 1824 the old building was so completely altered by the addition of twenty feet at one end (now to be the front), including portico and steeple, that an essentially new church resulted. In its two pairs of columns and the common lintel over the three doors, this reminds one of Carter's churches at Templeton and

Fitzwilliam. The steeple is also much the same as theirs save that it lacks the upper stage and the spire. Even the little elliptical window in the pediment is present. This church has Tuscan capitals, however, whereas Carter's are Ionic, and the Westmoreland church throughout is simpler in its ornamentation. The only sign today that it was originally a meetinghouse of the older type is the position of its windows, close up under the eaves. The upper row, incidentally, was lengthened when the church was divided into two stories in 1853.

Who was responsible for the design of the reconstructed church we do not know, but it was no vandal's hand that wrought the changes here. This building must evidently be added to the list of beautiful ones that trace their origin, directly or indirectly, to the genius of Elias Carter. Built in discord, dragged ignominiously over the hills, and deposited upon its present foundation by craft and greed, this church at last became one of the loveliest in New England.

Almost as fortunate has been the history of the First Church in Dedham, Massachusetts (Fig. 148), which stands today on the very site of the first meetinghouse built there by the infant town more than three hundred years ago. This was pieced out and amplified until its replacement in 1761 by a much larger pitched-roof house with three doors and a square belfry tower in the style of the time. This one served until 1820 when it was completely reconstructed. The rooftree was turned at right angles to its former position, and the long dimension of the old house became the width of the new. A considerable extension was made at what was to be the front, and a porch and spire were added. Nothing can now be seen of the eighteenth-century meetinghouse whose timbers are embedded in the present one, which is typical of the early years of the nineteenth century. Four severely plain pilasters are all that adorn its entrance bay. The simplest ornamentation at the cornices, and the urns on tower, belfry and lantern, are the only relief to the severity of the whole. The well-proportioned spire suggests that of Christ Church in Boston. The spacious setting with wide lawn in front and trees on either side adds to the attractiveness of this old church.

The two churches we have just described represent something of an extreme in that their reconstruction was so drastic as to amount essentially to a rebuilding. Most of the nineteenth-century modernizations were less ambitious. Let us now discuss a few typical examples of the scores of such buildings that still stand.

Few New England villages are more "beautiful for situation" than Thetford Hill, Vermont, high above the Connecticut River, looking east toward the White Mountains. At the end of the wide, tree-bordered village street, with a common down the middle of it, is a white meetinghouse of

148 First Church, 1761, Dedham, Massachusetts

149 *Congregational Church, 1787,*
Thetford Hill, Vermont

out and around the base of the old tower, and a modern belfry surmounts it. On the sides of the church are two rows of windows, joined by false blinds to give the appearance of one. The upper row are now well below the cornice, with a wide frieze between, but the scars of the original windows, still visible at the rear, show them to have been close under the eaves. The scars of the old front door, too, in the middle of the east side, and of the north door at what is now the rear are still to be seen, and show conclusively the changes that were wrought in converting the meetinghouse into a church. Inside is a gallery along three walls, but it is not the original one. The pulpit may be as old as the church. In the loft are to be seen some of the heaviest beams ever used in roof construction. The Thetford minister of today, gazing at the blank southern wall as he preaches, must sometimes envy his predecessor of 100 years ago who from his lofty pulpit on the western side of the meetinghouse could look out of the opposite windows upon the whole panorama of the White Mountains beyond.

Townshend, Vermont, has a meetinghouse (Fig. 150) that assumed a Gothic look in the middle years of the last century. It is in a lovely setting at the edge of the village green, and when it was built in 1790 was doubtless a simple square-towered meetinghouse, as its steeply pitched roof and general design still indicate. At some time early in the nineteenth century its front was built out around the tower, a fact shown by the marks on the clapboards. At this time the main entrance was changed from the

1787 (Fig. 149), the oldest church in Vermont, so the records say, that has been in continuous use. Originally standing near the center of the common, it was moved to its present site in 1830. At that time the present steeple was built and the bell hung. Again, in 1858, it was much altered. The steeply pitched roof of the original house and the top of the square tower that once stood at its southern end remain. All else is changed. A deep but simple porch has been built

*150 Federated Church, 1790,
Townshend, Vermont*

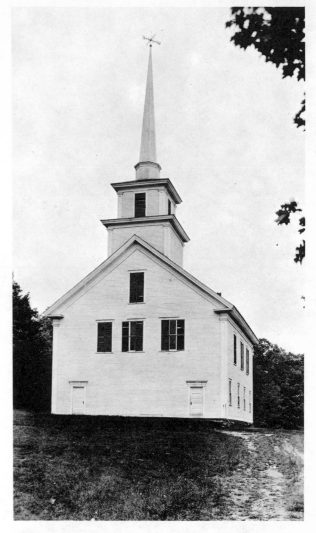

*151 Congregational Church, 1802,
Windham, Vermont*

side to the two doors at the front, as can be seen from the spacing of the windows and by the fact that a door to the vestry still enters at the old location. Sometime later the building was divided into two stories, a change visible externally in the elongated windows of the upper row; and probably at this time these windows gained their false pointed tops. The scars at the rear show the windows' original height and size. The belfry and spire may be original.

In the little hill town of Windham, Vermont, is a small meetinghouse built in 1802 (Fig. 151). Standing at an altitude of more than 2,000 feet, it is said to be higher above sea level than any other church in the state. The structure has undergone many changes. The roof is steeply pitched and the very short tower is now set back completely on it, leaving the great front bare and plain, save for the four windows above and the two small, widely separated doors. The

building now has two stories. At the side there are only three windows in the upper tier, though the scars of the rest of the original seven, close under the eaves, are plainly visible. No sign now remains of a side entrance, and it may well be that this was a Transitional meetinghouse and thus lacked such an entrance. The effect of the building, because of the absence of ornament and the few windows, is rather severe. Both church and town still maintain the house as they did in the old days.

The church at Amherst, New Hampshire, built in 1771 (Fig. 152), is said to have the oldest steeple in the state. It resembles the one on the meetinghouse at Brooklyn, Connecticut, put up the year before. The house, a typical structure, was built on the town's training field (now the common). The town sold it to the First Congregational Society in 1833, retaining title to the bell, clock, belfry, and tower. It still owns the clock. In 1836 the meetinghouse was moved across the road to its present site and remodeled. The door on the long side was closed, the front built out around the base of the tower, and the whole building raised so that a room could be added underneath. It was altered again in 1872. The Reverend Nathan Lord, called here in 1815, gradually lost his voice—a serious difficulty for a man who had to preach two-hour sermons—and finally resigned to become president of Dartmouth College.

The church in Hopkinton, New Hampshire (Fig. 153), was built on the

153 Congregational Church, 1789,
Hopkinton, New Hampshire

153

154 *Hopkinton Church in 1828*

common across the road as early as 1789, its present appearance notwithstanding. About 1800 a two-story porch was built in the middle of the long side, and in 1809 a belfry and steeple were added above it. A sketch made in 1828 (Fig. 154) shows this curious mixture of the eighteenth and nineteenth centuries. It suggests the

155 *Congregational Church, 1796, Rindge, New Hampshire*

plan of the meetinghouse at Exeter, New Hampshire (page 111). There well may be some connection between the two. In 1839 the Hopkinton church underwent a conversion to the Greek Revival mode and lost all of its original look save the steep roof.

The old church at Rindge, New Hampshire, built in 1796 (Fig. 155), was one of the largest of the country meetinghouses. It occupies a commanding site on a hill in the middle of the village. The tower is set back completely on the roof, but an examination of eaves and clapboards shows that the front has been extended to enclose the base of what was once a projecting tower. This was done in 1839, and the Greek Revival steeple, which replaced an earlier one, was doubtless added at that time. The church was then divided into two stories. Across the front, above the doors, are two tiers of windows, suggesting the possibility that this may once have been a "three-decker," with two galleries. For some time the lower floor was used as a town hall and for an academy, and the interior was further changed in 1871. The steeple appears too short for the building. It is said that ten feet of it were sacrificed when a new hand-pumped fire engine could not put a stream of water to the top.

The first Presbyterian church in New England was organized at Derry (now East Derry), New Hampshire, in 1719 by men from the north of Ireland. The present meetinghouse, built in 1769 (Fig. 156), is now something of an architectural puzzle. To begin with, the tower was a later addition, for it lacks the decorated cornice of the church itself. Then, in 1824, the building was cut in two and 24 feet of length were added between the halves. The clapboards show no sign of the patching, and so we may conclude that new ones were put on after that time. There is a scar of a large door, however, in the middle of the south side, suggesting that the main door was still there after the church was lengthened. On the opposite side of the building, as might be expected, is the mark of a pulpit window. The situation is complicated by the presence of a window scar in the middle of the large door scar! Evidently the orientation of the house was not changed until some time after it was lengthened, when this window was added to the six in the lower tier. The pulpit then was placed at the east end, as the scar of a pulpit window there shows, and the main entrance was now at the tower end. The steeple was probably added in 1824, for its design is characteristic of this period. The lantern stage resembles one of those in the Newburyport steeple, not far away. Its effect is marred by a weak stage above, too narrow for good proportions. Perhaps this was the work of another hand.

But even more changes were made in the old house. In 1845 it was divided into two stories, and the seven pairs of windows on each side reduced to four. The pulpit was now moved again, to the tower end, and the pews reversed so as to face it and the entrance, according to the fashion of the day. Tiring of this in time, the church built the present small door on the side at the rear, to avoid having to reverse the pews again. Town meetings

156 *Congregational Church, 1769, East Derry, New Hampshire*

155

were held for many years on the lower floor. The windows in the auditorium above—another change—are of colored glass. Many years ago the church became Congregational. In the cemetery nearby are the graves of its first five ministers.

One would never guess that the present large and ornate church at the head of the Central Square in Keene, New Hampshire (Fig. 157), began as the meetinghouse of 1786. Such is the case, however, though only the frame survives in the present building, giving it the steep roof pitch that shows its age. As first erected near the south end of the square, the meetinghouse was a typical eighteenth-century structure. In 1826 the town fathers allocated the building to the Unitarians for thirteen Sundays in the year. They soon withdrew and formed

157 First Congregational Church, 1786,
Keene, New Hampshire

158 Congregational Church, 1730,
Kittery Point, Maine

156

their own church, the reverse of what usually happened in such controversies.

The town thereafter sold its rights in the house to the Congregational Society, which moved the building across the street and faced it south, where it stands today. At this time it was completely altered to the new church plan in the usual manner. A picture of it at this stage shows it with shallow entrance bay, four columns, a square tower, a square belfry, and above this two octagonal stages and a spire. In 1860 there was need for much more space and the building was raised so that a story could be added underneath. It was also widened, as can be seen by the flat extension of the roof on either side. At this time, too, the building underwent a great elaboration of its design, although the basic plan was not abandoned, as it was in many Victorian modernizations. Corinthian columns and pilasters were added, pediment and cornices enriched, and the steeple given a much greater wealth of detail.

The little church at Kittery Point, Maine (Fig. 158), built in 1730, is the oldest one in the state. It is perfectly plain, with one door at the front and two windows on each side. All outward indications of antiquity disappeared many years ago. The original door on the long side was closed in 1840, the main entrance put at the end, with the pulpit opposite, and the steeple taken down. In 1874, when the church was turned to face the new road, it was further altered. Within, at the narrow end opposite the door, stands the paneled pulpit, said to be original, and two of the old spindle-top square pews. In this church worshiped Sir William Pepperell, conqueror of Louisburg in 1745, and owner of much of the region hereabout, whose ancient house is down the road a little way. In the cemetery across the road is buried the poet Celia Thaxter.

The frame of the church at York Village, Maine (Fig. 159), was raised in 1747, and its age appears in the steep pitch of the roof; but everything else about the church is Victorian, the result of various alterations, the most drastic occurring in 1882. But all marks of age can hardly be hidden in an old building, and there are two left here. One is the weathercock on the spire. The other may be found by climbing the stairs to the steeple, for here remain in place a few of the old yellow clapboards that once covered the gable end of the house. This is one of the few cases where any remnant of color, once so common in New England meetinghouses, is still to be seen. Chocolate, red, and Spanish yellow were favorites.

Here in the early days preached the Reverend Samuel Moodey. Of him it is told that on a Sabbath, when some of his flock began to doze, he paused in his sermon and shouted "Fire! Fire!" "Where?" asked the rousing congregation. Pointing an accusing finger at them the preacher thundered, "In hell, for sleeping sinners!"

The First Parish Church of Kennebunk, Maine (Fig. 160), built between 1771 and 1773, dominates the village from its location where two main roads meet. It still has the projecting tower of an eighteenth-century meetinghouse, but otherwise has under-

159 Congregational Church, 1747, York Village, Maine

157

160 First Parish Church, 1771, Kennebunk, Maine

gone many changes. In 1803 the building was sawn across and an addition of 28 feet inserted. At this time, too, the house seems to have been turned so that the end rather than the long side faced the road, and the main entrance was placed in the tower. The steeple was then added in the style of that day. In 1838 the house was divided into two stories. A Palladian pulpit window at the rear, now closed, may date before this change. There are still a number of unsolved problems about this handsome church; for example, there are two tiers of eight windows on the south side, though only seven on the north; and the windows are not evenly spaced.

The old Baptist meetinghouse in Yarmouth, Maine (Fig. 161), was raised in 1796. The windows on the front are unusual in a church of this type for they have bluntly pointed tops with delicately interlaced sashbars. Above the belfry is an octagonal stage with windows like those on the front of the building. At first, apparently, there was a square tower projecting somewhat from the front, with a single door into it. In 1825 it was voted to enlarge this "porch" to make more room, and at that time, presumably, the two other doors and windows were added to form the present entrance bay. In 1837 the building was lengthened by cutting it across and inserting a section, and the interior was altered by removal of the galleries, pews and pulpit. The original side windows were taken out in 1850 and

the present three large windows installed. The building was used as a Baptist church until 1887; later, it was given to the town as a Memorial Hall.

The conversion of an old square-towered meetinghouse into a church was rarely accomplished with as much success as at Sheffield, Massachusetts (Fig. 162), in the southwestern corner of Berkshire county, a region notable for its old churches. This building stood a little east of its present site, in what would now be the middle of the highway, and seems to have been of the usual type for that date. It had a tower at the end, either originally or as an addition. The roof is very steep. In 1819 the house was moved to

162 Congregational Church, 1760, Sheffield, Massachusetts

161 Old Baptist Meetinghouse, 1796, Yarmouth, Maine

163 *Community Church, 1781,*
North Orange, Massachusetts

In this house, at a town meeting in 1773, was unanimously adopted the so-called "Sheffield Declaration," in which it was resolved, first, "that Mankind in a State of Nature are equal, free and independent of each other, and have a right to the undisturbed Enjoyment of their Lives, their Liberty and Property," and, second, "that the great end of political Society is to secure in a more effectual manner those rights and privileges wherewith God and Nature have made us free." Protests were also made in it against invasion of the rights of citizens, their taxation without representation, and their removal for trial to a place distant from their habitation. One can hear, in this document, phrases of a more famous Declaration.

The Community Church (Congregational-Universalist) of North Orange, Massachusetts (Fig. 163), was built in 1781 as a typical meeting-house. In 1832 it was turned so that the gable end faced the road. The pilastered front was built out around the tower and the building divided into two stories. In 1865 an extension of 14 feet was added at the rear. The pulpit is now at the front.

The church in West Granville, Massachusetts (Fig. 164), is of much interest. It was built in 1782 and architecturally is one of the most unusual in New England. The location of the original main door and the pulpit window opposite may be seen in the patched clapboards. It probably had no tower at first, but porches at each end; the scar of the one at what is now the rear can still be seen. The roof is very steep and the upper windows are close under the eaves. Remarkably,

its present location and converted in the usual way, the old south door being closed and the pulpit put in the west. At the east end, the front was brought forward so that it enclosed most of the base of the tower. In the upstairs vestibule one can see traces of the windows that were originally in the east wall before the addition was made. The octagonal belfry and the stage above are not unlike those of a Hoadley steeple. Within, the gallery has been removed and little original work is left; but one can find evidence, in the plastering, of the position of the original door in the middle of the south side. In the cellar the cornerstone bears masonic emblems and states that the church was built in 1760 and remodeled in 1819.

the building has an overhang, much as in some old dwelling houses, the only such example in a New England church. The change to the new church design was doubtless made early in the nineteenth century, for the three-doored porch and the tower set part-way back on the roof seem to be of that period. There is a scar of a corresponding pulpit window at the opposite end. The turret-like structures at the front corners, together with the pinnacles on the belfry and the window over the middle door, were probably added in the era of Victorian Gothic. The church thus combines three different architectural styles. There are no side galleries now and the one at the front, over the entrance, has been made into a room. Part of the wall of this room consists

of panels, probably from the old pews. The floor of the auditorium has been raised about four feet to accommodate a furnace below. Beside the meeting-house stands an old academy building, now used as a parish house.

The oldest meetinghouse in the Connecticut Valley is at Longmeadow, Massachusetts. Built in 1767, it has had a checkered history. When built, it was typical of its time except that the bell was hung in the square tower instead of in a belfry above it. When the change to the church plan was made in 1828, as we know from pictorial evidence, the main door on the south was closed and porches were built on the new front (west), one in each of the angles between tower and church, an unusual arrangement. There were now three doors, one in

164 Congregational Church, 1782, West Granville, Massachusetts

165 *Congregational Church, 1767,*
Longmeadow, Massachusetts;
Victorian Gothic appearance, 1874

each porch and one in the tower. It was probably at this time that a steeple, with two octagonal stages, a spire, and a weathercock, was built on the tower. So the church remained for almost half a century. In 1874 it was moved to a site near the old burying ground and there, as complacently reported, it was "wholly clothed upon with new beauty under the advice of a competent architect." This "new beauty" was Victorian Gothic (Fig. 165). Change was as great within. Taste improved, however, and in the 1930s the edifice was moved once more, to the head of the common, and largely rebuilt, though not in any of its earlier forms. It now has a four-columned portico, an attractive steeple, and a spire such as might have been built in the early nineteenth century (Fig. 166). Little of the original meeting-house remains except the frame; but overhead still swings the handsome weathercock, a well-loved landmark of the valley.

The Reverend Stephen Williams, minister when this church was built, lived to be ninety and preached here for sixty-six years. The son of John Williams, the minister at Deerfield. When ten years old he was carried captive into Canada after the sack of that town in 1704. After his return he entered the ministry. When the Revolution broke out he prayed for the king on the first Sabbath, to the disgust of

166 *Longmeadow church today*

167 *Unitarian Church, 1797,*
Sudbury, Massachusetts

168 *Congregational Church, 1766,*
Shrewsbury, Massachusetts

his congregation, who slammed down their seats and sat during the rest of the prayer.

The town of Sudbury, Massachusetts, has a church of 1797 (Fig. 167), now considerably changed. It is unusual in that there are tiers of four equally spaced windows on each side. This indicates that the main door was not originally on the side, since in such cases, when the door has later been replaced by a window, there is necessarily an odd number of windows. A small door, obviously not original, is now in the middle of the east side. On the north end is the scar of the old pulpit window. Our conclusion is that the house was originally Transitional in type with the entrance through a tower on the south and with the pulpit on the north. This is borne out by a vote of the town that the church should have "a porch at one end with a steeple or spear on the top of said porch." Some changes were made in 1820, and at that time, probably, the entrance bay with three doors was built out around the base of the tower, flush with its front. The building was divided into two stories in the 1840s.

The church at Shrewsbury, Massachusetts (Fig. 168), was built in 1766 as a plain meetinghouse, except for an elaborate porch on the south side. Most such porches, of which there were a good many in New England, were demolished when the meetinghouse was turned into a church, but at least one still exists. It is at Shirley Center, not far away, and it owes its preservation, after its removal from the meetinghouse, to the fact that it was added to a nearby broom shop

(Fig. 169). Like many old meeting-houses the one at Shrewsbury lacked tower and steeple for many years. In 1807 these were added, replacing the small porch at the west end, and a bell was hung. John Ames, who built other meetinghouses in the vicinity, probably built this one. In 1834 the high pulpit and square pews were taken out, the building turned with the tower end facing south, and then raised so that a vestry could be built underneath. Here town meetings were held until 1872. Probably at this time the present deep porch was built out around the base of the tower. During the later nineteenth century, colored glass was put in the windows and other Victorian "improvements" were made; but a few years ago, fortunately, the church was restored to something like its old estate. The steeple blew off in 1938 but was soon restored.

The Reverend Joseph Sumner, in whose ministry the Shrewsbury meetinghouse was built, was a remarkable man. Six feet four, with a commanding presence, and always wearing a wig, he was indeed "a Saul among his people." A small boy, beholding him for the first time, ran and told his mother that he had just seen God. General Artemus Ward, one of Sumner's parishioners, was Shrewsbury's most famous son, serving not only in the French and Indian War and in the Revolution, but later as high sheriff of Worcester County. As such he routed Daniel Shays and his rebels.

The old meetinghouse at Townsend, Massachusetts (Fig. 170), a typical eighteenth-century structure, was built in 1771. It was moved to its pres-

169 Porch of meetinghouse, 1773, Shirley Center, Massachusetts

170 Methodist Church, 1771, Townsend, Massachusetts

165

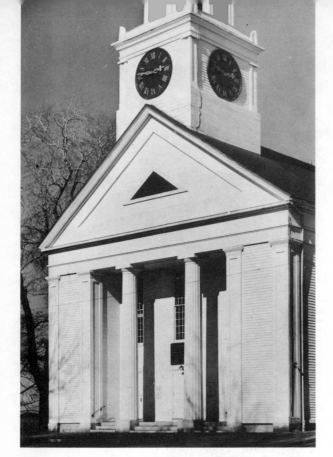

171 Unitarian Church, 1755,
Groton, Massachusetts

In one group of churches, chiefly in northeastern Massachusetts, eighteenth-century meetinghouses have been changed to the Greek Revival style in a fashion different from the usual one. The door and pulpit window on the long sides were closed, as in other cases. The front was then brought forward, but the base of the tower, instead of being enclosed on each side by these additions (as usually happened), was removed to leave a recess. At the front of this, under what is left of the tower above, are two columns and at the back of it are doors into the church.

The most notable example of this type of alteration is the meetinghouse at Groton, built in 1755 (Fig. 171). Barber's *Historical Collections* gives a picture of what the structure was like in 1838 (Fig. 172). The tower projected from one end, surmounted by what looks like the present-day steeple. In the middle of the long side was the main door with a large porch. In 1839 the house was turned so that its new entrance at the end now faced the road. The building was divided into two stories, and the lower floor

ent location from Meeting House Hill in 1804, and at this time, probably, the tower and steeple were added. The latter is much like that at Ashfield, suggesting that John Ames, who lived in Marlboro, not far away, may have designed both. The house has been divided into two stories, church above and (formerly) town hall below. Originally there were two rows of seven windows on each side, but the second, fourth, and sixth were removed. The old front door is still on the long south side, and a scar of the pulpit window may be seen on the north side. Congregationalists built the house but withdrew in favor of the Unitarians in 1829. The Methodists took over the building in 1852.

172 Groton Church in 1838

was used as the town hall for twenty years. Groton was once the county seat and from 1776 to 1787 the Courts of General Sessions and of Common Pleas for Middlesex County sat in this meetinghouse. The interior of the church was altered again in 1877 but partly restored in 1916.

Other churches, all in this part of the state, were remodeled in the same way as the one at Groton. These are at Hamilton (built 1762), Groveland (built 1790) and Phillipston (built 1785). The Phillipston church is typical of the group (Fig. 173). Its steeple, however, is relatively modern.

The Unitarian church of Beverly, which was built in 1770, has undergone so many changes that little of the original remains today save the frame; but the steep pitch of its roof indicates the antiquity of the building. The house was enlarged in 1795; remodeled in 1835, when the clock was placed in the tower; remodeled again in 1867, when the Greek Revival front was added; and further altered in 1888. The date on the tower is that of the organization of the church.

The meetinghouse of the First Parish church of Billerica, Massachusetts, built in 1797 (Fig. 174), was altered to the Greek Revival style in 1844. It was then turned through 90 degrees so that the new entrance faced the road, and a Doric portico was added in front of the three-doored entrance bay. Barber's picture of 1839 shows a large porch on the long east side, and a clock tower and steeple at the north end. This steeple resembles the present one, which thus may well be original, but turned to the east. The interior is much changed.

173 Congregational Church, 1785, Phillipston, Massachusetts

174 Unitarian Church, 1797, Billerica, Massachusetts

175 Unitarian Church, 1788,
Milton, Massachusetts

176 Congregational Church, 1732,
Burlington, Massachusetts

The Unitarian church at Milton, Massachusetts, built in 1788 (Fig. 175), obviously has been changed from the square-towered meetinghouse plan to that of a church, as shown by the steep pitch of the roof and the uneven spacing of the side windows. Originally it had its long side, with main door, facing the road; but in 1835 it was turned and an entrance bay built out around the base of the tower. The steeple shows a marked resemblance to those of the old church at Wethersfield, Connecticut, and of Trinity church at Newport, Rhode Island. Extensive changes within were made in 1871, when the side galleries were removed and the ceiling so lowered that the upper windows do not open into the auditorium.

Burlington, Massachusetts, was formerly the second parish of Woburn, and its present church, built in 1732 (Fig. 176), was its first meetinghouse. This structure has undergone an unusual series of alterations and today presents an appearance unlike any other. At first it was a typical eighteenth-century structure. In 1846 the old steeple was removed, the building was lengthened 10 feet and two Doric columns were built in front, so that the appearance was for a time much like that of the church at Groton today. In 1888 more radical changes were made. The church was now larger than necessary for Sunday services. The interior was rearranged so that by the use of moveable partitions, rooms could be kept separate or thrown together as needed. On the south side, but considerably east of its center, a two-story porch, rather deep and with a small portico, was built out and the main entrance placed in it. Over it was added a Victorian steeple replacing the one of 1846. Despite all these changes, the original frame with its tremendous beams is still intact. Further changes are now contemplated, and we may hope that they will help restore one of the building's earlier states.

In the cemetery across the road, in use since 1730, is the portrait stone of the Reverend Thomas Jones, minister of this church, "who died suddenly on the Lord's Day, March 13, 1774."

One of the oldest meetinghouses in New England is that of what is now the First Baptist Society in Westwood, Massachusetts (originally the Clapboard Trees parish of Dedham). This was built in 1730 (Fig. 177). In 1807, when it was in need of repair, some of the members wanted to rebuild it on the old site, others to build a new structure nearer the village center. The first group prevailed, and erected the present First Parish church, which soon became Unitarian. The second group got their own way, too, for they bought the old house and moved it to their preferred site, where they organized a Baptist church. In 1834 it was lengthened 25 feet, the door moved from the long side to the end, and a belfry built on the roof. In this condition the Clapboard Trees meetinghouse has lasted more than a century and a quarter, strong in frame and vigorous in spirit, only a year younger than Boston's Old South itself.

There are many remodeled meetinghouses in Connecticut, too. The one in the village of Abington, in the town of Pomfret (Fig. 178), seems at first glance to be simply another Greek

177 First Baptist Church, 1730, Westwood, Massachusetts

169

178 Congregational Church, 1751, Abington, Connecticut

Revival building. Built in 1751, it is actually the oldest ecclesiastical structure in the state. Its dimensions at first were 48 by 39 feet, the same as those of the present auditorium. In 1802 the pulpit was moved from the north side to the east end, where a scar of the pulpit window in the clapboards can be seen, and the main entrance was changed from the south side to the west end. Here the front was built out on either side of the square tower. In 1834 the whole structure was remodeled in Greek Revival style. The present ceiling is somewhat lower than the original one, and is coved (curved) at the sides to hide the old braces. In the loft can be seen the position of the old ceiling and also the upper portion of the original

plastered side walls. Here, too, one can see the heavy oak braces between wall posts and roof trusses. That these were once exposed to view is proved by the fact that they were not left rough but that their corners were carefully planed off, or chamfered. The wall posts are also chamfered, showing that they, too, were once visible to the congregation.

The 1790 Congregational Church at Centerbrook, Connecticut (Fig. 179), is another much modified old structure. The roof is very steep and the upper windows are close under the eaves, both, as we have seen, being marks of an eighteenth-century house. Of the side windows, the central one is rather widely separated from its neighbors. Around this, on the west side, can be seen in the clapboards the patches that mark the position of the old front door. On the opposite side the location of the old pulpit window is also evident, and there is the scar of a door at the north end. All this indicates that the building was at first a typical meetinghouse with main entrance on the broad side and doors at each end. From the records we learn that the house was turned in 1839 so that the narrow end faced the road. The main door was closed, tower and steeple were removed, and a new belfry and front door added. In 1888 the projecting tower and the present belfry were built, the final step in the mutation of a colonial into a Victorian building. Almost everything within is altered. The main structure, however—walls, windows and frame—is still intact. We may hope that it will one day be restored to its former state.

179 Congregational Church, 1790, Centerbrook, Connecticut

East Haven, Connecticut, has the oldest stone meetinghouse in New England, begun in 1772 and finished two years later (Fig. 180). George Lancraft, a Dutch architect, was its builder. Like the other structures discussed, it has been substantially altered. Some of the changes involved parts of the stone walls themselves. In 1850 the door on the long south side, and the pulpit window opposite, were closed, the upper windows lengthened somewhat, and two new doors opened on the front. The present steeple was built in 1859.

The erection of such an expensive meetinghouse taxed the resources of the town to the utmost. Even though most of the stonework was done by the people themselves, it was estimated that the stone shell of the building, up to 1774, had cost an amount equivalent to three-fifths of the whole grand list of property in East Haven. This church is a monument to the skill, determination, and faith of its builders.

The Congregational church at Hampton, Connecticut, built in 1754 (Fig. 181), evidently had a tower at first, since in 1794 it was voted to make a door from the steeple into the gallery. The building was turned in 1838 so that its end instead of its broad side faced the road. This fact, together with its age, the steep pitch of its roof, and the unequal spacing of its windows (indicating that the main door was originally on the side) makes it clear that this began as a typical eighteenth-century meetinghouse. In 1838, evidently, the old tower was removed, the present steeple built on the roof and the columned portico

180 *Congregational Church, 1772, East Haven, Connecticut*

181 *Congregational Church, 1754, Hampton, Connecticut*

171

182 Congregational Church, 1814, Canton Center, Connecticut

added on the front. Very little of the present interior is original, though below the windows the walls are finished with what seems to be the old pew doors.

Not all the modernized churches were originally of the meetinghouse type. A number of those built in the early years of the nineteenth century were later changed either to the style of the Greek Revival or the Gothic. The church at Canton Center, Connecticut (Fig. 182), is a notable example. This was built in 1814, and evidently conformed to the fashion of the period in having an entrance bay with three doors and a tower set back partly over the roof. The major external change has been in the windows, for the upper row on either side have disappeared, giving the church a curious appearance. The reason for this is obvious when one enters, for the galleries have been removed and the ceiling is a vault of stained wood curving down on the sides. From this ceiling project downward a series of false trusses of Gothic design. As an example of the architectural changes that could be produced in a Victorian modernization, this interior would be hard to equal.

The Congregational church in Barrington, Rhode Island, built in 1806 (Fig. 183), is another nineteenth-century church that has been radically changed. The remodeling was done in 1851. Unequal spacing of the side windows suggests that the front has been brought forward, and that the tower originally projected its full depth from the building. The entrance apparently was through this tower, so that the church was probably of the type we have called Transitional. In 1888,

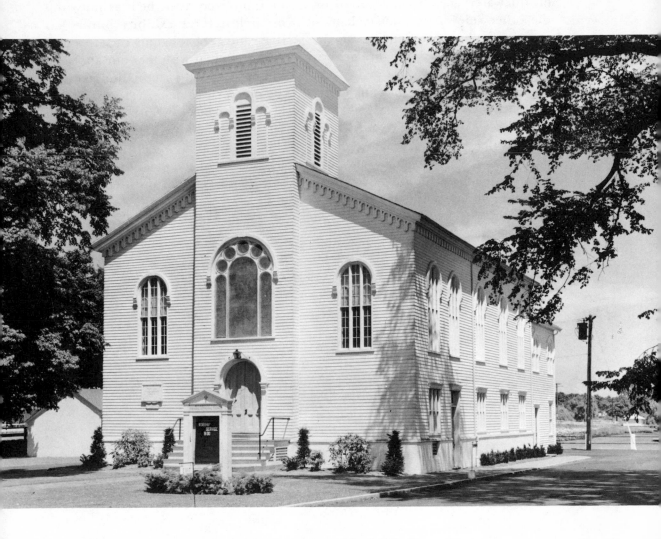

183 United Congregational Church, 1806, Barrington, Rhode Island

when the church was extended at the rear, the general appearance of the outside was modernized. The spire was blown off in 1938. This church is on tidewater; members who lived on the other side of the estuary had to come over by boat, landing at the church wharf, until the bridge was built in 1890.

In scores of other meetinghouses and churches, changes much like the ones described in this chapter have been made. They are evidence of activity in the church organizations which used these buildings, for only a dead church remains unchanged.

The alterations tell us something of human frailty and fallibility, but more of human aspiration. These old structures have never been regarded by those who used them as museums or architectural exhibits but as active centers of religious life. In many cases we might wish that our ancestors had used more discrimination in carrying out their changes. Yet we do these men and women wrong if we do not recognize their dedication to something that was far higher than any material structure—"a house not made with hands, eternal in the heavens."

Eight 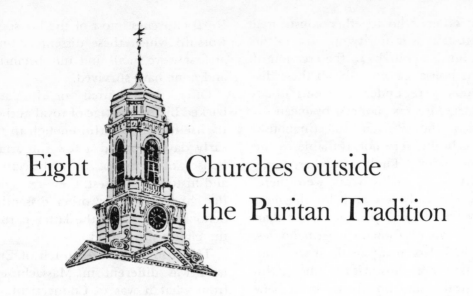 Churches outside the Puritan Tradition

THE Puritan experiment in New England was one of the most determined attempts ever made to establish an ideal society. To the Puritan mind the theocratic principle seemed perfectly logical. Although minor differences as to methods of ecclesiastical and political organization were to be found among various groups who left the old England to found a new one in the wilderness, there was a surprising unanimity in the minds of these men as to the general type of social order they proposed to set up. In it the church was not merely to be established by the state; it was, essentially, to *be* the state; the godly were at last to be given an opportunity to govern the affairs of men and thus to establish what, it was fervently hoped, would prove an approximation to the Kingdom of Heaven.

The diversity of the human species, however, was a factor which these builders of Zion failed to take into account. Never, save at the very start, did the Puritan theocracy command a sufficiently general acceptance of its doctrines to insure the harmonious functioning of a church-state. Not only did unsympathetic dissenters from abroad invade the peace of New England, but in the very household of the faith there soon began to appear those who were unable to fit their minds and consciences into the mold of the established order.

Among the disturbers of Israel were the Baptists, Episcopalians, and Quakers; but before long, and especially after the Great Awakening, there were added to these a score of sects: the New Lights, Rogerines, Perfectionists, Christians, Dorrellites, Sandemanians, and others who together constituted a substantial minority opposed to the established church. In the erection of their houses of worship, all these dissenters were under a serious disadvantage, for tax moneys, by means of which the Puritan meetinghouses were built, were not available to the unorthodox. Their churches, especially in the earlier years, were therefore relatively few and, for the most part, smaller and less impressive than the Congregational meetinghouses. Nevertheless, many of them were important both historically and architecturally, and no discussion of New England churches which did not include them would be complete.

Roger Williams was the first to challenge the authority of the Puritan theocracy. Undoubtedly he was a difficult and cantankerous man, and the blame for his rupture with the Puritans cannot be laid entirely on their shoulders. In his insistence that the civil power could have no authority over the consciences of men, however, he was so far in advance of the philosophy upon which the theocratic experiment of Massachusetts had been founded that his presence there soon became intolerable. About the little settlement that he established at the head of Narragansett Bay there soon gathered other refugees—Anabaptists, Antinomians, Quakers, Jews, and Episcopalians—all of whom found scant hospitality in the other New England colonies. Rhode Island never wavered, however, in maintaining for all her people complete freedom of conscience and religious belief, joined to a direct popular control of their political institutions. Save for the Epis-

copal churches, most of the houses of worship which these dissenters built at first were small and unsubstantial, and none have survived.

Only the Church of England, backed by the prestige of royal authority itself, was powerful enough in the early days to build a few important houses of worship. In architectural and historical interest, these exceeded the churches of any other dissenting denomination until the latter part of the eighteenth century.

The history of the Church of England was different in Massachusetts from what it was in Connecticut. In Boston, by virtue of its position as the capital and metropolis of New England, there was always a considerable group of merchants and officials whose chief ties were to the mother country and who were predominantly Episcopalian. When Governor Andros forced his way into the Old South meetinghouse in 1687, however, to hold Episcopal services there, he deeply offended the Boston Puritans and for a long time they did not forgive the Church of England. Soon afterward, to be sure, under the smile of royal patronage, King's Chapel was built and in due time a few similar houses of worship were erected in the Bay colony. But for many years the Church of England remained an alien intruder, forced upon an inhospitable people. It was supported chiefly by sea captains, military men, officials, and some of the wealthier merchants. Never in all the years up to the Revolution did the Church of England in Massachusetts really get out of sight of salt water.

Connecticut was at first equally inhospitable to the church of its fathers, but was more fortunate in being able to avoid intimate contact with it. When the Church of England did appear there, it was not as an intruder. It grew up among the Puritans themselves, and was therefore largely free from the stigma so long attached to it in the older colony. Its beginnings were dramatic enough. A few feeble missionary efforts had been made by the Society for the Propagation of the Gospel early in the eighteenth century, particularly around Stratford, but these had accomplished little. Suddenly all was changed. In 1722 almost the entire faculty of Yale College, consisting of the Reverend Timothy Cutler, the rector, and the Reverend Mr. Brown, the tutor, together with the Reverend Samuel Johnson, minister of West Haven, announced their adherence to Episcopacy, resigned their respective offices, and departed for England to take holy orders.

The sensation produced by this apostasy can hardly be imagined today. "I suppose that greater alarm would scarcely be awakened now," wrote President Woolsey of Yale, a century and a half later, "if the theological faculty of Yale were to declare for the Church of Rome, avow their belief in transubstantiation, and pray to the Virgin Mary."

Dr. Cutler returned from England to become rector of the newly founded Christ Church in Boston. Mr. Johnson came back to Connecticut and was the virtual founder of the church in that colony. To and fro he went, establishing and fostering new churches wherever groups of the faithful were

to be found, until before the Revolution there were no less than forty-two parishes of the Church of England in Connecticut. These churches were soon independent of missionary support, and since their membership was drawn almost entirely from the native population, they held a much more acceptable position in the life of the people than did their sister churches in Massachusetts. It is therefore not surprising that when the liberal reaction against the rigors of Calvinistic theology set in after the Revolution, most of the dissenters in Connecticut should have turned to the Episcopal church instead of to Unitarianism, which swept over much of Massachusetts.

Although the Church of England in Massachusetts thus lagged behind its development in Connecticut so far as numbers and enthusiasm were concerned, it excelled in the size and excellence of its church edifices. The wealth of their communicants and the many tokens of royal favor and gifts from overseas made these houses of worship among the most elaborate and beautiful of the early days. Their relatively poor fellow churchmen elsewhere in New England could not afford such magnificence, and the Colonial buildings that came from their hands are of comparatively minor interest.

King's Chapel, in Boston, as we have seen, was the first house of the Church of England to be erected in the New England colonies. It was completed in 1689, a small wooden building, doubtless with a square tower in front. In 1710 this was enlarged to twice its former size. Before

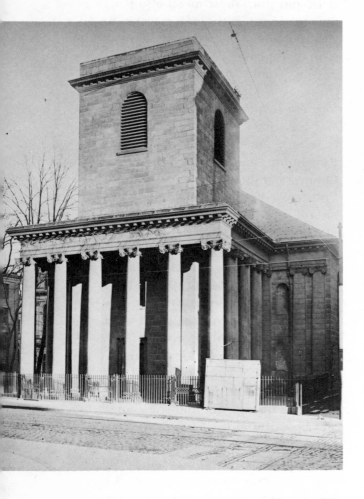

*184 King's Chapel, 1749,
Boston, Massachusetts*

many years even this was outgrown, and in 1749 the present church (Fig. 184), built of Quincy granite, was erected. Its architect was Peter Harrison of Newport (1716–1775). The body of the church is oblong, with a plain tower in front, the roof sloping back so that above the cornice the tower stands free. In 1790 the colonnade, now such a conspicuous part of the structure, was built around the base of the tower. At the rear, a chancel projects from the body of the church. There are two tiers of windows, the upper much longer than the lower.

Within there is a quiet beauty of design and ornament that makes King's Chapel one of the most satisfying churches in New England. Corinthian columns rise in pairs through the galleries to the vaulted ceiling. The box pews with doors have been retained, and the wine-glass pulpit built in 1718 for the earlier chapel is still in use (Fig. 185). Save for the removal of the Governor's pew and the royal emblems, little change has been made in the interior since the

185 Pulpit, King's Chapel

Revolution. Even the altar has been left in the chancel, although it is no longer the focal point of the church, since King's Chapel, the first parish of the Church of England to be established in New England, was also the first church in the United States to make public acceptance of the Unitarian faith.

The oldest church building in Massachusetts still used by the Episcopal Church is St. Michael's of Marblehead, erected in 1714 (Fig. 186). This wooden building has survived the vicissitudes of time, the riots of the Revolution, and the threat of fire and neglect.

Originally it was 48 feet square, with two rows of windows on three sides, the upper ones round-topped. There probably was no gallery. The

squat bell tower, as now, was on the west side. The roof had *two* gables, with a trough between them. In 1728 the house was extended to the north by one window bay and the present hip roof built over the gables. Parts of the original gable roofs, with their shingles, can still be seen in the loft. In 1832 the altar was moved to the north, the original box pews were replaced by the present slips, a new pulpit and reading desk installed, and the single row of pointed windows substituted for the earlier double row. The first bell came from England; when the news of the signing of the Declaration of Independence reached Marblehead, a crowd broke into the church and rang it until it cracked. It was recast in Paul Revere's foundry in 1818. Although it cannot be said that St. Michael's is a handsome church, it does have a quaint simplicity. The original plan was to build a steeple over the tower, and this would doubtless have improved its appearance. Its setting is poor today, but in this town of narrow, twisting streets, the building has always been crowded by its neighbors.

St. Michael's, like other Episcopal churches, was not popular with the Puritans, who objected to its celebration of Christmas and other church festivals. At the beginning of the Revolution, the rector declared himself a Loyalist and had to leave for Nova Scotia. After the war the church was closed for a time. An attempt was made in 1799 to take over the build-

186 St. Michael's Church, 1714, Marblehead, Massachusetts

ing for use as a Congregational church, but this did not succeed.

Almost as old as St. Michael's and far more important architecturally is Christ Church, Boston, built in 1723 (Fig. 187). This parish was organized to accommodate church members living in the northern part of the town. The Reverend Timothy Cutler, one of the Connecticut group of converts to the Church of England, became its first rector. It is the oldest surviving church in the city, and stands today much as it was at first. Tradition says it was designed by William Price, a print dealer of Boston. The structure is of brick. In the projecting tower at the front of the building is hung a peal of eight bells, cast in England by Abel Rudhall of Gloucester in 1744. Above this are two square stages, topped by a spire. This tall steeple was blown off in the hurricane of 1804, and rebuilt several years later under the direction of Charles Bulfinch. It is said that he followed the original design, though the height of the spire was reduced by 16 feet. In a recent hurricane it was blown off again but soon restored. The influence of the design of Christ Church is evident in that of Trinity Church at Newport, Rhode Island, and was probably felt elsewhere.

The interior retains its original form, and is reminiscent of that of King's Chapel, although the ornamentation is less rich. Here are the square pews and pulpit, much as they were a half-century before the Revolution.

187 Christ Church, 1723,
Boston, Massachusetts

There are galleries on three sides with columns supporting them and continuing through to the vaulted ceiling. On the walls are tablets commemorating notable members of the parish in the early days. To the crypt underneath was brought the body of Major Pitcairn, the British officer who ordered the rebels, drawn up on Lexington green, to disperse, and who later went to his death leading the redcoats up Bunker Hill. The chandeliers and the statuettes over the organ, originally intended for a Canadian convent, were captured by a privateer in the French and Indian War of 1746 and given to the church.

As to whether this is the church where the lanterns were hung out for Paul Revere, "on the eighteenth of April in 'seventy-five," there has been some doubt. The true "Old North Church" was not this one at all, but one of the Boston meetinghouses, that of the Second Church, to be distinguished from the later "New North." It would seem that such a church would have been more likely to be involved in an anti-British plot than a Church of England, the members of which were presumably loyal subjects of the king. Nevertheless, on the basis of all the evidence, especially of Paul Revere's frequent attendance at this church, and the fact that its sexton warmly supported the Patriot cause, many historians believe that Christ Church was the one where the lanterns were hung on that fateful night.

The increasing number of adherents to the Church of England in the Boston region led to the building of several Episcopal churches later in the eighteenth century. In Cambridge there gathered a group of wealthy families—the Vassals, Lees, Olivers, Apthorps and others—who built the beautiful mansions on Brattle Street, or "Tory Row." Most were adherents of the Church of England or desired to be, and in 1761, again with Peter Harrison of Newport as designer, they built Christ Church (Fig. 188) near what is now Harvard Square. The tower at the front projects for its full depth, has doors on three sides, and carries a plain belfry. On each side is a single row of windows, now seven in number, for in 1857 the church was lengthened by 23 feet. Almost the only external ornament is on the cornices and the wide frieze. Within, there is much greater richness of detail. The chief changes have been the extension of the chancel, alteration of the square pews to slips, and replacement of the original pulpit.

Promising as its start was, the early years of Christ Church were unhappy. The first rector, East Apthorp, left after a bitter dispute with the Reverend John Mayhew of Boston over the question as to whether missionary funds from England should be spent to establish more Episcopal churches or to help convert the Indians. Soon afterward came the Revolution, and since most of the church members were Tories, their enforced departure was a serious blow to the parish. In the early days of the siege of Boston a militia company from Connecticut were quartered in the church. They

188 Christ Church, 1761, Cambridge, Massachusetts

melted down many of the window weights and organ pipes to make bullets. Washington himself forbade further vandalism. He is said to have worshiped in the church on one occasion. Later, intruders greatly damaged the interior. The church remained in a ruinous condition for a long time, and even when services began again after the war, there was no settled minister for thirty years. The building was partially restored in 1824, and, as we have seen, enlarged thirty-three years later.

Portsmouth, New Hampshire, was another early center of Episcopalianism. It was in 1732 that Queen's Chapel was erected on the crest of Church Hill in Portsmouth, and named in honor of Queen Caroline, the consort of George II. Her Majesty presented the church with a prayer book, a silver service, and a copy of the "Vinegar" Bible ("vineyard" misspelled). The bell was captured from the French at Louisburg in 1745, and presented to the church by the officers of the New Hampshire company that served in the siege. The Reverend Samuel Fayerweather, rector of the Narragansett church in Rhode Island, visiting Queen's Chapel in 1760, found it to contain a "small but a Gay and Shining Congregation in Respect to Dress and Appearance." Washington attended a service here during his visit to Portsmouth in 1789. In 1806 Queen's Chapel burned.

Its successor, the church we know today as St. John's (Fig. 189), was

189 St. John's Episcopal Church, 1807, Portsmouth, New Hampshire

erected the following year. It is a plain brick structure, anticipating in the simplicity of its design the Greek Revival buildings of twenty years later. There is no portico, and the tower is set well back on the roof. Above it rises a pleasing octagonal lantern with large windows, as befits a seaport town. In the belfry still hangs the old French bell, recast after the fire. The interior has been altered more than in most old Episcopal churches, and the square pews and wine-glass pulpit with its sounding board are gone. Most of those who in the old days held authority from the Crown in the Province of New Hampshire worshiped in Queen's Chapel and many of them are buried nearby.

In 1702 a group of churchmen on the western shore of Narragansett Bay applied to the Society for the Propagation of the Gospel for aid in establishing the services of the Church of England among them, and in 1707 the Reverend Christopher Bridge arrived. In the same year St. Paul's Church was built for this parish in what is now the town of Wickford, Rhode Island (Fig. 190). This simple little building is the oldest Episcopal church in New England.

It was first erected some five miles from its present location, not far from the old Pequot Path that later became the Post Road. It throve for a time, serving a large but widely scattered congregation. Here preached for thirty-six years, beginning in 1721, the doughty Reverend Doctor James MacSparran, the "Apostle of the Narragansett Country." Indians and Negro slaves attended his services and were baptized, somewhat against the oppo-

190 *St. Paul's Episcopal Church, 1707, Wickford, Rhode Island*

sition of the slave-holding members of his congregation. During the Revolution, services at St. Paul's were suspended, and for a time the church was used as a barracks by American soldiers. After peace had come again the little parish strove to recover its earlier vigor; but its flock had become widely dispersed, and in 1799 the parish decided to remove the church to the village of Wickford. On a remote country lane, the original site of the church—the "Old Platform"—may still be recognized. Near it are the graves of the Narragansett churchmen who during nearly a century were buried there.

St. Paul's in its new setting again throve for a time, but in 1848 it was abandoned when the parish built a new church nearer the town center. Friends of the old structure assumed the task of preserving it, and today, more than two and a half centuries old, it is the property of the Diocese of Rhode Island, which carefully

185

maintains it. Services are occasionally held here in the summer.

The Old Narragansett Church, as it is now commonly known, is unique among the Episcopal churches of New England in conforming essentially to the Puritan meetinghouse plan of architecture. It is an oblong, pitched-roof building, perfectly simple in form with a single door on the broad south side and a pulpit opposite. The only external ornamentation is around the bold doorway. The upper row of windows is close under the eaves, and directly back of the pulpit are two round-topped pulpit windows. The interior is plain (Fig. 191). The timbers of the frame project into the room as in the older Puritan meetinghouses, and the walls are plastered. The ceiling ascends into a graceful vault. The

186

oblong, square-doored pews are not original, but were installed after the church was moved to its present site. At the eastern end stands the altar. The orientation of the building was reversed in the moving, and the altar was probably once at what is now the west end. The original wine-glass pulpit with its ascending steps was removed many years ago. At first the church was without bell or spire. A square belfry tower was built at the west end about 1811, and a bell placed there in 1820, so that the church must then have presented a rather striking resemblance to a typical Puritan meetinghouse. The workmanship of the tower was evidently inferior, however, for on a windless night in 1868 it collapsed of its own weight. It was not replaced. Both without and within, therefore, St. Paul's today presents very much the appearance it must have had when its timbers were raised in the Narragansett wilderness.

Trinity Parish at Newport, Rhode Island, was from the start a larger and more thriving one than Saint Paul's, for Newport soon became an important commercial town and was the home of many communicants of the English church. We know nothing of the first building, erected in 1702; doubtless it was not large. The present Trinity Church (Fig. 192), one of the glories of the older part of the town, was built in 1726 and seems to have followed closely the lines of Christ Church at Boston, erected only three years before. Its designer was Richard Munday. The body is relatively long, since in 1762 it was sawn across and lengthened by 30 feet. The tower is at the west end. The steeple,

191 Interior, St. Paul's Episcopal Church, Wickford, Rhode Island

probably built about 1760 (the first had blown down in 1731), is thought to have been copied from that on Christ Church, Boston. In the highest of the three square stages are the windows characteristic of the steeple lookouts of seaport towns. The main doorway is in the tower, with others on the sides.

Within, the church seems to have been altered but little. Like the exterior, it reminds one of Christ Church, Boston. Square columns support the gallery and rise through it to the vaulted roof. All of the old square pews have been retained, and the one in which Washington worshiped in 1781 is marked. There are seats for slaves and prisoners in the gallery. The original "three-decker" pulpit (Fig. 193), in which successive portions of the service were read at progressively higher altitudes until the climax was attained with the delivery of the sermon, is unique in New England. Here Bishop Berkeley preached during his visit to Rhode Island from 1728 to 1731. Here, also, Samuel Seabury, the first Episcopal bishop in the United States, preached his first sermon after his consecration. The pulpit stands in the middle of the aisle. During some restorations in 1928, the relatively modern altar was taken out and the original oak communion table replaced.

While Newport was held by the British during the Revolution, the soldiers of the King worshiped here; but after the evacuation of the town the Americans tore out the royal insignia and used them for targets. Although hemmed about with newer structures, Old Trinity, with its pop-

192 Trinity Episcopal Church, 1726, Newport, Rhode Island

193 Pulpit, Trinity Episcopal Church

194 Trinity Episcopal Church, 1815,
New Haven, Connecticut

ulous graveyard, stands as a symbol of the valiant and prosperous days of the eighteenth century when commerce with the Barbadoes in rum and sugar, the slave trade with Africa, and a good deal of privateering, made Newport one of the most important towns on the Atlantic coast.

Episcopal churches in the early days, as we have seen, were more numerous in Connecticut than elsewhere. Most of the parishes had church buildings. Depending largely on an agricultural population for support, however, and in most cases without liberal gifts from munificent patrons abroad or wealthy merchants and aristocrats at home, these churches were unable to erect such impressive sanctuaries as were

built in many of the seaboard towns of the rest of New England. All but one were of wood, and only a few have survived to the present day.

Some time elapsed before the considerable group of churchmen in New Haven could organize themselves into a parish and build a church, on account of the opposition of the Puritans, and perhaps especially because of the location of Yale College in that town. Finally, in 1752, Trinity Church was built. An old picture of it shows it to have conformed to the common plan of the time. Surmounting the tower at the front was a belfry and rather tall spire—the first, it is said, to be built in New Haven. The successor to this church (Fig. 194), built in 1815 by Ithiel Town, stands today on the New Haven Green along with Center Church and United Church, a much admired group of beautiful and historic buildings. Town had been in charge of the building of Center Church the year before, but this new structure—of stone, and Gothic in style—was quite different. It has rightly been praised for its beauty and purity of design. The windows are long and pointed, and the tall tower projects a little from the front and carries no spire. Its top portion was once of wood but is now entirely of stone. At first there were wooden pinnacles at the corners; these also are now of stone. A chime of bells hangs in the tower. The interior, finished in dark wood and with vaulted ceiling and stone piers, is very impressive. There is no other place where the best of the Episcopal and the Puritan church designs, both exterior and interior, can be compared so well as in Trinity Church and its two Congregational neighbors on the New Haven Green.

Most of David Hoadley's churches are Congregational meetinghouses; but he built a lovely Episcopal church in Bethany, Connecticut, in 1809 (Fig. 195). It has a plain front with a single, well-designed entrance. The upper windows are round-topped, with interlacing bars. The octagonal belfry and dome somewhat suggest those of Hoadley's church at Orange. The original front doors and fanlight were removed long ago, and the present ones are restorations. There have been no major changes in the interior, which shows much pleasing ornament.

Trinity Church in Brooklyn (Fig. 196) has one of the most interesting origins of any Episcopal church in New England. When a new meetinghouse was to be built in this town several years before the Revolution, Colonel Godfrey Malbone, son of a wealthy Newport merchant and a staunch Episcopalian, was to be taxed £200 for its construction—one eighth of the entire cost. He vehemently objected, but there was no relief except for him to claim allegiance to another religious organization. There being no other in Brooklyn, Colonel Malbone determined to establish an Episcopal church. Gathering together about twenty heads of families of like persuasion, he organized Trinity parish in 1769, and began the erection of its church the next year, meeting most of the cost himself. The church was opened in April of 1771.

While the church was going up, the colonel gathered the people of the new parish and the surrounding

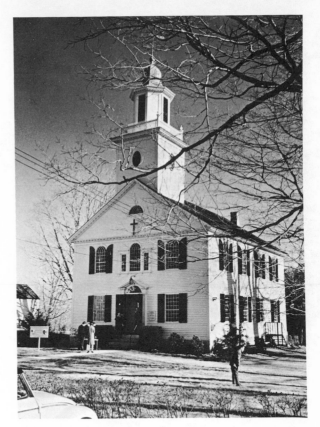

195 *Christ Episcopal Church, 1809, Bethany, Connecticut*

189

196 *Trinity Episcopal Church, 1770, Brooklyn, Connecticut*

*197 Interior, Trinity Episcopal Church,
Brooklyn, Connecticut*

churchmen and read the services to them himself. At the outbreak of the Revolution the new church was closed for a time. The colonel's death in 1785 was a severe blow, but the church survived and continued for many years. There is a touch of romance in the story, too, for Daniel Putnam, the son of Israel Putnam (one of the pillars of the Congregational church), married Malbone's daughter, and became senior warden of Trinity.

The "Malbone Church," as it is commonly called, stands today in essentially its original condition, about a mile out of the village and off the main road. The site is lovely, commanding an extensive view of the rolling country of northeastern Connecticut. A stone wall surrounds the churchyard on three sides.

In several particulars the building itself is remarkable. The plan is said to have been made from the colonel's recollections of other edifices, but there is little resemblance between Trinity and any other Episcopal church now standing. Its hip roof suggests the square meetinghouse design of the earliest type. The building is perfectly plain, save for the ornamented doorway on the west. There are two rows of windows, the blinds on which are relatively recent additions. Apparently the interior (Fig. 197) is much as it used to be, with a gallery along three sides and the original pews. The pulpit at first was further toward the west in the main aisle, and had a sounding board suspended from the point where there is now a small circle in the ceiling. The church is kept in good repair. Once a year, on All Saints' Day, a service is held in memory of those who built this temple to the Lord in a hostile land, and who are buried in the churchyard.

In the town of Woodbury was established, in 1740, the Parish of St. Paul's, which has played a part of no little importance in the life of the Episcopal church in Connecticut and eventually in the United States. When the town built a new meetinghouse in 1747, the old house, then used as a town hall, was made available to the communicants of the Church of England. To the parish of St. Paul's, in 1771, came the Reverend John Rutgers Marshall, who had gone from Connecticut to England to take holy orders. He resided in the Glebe House, still standing at the foot of the hill below the church that was later built under his guidance.

At the end of the Revolution, the situation of the American Episcopalians was difficult in the extreme. Since they had severed their relations with England, the services of the established church evidently could not be conducted in the same manner as before. Further, since there was no American bishop, there was no means of obtaining ordination except by going to England. Under these conditions, a secret gathering of ten of the fourteen clergymen in Connecticut was held on March 25, 1783, on Mr. Marshall's invitation, at the Glebe House in Woodbury. Samuel Seabury was chosen to go abroad for consecration as the first American bishop. Not being able to subscribe to the British oath of allegiance, he was secretly consecrated by Scottish bishops at Aberdeen, in November, 1784, and immediately returned as Bishop of Connecticut and the first bishop of the American Episcopal Church, bringing with him the benefits of the Apostolic Succession.

In 1785 St. Paul's parish began to build the church (Fig. 198) in which it still worships. An old drawing shows that at first it resembled many early Episcopal churches in having the tower projecting for its full depth from the front, and two rows of round-topped windows. The steeple, however, was of a design unusual at that time. It consisted of an open-arched, octagonal belfry on the tower, an octagonal lantern above this, and a spire. Tower, belfry, and lantern had balustrades about their tops. In our discussion of the work of David Hoadley, we noted that he may have seen and been influenced by this steeple of St. Paul's, which through him may therefore have had an important influence on meetinghouse design in Connecticut.

The church was not completely finished until 1814 and not consecrated until 1822. It underwent a good deal of alteration in 1855, when the front was brought forward almost to the face of the tower, and a door placed in each of the additions thus made. Later the spire was replaced by a dome and two of the balustrades were removed. Later still, the façade was decorated with scrollwork. A few years ago this was removed, the dome was replaced by a spire, and the interior partially restored so that the appearance of this historic church has been much improved. The parish house is a recent addition.

198 St. Paul's Episcopal Church, 1785, Woodbury, Connecticut

199 St. Peter's Episcopal Church, 1802, Monroe, Connecticut

200 Union Episcopal Church, 1773, West Claremont, New Hampshire

St. Peter's Episcopal church in Monroe, Connecticut (Fig. 199), was built in 1802, when the town was a part of Huntington, and much resembles St. Paul's church in that town. As in so many old Episcopal churches, the tower projects somewhat from the front of the building. Over the rather elaborate doorway in the tower is a large Palladian window. There used to be a balustrade around the tower. The church was raised four feet, in 1932, to permit the building of rooms beneath.

Inland Massachusetts, for reasons already discussed, has comparatively few old Episcopal churches. In New Hampshire, however, the case is somewhat different. At West Claremont (Fig. 200), on the edge of the Connecticut Valley, is the oldest Episcopal church in the state. Begun in 1773, its completion was delayed until 1789 by the Revolution. The exterior was gray for many years, with red—New England thrift!—on the rear wall. It now is white. On each side is a single row of long, round-headed windows, with sixty panes to each. The rear third of the house, including two windows, was added in 1821, and the line of division can easily be seen. The projecting tower rises only a little above the peak of the roof. Tower and belfry were added in 1801. Within, the church has been little changed and is a sight to warm the antiquarian's heart (Fig. 201). The square pews with spindle tops are still in place, two rows of small ones down the center and a row of large ones on either wall. The small ones are elevated by a single step above the floor and the large ones by two. Each pew door is made of a single wide board. The gallery at the rear was closed off in 1845. Governor Wentworth is said to have provided the plan for this church and also to have promised the nails and glass for its construction, but as a Loyalist he was forced to leave New Hampshire before his promise could be fulfilled.

The early settlers of Claremont were mostly Episcopalians from Connecticut. After they appealed for help to the Society for the Propagation of the Gospel, a clergyman was sent them but he was rather roughly treated by the patriots. It is said that Congregationalists, none the less, joined Episcopalians in building this church (whence its present name of "Union" Church) on the understanding that its clergyman should be a Congregational minister but ordained by the Church of England. When this solution proved impractical, the Congregationalists built their own meetinghouse, and the Union Church became Episcopalian.

Across the lane from this church is a small brick Roman Catholic chapel, "Old Saint Mary's," built in 1823. It was erected by a former rector of the Episcopal church who, with his son, was converted to Catholicism. The lower story was the chapel, and the upper one was used for some years as a school. The churchyards of the two parishes—Episcopal and Roman Catholic—are side by side, with no fence between them.

No other non-Puritan denomination in New England erected many churches comparable to those of the Episcopalians in size or architectural distinction. Numerically, the Baptists were the most important of these

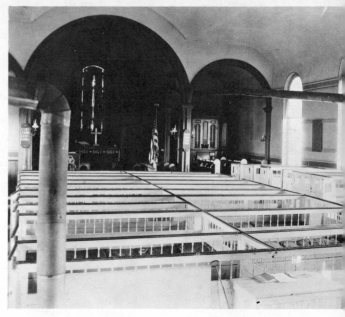

201 Interior, Union Episcopal Church

bodies, and at first the largest part of the population of Rhode Island was of the Baptist faith. In general, they were not a wealthy folk, nor did they attach particular importance to the character of the houses in which they worshiped. Their early meetinghouses have not survived. In Newport and Providence, however, the two chief towns of Rhode Island, Baptist meetinghouses of importance have come down to us.

In 1729, the year in which the Old South Church of Boston was built, the congregation of Seventh Day Baptists in Newport built a small meetinghouse without tower or spire. It measured only 38 by 26 feet. Its exterior was plain, its roof the pitched type then coming into fashion. A fireproof shelter of brick now protects this old meetinghouse, which has been moved to where it serves as part of the headquarters of the Newport Historical Society. Within, the ceiling is vaulted,

193

resembling that of St. Paul's Episcopal church at Wickford. The pulpit (Fig. 202) is much like the one at Cohasset, Massachusetts, built a number of years later. The face of the gallery is richly decorated. Originally there were square pews on the floor. Panels from their sides now form a dado about the wall.

Larger and more splendid is the First Baptist Church of Providence, built in 1775 (Fig. 203). This was the third meetinghouse of the church founded by Roger Williams, the oldest Baptist church in America. For sixty years the members had no house of worship, but met in one another's homes or out of doors. The first church was erected in 1700, the second and larger one in 1726. The congregation prospered with the years, and Nicholas Brown, founder and benefactor of the university that now bears his name, with his brother and other members of his family, worshiped there and generously supported the church. In 1771, Rhode Island College, as Brown was at first called, moved to Providence from the town of Warren, thus

203 First Baptist Church, 1775, Providence, Rhode Island

202 Pulpit, Seventh-Day Baptist Church, 1729, Newport, Rhode Island

necessitating a larger meetinghouse for the accommodation of the increased congregation. In 1775 this new one was erected "for the worship of Almighty God, and to hold commencements in." The cost of its construction was high for those days: £7,000.

The building is unique among New England churches of the eighteenth century in that it is neither a typical meetinghouse, oblong with the main entrance on the side, nor quite of the church type which succeeded this, but something of a compromise between the two. The structure is square, measuring 80 feet each way, with doors on all four sides. The peak of the low-pitched roof runs east and west, and at the west end projects the tower. The base of the tower is enclosed by a deep but narrow porch. Through this, but at a level considerably below the foundation line of the house, is the main door of the church. This arrangement was necessitated by the height of the foundation and the fact that the ground slopes steeply. Two rows of round-headed windows encircle the entire church. In the position of the pulpit at the east end, opposite the tower and main entrance, the building conforms to the later church design; but in its width and its numerous entrances, it resembles the older meetinghouses.

This church is the first one in New England in which the direct influence of an English architect can be clearly seen. Joseph Brown, the chairman of the building committee, possessed a copy of James Gibbs' *Book of Architecture*, published in 1728, which contained many drawings of Gibbs' churches. The spire of the Providence church quite obviously was copied from Plate XXX of this book. Gibbs had made four designs for the spire of St. Martin's-in-the-Fields, in London, and the three that he did not use there appear in the plate. It is the central one of the three which the committee decided to reproduce. The very copy of Gibbs' book that in all probability was used by the building committee is today in the Providence Athenaeum. The spire is far more elaborately ornamented than that of any other New England meetinghouse of the time, and resembles the type that distinguished the large city churches of the early part of the nineteenth century, such as that of the Park Street Church of Boston.

The interior of the church has been considerably changed. The three galleries, with five columns continuing through them to the vaulted ceiling, are much as they were, and the five doors (there are two at the east end), with their elaborate casings, are original. In 1832, however, the 126 square pews on the floor were removed and replaced by slips, and the old pulpit and sounding board were taken out. A Greek Revival pulpit took the place of the older one, and the Palladian pulpit window was sealed up. Soon afterward, the square pews in the galleries followed those on the floor into oblivion. In the middle of the west gallery now stands an organ, installed in 1834. To make room for it, the so-called "upper gallery," supported on columns above the main one and providing accommodation for Negroes, was removed. Still later the baptistry was built out at the east end and the pulpit of today—the third which the house has had—was placed just in front of it. Despite all these changes, the interior is a beautiful one, reminding us more of the Episcopal churches of the eighteenth century and of a few Puritan churches of the early nineteenth century than of a Yankee meetinghouse of Revolutionary days.

The Baptists have built a few notable churches elsewhere, as at East Poultney, Vermont, and Yarmouth, Maine. At the other end of the architectural scale stands the tiny "Elder Ballou" meetinghouse in Cumberland, Rhode Island (Fig. 204), built about 1740 by a congregation of Six Principle Baptists. It measures only 27 by 25 feet. There are doors on the west, south, and east, and a pulpit at the north, with a pulpit window behind it. Two tiers of small windows encircle the house, the upper directly beneath the eaves. Within, there is a small gallery on three sides. On the floor are the simplest of pews, and in the gallery, backless benches only. The timbers of the frame project into the room from the plastered walls. In front of the pulpit, which is simply a plain bench (Fig. 205), is the Elders' seat with hinges for a communion table in front of it. The whole structure is of the utmost plainness and severity, and is a good example of a rude early meetinghouse. The doctrines of the Six Principle Baptists, which go back to Roger Williams himself, are found in the first two verses of the sixth chapter of Hebrews: Repentance, Faith, Baptism, Laying on of Hands, Resurrection of the Dead, and Eternal Judgment. The denomination today is very small, but it still has several

204 Elder Ballou Meetinghouse, 1740, Cumberland, Rhode Island

197

205 Interior, Elder Ballou Meetinghouse

206 *Maple Root Church, 1797, Coventry, Rhode Island*

207 *First Presbyterian Church, 1756, Newburyport, Massachusetts*

churches in Rhode Island. One of them is the "Maple Root" church in Coventry (Fig. 206), built in 1797. It is very simple, and much like a small eighteenth-century Puritan meeting-house.

Presbyterian churches are rare in New England, but in early days there was sometimes a closer relationship between certain of the Puritan churches than was compatible with their complete independence. This was shown, for example, in the adoption of the Saybrook Platform in 1708 by delegates from the Connecticut churches. Some churches were even called, rather loosely, Presbyterian. Of true Presbyterian churches, however, that maintained definite relations with the denomination as a whole, only one, the First Presbyterian church of Newburyport, Massachusetts (Fig. 207), more commonly called the "Old South" is of marked interest.

The coming of George Whitefield, the great evangelist, to Newburyport in 1740 led to a religious ferment, the result of which was the withdrawal of thirty men with their families from the First Church and another thirty-eight from the Third Church (both Congregational) and their organization into a new church that ultimately became Presbyterian in affiliation. Their first chapel, built in 1743, was succeeded by the present church in 1756. The building was constructed on the meetinghouse plan with the main door on one long side and the pulpit opposite. It was one of the largest in New England, 90 feet long by 63 feet wide. There was a tower at one end and a porch at the other. Over the tower rose a graceful steeple with an open, arched belfry of eight columns surmounted by a dome and spire. The later architectural history of the building is not entirely clear, but in 1829 there was a radical change in which the main door seems to have been closed and the entrance put through the tower. The steeple was replaced in 1848 by one of Greek Revival style. Over this was an octagonal, windowed lantern, and above, until recently, a spire.

In 1856, a century after its erection, the church was again made over. The body of it was built out around the square tower, and an entrance bay with three doors added at the front. The pulpit was moved to the opposite end and new galleries were built. In recent repairs the old spire was replaced by the present low dome, and the pinnacles, formerly over the columns, removed. Since 1759, the same copper weathercock has turned in the wind. Originally there were 140 square pews inside, with the Elders' pew in front of the pulpit and the deacons' seat in front of that. The tything men occupied the rear seats and carried their official rods (still preserved as relics) to strike awe into the hearts of noisy youth. The pews were replaced by slips in 1856.

In this church Benedict Arnold and his men, on their way to Quebec, stopped to worship in September, 1775. On the first Sunday after the Battle of Lexington, the minister made an appeal for the Patriot cause, and Captain Ezra Hunt formed here what is said to have been the first company of volunteers in the American army. But it is the man whose inspiration led to the building of this church—George Whitefield—whose name is most often associated with it today. Many years after his first visit to America, after crossing the Atlantic thirteen times, Whitefield returned to Newburyport, broken in health but still full of missionary ardor, and here he died in September, 1770. Before his death he besought his friend, the Reverend Jonathan Parsons, pastor of the Old South, that he might be buried under the pulpit of this church. There in a crypt, his body was laid to rest, as was later that of Parsons. Many years ago, while the crypt was open to visitors, someone stole one of Whitefield's arm-bones. It was later returned, and the crypt was then sealed. In 1856, when the position of the pulpit was changed, a new crypt was built beneath it and the remains were transferred thither.

There are few old Methodist church buildings in New England, and only one, perhaps, for its historical interest, deserves mention here. This is the church at Readfield, Maine, built in 1795 and dedicated in that year by Jesse Lee, the indefatigable propagator of Methodism. This simple building was moved in 1824, and has been much altered. It is of no architectural interest. The remarkable fact in its history, indicating the vigorous spirit of frontier Methodism, is that in 1798 Lee brought together in this rather isolated place, with the very primitive means of transportation and entertainment available, a Methodist Conference of all New England that was attended by almost two thousand people.

"The oldest Universalist church in the world" is the claim made for a building standing in Oxford, Massa-

208 Old Universalist Church, 1792,
Oxford, Massachusetts

209 German Lutheran Meetinghouse, 1772,
Waldoboro, Maine

chusetts. This church was organized just after the Revolution, and the building erected in 1792 (Fig. 208). Hosea Ballou, a founder of Universalism, was installed as its minister in 1794. The building seems to have been Transitional in style at first but was greatly changed in 1845 and later divided into two stories. Services were discontinued long ago and today the lower floor is occupied by stores. In 1815 the steeple was blown down. It was rebuilt and for a long time it had the only bell in town. Clara Barton, organizer of the American branch of the Red Cross, was brought up in this church.

Lutherans have never been very numerous in New England, and there is only one meetinghouse built by them that is old enough to be included here. It stands in Waldoboro, Maine, where it was erected in 1772 (Fig. 209). A group of German Lutherans, encouraged by promises of prosperity, came over in 1748, and others followed. Externally, the building somewhat resembles a Puritan meetinghouse of the eighteenth century. At one end is a two-story porch, and within, at the other end, is a high pulpit. There is no deacons' seat in front of it, for deacons have a relatively unimportant place in Lutheran churches. The pews are square and unpainted. Regular church services have long been discontinued, though a few are held in the summer. In the cemetery is the grave of an early pastor, Frederick Augustus Rodolphus Ritz.

No small part in the history and religious life of New England, particularly in earlier years, was played by members of the Society of Friends, as the Quakers are properly called. Long persecuted but finally accepted, they introduced a leaven of gentleness into the tough lump of Puritanism and their influence is still important. The Friends made no great contributions to meetinghouse architecture. The houses they erected, however, have a simplicity and charm that to many is as attractive as the columned portico or ornamented steeple of the Puritan church.

Of the Friends meetinghouses built here before 1830 about a score have survived. There are none in Vermont or Connecticut. Most are found in Rhode Island and adjacent southern Massachusetts, in northeastern Massachusetts and nearby southeastern New Hampshire, and in Maine. Typically, they have two doors, one for men and one for women. Within, there are benches or pews on all four sides, facing the center. There is no formal pulpit, but a plain table behind which a speaker may stand. In the old days there was always a moveable partition in the middle of the house so that men and women could meet separately if they desired. There is a gallery on four sides. Ornament is almost completely lacking. The construction of the house was not standardized, and dimensions of benches and stairs are often different on the men's side from those on the women's. Indeed, in the meetinghouse at Adams, Massachusetts, there is a plaque calling attention to the fact that the building "displays a variety of handiwork—a symbol of the Quaker convincement that each man must be guided by his own inner light." Adjacent to the meetinghouse is usually a cemetery in which, in the democracy of death, the stones are uniform in size and shape. In a few of the old houses there still are regular services on First Days, and in most of them there is one yearly Meeting.

Although few notable historical events have been connected with these structures, one should not assume that the men and women who met there were never stirred to action. The fortitude with which they faced persecution in the early years makes one of the great pages of New England history. Edward Wanton, an official participating in the hangings of some Quakers in Boston, was so impressed by their demeanor that he became one himself. He organized a Meeting in his home town of Scituate and gave land for a meetinghouse, which he helped build in 1706. Some years later this was moved up the river—perhaps on the ice—to where it now stands beside a much-travelled highway in North Pembroke (Fig. 210).

210 Friends Meetinghouse, 1706, North Pembroke, Massachusetts

211 Friends Meetinghouse, 1810,
East Sandwich, Massachusetts

202

212 Friends Meetinghouse, 1776,
South Uxbridge, Massachusetts

In East Sandwich, on Cape Cod, overlooking the marshes and Cape Cod Bay, stands a large and well preserved meetinghouse of 1810 (Fig. 211). A floor was later added at the gallery level and the upper story used for social purposes. Here may be seen the old windlass once employed to raise and lower the partition that divided the congregation. There is now only one Meeting a year, on the first First Day of the Eighth Month.

In South Uxbridge, Massachusetts, the Friends meetinghouse of 1776 (Fig. 212) is unusual in being built of brick. The supply on hand when the building was erected proved too small to finish it, and since the brick-maker had enlisted in the Continental army, the upper gable ends were not finished until he returned. The bricks he then made were slightly different in color from the earlier ones, and the line between the two can still be seen.

The meetinghouse was in constant service until about fifty years ago, the attendance sometimes being so large that the unfinished gallery had to be used. During a recent restoration it was found that the present single-doored porch was not original, and that here, as in other Friends' houses, there used to be two doors. This Uxbridge Meeting numbered among its members the most eminent citizen of nearby Rhode Island, Stephen Hopkins, who had been a member of the Continental Congress, a signer of the Declaration of Independence and Governor and Chief Justice of the state. This great man persisted in keeping ownership of a slave. Several committees labored with him to free this slave. When he finally refused to do so, the Meeting "put him from under their care" and "drew up papers of denial against him."

Much as the Friends disliked war, one of their meetinghouses, that on Quaker Hill in Portsmouth, Rhode Island, built about 1700 (Fig. 213), found itself involved in the Revolution. The British at one time held an important fort nearby, and used the house as a barracks for Hessian troops. The Battle of Rhode Island (August 29, 1778) was fought not far away. In this house, after the war, was founded the Friends Boarding School, which moved to Providence in 1819 to become the famous Moses Brown School. Today, the meetinghouse serves an active Friends organization which uses the old building efficiently. The outside seems little changed, but one of the rooms within has pews and a pulpit, making it look much like the auditorium of a small church.

Southeastern New Hampshire was the home of many Friends in the early years, and some of their meetinghouses still stand there. In Dover, at one time, a third of the population were of this faith. In this place stands a large meetinghouse (Fig. 214), built on the Dover Point Road and moved here when the population shifted. Services are held in it on every First Day. In this house the poet Whittier's parents were married, after the simple Quaker fashion, and here he himself often worshiped.

There are various minor sects in New England, of some interest in religious history, of which a few old meetinghouses still survive. There is opportunity here to mention only two of these.

A group of Covenanters from Scot-

213 Friends Meetinghouse, 1700, Portsmouth, Rhode Island

203

214 Friends Meetinghouse, 1768, Dover, New Hampshire

215 Reformed Presbyterian Church, 1831,
West Barnet, Vermont

204

216 Shaker Meetinghouse, 1792,
Canterbury, New Hampshire

land settled in the region of what is now Caledonia County, Vermont, late in the eighteenth century. At West Barnet, the "Walter Harvey meetinghouse" of 1831 (Fig. 215) is the last of the Old Covenanter churches in New England that is still active. Their stern creed requires its adherents to sing metrical versions of the Psalms without instrumental accompaniment, and to refrain from voting in national elections, since God is not acknowledged in the Constitution of the United States. They celebrate the Lord's Supper only twice a year. At this feast, tokens that were distributed earlier are collected from members, a reminder of the days when the Covenanters, before they came to America, were often persecuted, and had to make sure that no outsiders or spies gained access to their rites.

Late in the eighteenth and early in the nineteenth century, the Shakers established a number of communities in various parts of New England. This sect, named from its ritualistic dances, developed thrifty and successful farmers and gifted craftsmen. Only two communities are still active: at Canterbury, New Hampshire, and Sabbathday Lake (New Gloucester), Maine. The Shaker meetinghouse at Canterbury (Fig. 216) is typical. It is a plain, white, gambrel-roofed building of two stories, with two front doors. The chapel is on the first floor and other rooms occupy the second. During the erection of this building, the men worked in reverent silence, with as little noise and talking as possible.

As denominations and minor sects increased in number, meetinghouses were sometimes built to serve more than one of them. In many of the smaller towns, particularly in the northern states of New England, and especially where the Congregational church was not the dominant one, members of several denominations often joined to build such a union church. Usually the Sabbaths were allocated to each in proportion to the number of its members. Less commonly, a nondenominational church was organized. The building was erected by a committee or by a meetinghouse society, and occasionally by the town itself. The last was the case with the Old Town House at Bridgewater Hill, New Hampshire (Fig. 217), built in 1806 to serve for town meetings and for the religious services of all the denominations in town. As was often the case, the meetinghouse here was located near the geographical center of the town, but this is now several miles from the center of population. Originally it was a typical meetinghouse, but in 1881 it was reduced in size and the interior much altered. Town meetings were still held here until a few years ago, but the only gatherings in the old house now are those celebrating Old Home Week each summer.

There are a few old Indian meetinghouses standing in New England. Attempts to convert the aborigines to Chistianity were made by various people, notably John Eliot, who established a community of "Praying Indians" at Natick, Massachusetts, in 1650. Richard Bourne moved to Cape Cod and organized an Indian church in what is now the town of Mashpee. A meetinghouse (Fig. 218), standing in a rather isolated place in sandy, pitch-

217 Old Town House, 1806,
Bridgewater Hill, New Hampshire

205

218 Old Indian Church,
Mashpee, Massachusetts

pine woods, bears the legend "Old Indian Church, built in 1684, remodeled in 1717, rededicated in 1923." There was probably a meetinghouse here in 1684, but this one, old though it is, clearly does not go back to the seventeenth century, though some of the frame may be old. Around it is a cemetery where people of Indian blood have been buried for many years.

At Mohegan, Connecticut, stands a small church (Fig. 219) built by subscription in 1831 for the remaining members of the Mohegan tribe. It is still active as a Congregational church. Every year the Indians here take part in a "brush arbor" ceremony that goes back to the days when they worshiped the gods of the harvest.

The churches so far discussed in this chapter have been somewhat outside the Puritan tradition, but all of them have been Protestant. For many years no churches of any other faith existed in New England, or, indeed, would have been tolerated. The Roman Catholic church, now dominant in parts of New England, had few communicants until after the Revolution. The early Catholic churches were of little historical or architectural interest, but one is notable—St. Patrick's at Damariscotta Mills in the town of Newcastle, Maine. Built in 1808 (Fig. 220), it is the oldest Roman Catholic church building in New England. A number of Irishmen settled in

219 Congregational Church, 1831, Mohegan, Connecticut

220 St. Patrick's Roman Catholic Church, 1808, Newcastle, Maine

221 Touro Synagogue, 1763, Newport, Rhode Island

this part of Maine in the late eighteenth century, and two of them, Matthew Cottrill and James Kavenagh, became prosperous. At their invitation in 1798, Father (later Bishop) John Cheverus visited the Newcastle region, and continued to return every summer for twenty years. He also ministered to the Penobscot Indians, who became strongly attached to him. Father Cheverus had fled the French Revolution and come to Boston in 1795, where his personality and scholarship won him many friends among clergymen and writers. With his encouragement, St. Patrick's was built and it was he who dedicated it on July 17, 1808.

It is a small, simple church, built of native brick. Its windows, plain at first, have been replaced by stained glass and the original benches by pews.

Above the altar (of the sarcophagus type) is a painting of the *Descent from the Cross* done by a member of the Rubens school, and given to the church by Father Cheverus. The square bell tower in front of the church was added in 1818 to carry the Paul Revere bell presented to the church by Matthew Cottrill. This is thought to be the only Revere bell in a Catholic church. The spire was added in 1894.

Another religious group, the Jews, were also few in number in early New England. Rhode Island, however, with her tradition of complete freedom for all religions, soon attracted a good many of them, most of whom settled in Newport. Their present synagogue, Temple Jeshuat Israel, was built, of brick, in 1763 (Fig. 221), and is commonly called the Touro synagogue after Isaac Touro, the congregation's first permanent rabbi. It is the oldest one in New England and perhaps in the United States. Peter Harrison was its architect. The building is so oriented that worshipers before the ark face eastward toward Jerusalem. The small entrance porch leads into a much-admired interior in which is combined the Georgian style of the eighteenth century with the synagogue design in the Sephardic tradition of Spanish and Portuguese Jews. The galleries on the three sides are reserved for women. During the Revolution the prosperity of Newport declined, and that of the synagogue with it, and the building was closed for a time. In 1781, town meetings were held in it, and from 1781 to 1784 the Rhode Island General Assembly met here, as well as the Supreme Court of the state. The synagogue was restored and reopened in 1883, aided in part by legacies from Isaac Touro's two sons.

Although the organizations discussed in this chapter do not trace their origin directly from the ones first established in New England and dominant so long, their thriving presence shows how large a share of religious life was centered in churches drawing inspiration, in some measure, from sources outside the beliefs and practices of the founding fathers. They had an important part in the vigorous spiritual life that contributed so much to the strength and influence of New England. These six states—small in area and population but great in many other ways—have been of immense significance in the history of our nation. Although their relative

strength has long been declining, and much of the old stock that was nourished in this rugged land is now dispersed beyond its borders, the descendants of the men and women of New England's first two centuries still powerfully influence American character. The Yankee was unique in the particular combination of qualities that distinguished him. He was thrifty, ambitious, industrious, keen of intellect, eager for education, talented and resourceful in invention, by nature a trader, shrewd in business, and possessed of a certain sharpness of mind and stubbornness of will that carried him far. It is not strange that as the agricultural way of life began to give place to commerce and industry, he became a power in the land, and, in the rising tempo of New England life, made this small corner of the nation for a time its industrial and intellectual capital.

But the New Englander contributed something more vital and important still—the Puritan tradition. Derived in large measure from the religious faith of his fathers, this is a subtle quality, involving a degree of moral sensitivity and a feeling of responsibility not only for one's own conduct but for the welfare of society as a whole, that has become famous as the "New England conscience." It served as a leaven to sweeten the raw mass of an expanding frontier nation and to remind it of its moral heritage. In the great humanitarian movements of the nineteenth century—for better education, child welfare, prison reform, temperance, the abolition of slavery, and many others—it is no accident that most of the leaders were men and women of New England stock. To be sure, in the inevitable reaction, the words "reform" and "Puritanical" have often come into ill repute and are subject to much ridicule; but this in part is an uneasy tribute that the present pays the past. American culture, crude and selfish as it has often been, would have matured with much more difficulty had it not been for the Puritan tradition. This is still powerful in the hearts of those who cherish a New England heritage. An altruistic concern for others, formerly directed to the saving of their souls but now expressed in services of a much wider sort, is a typical American trait, we like to think, even though the people who display it may have shaken off formal allegiance to the faith of their fathers.

The history of the United States cannot be understood without a knowledge of the history of New England, and the driving force of New England history lies in its Puritan tradition. As we have seen repeatedly in these pages, this underwent progressive changes as the years passed, changes that were expressed not only in the religious beliefs and practices of the Puritans themselves, but even in the style and construction of the buildings in which this religious life so typically found expression. Here, as in all human history, architecture and religion have been closely related, and a knowledge of one helps us to understand the other. Scholarly interpretations of Puritanism by philosophers and historians often tell us less about the inner character of the Puritan than does a white steeple rising beside the street of a New England village.

Appendix

CHECK LIST OF NEW ENGLAND
MEETINGHOUSES & CHURCHES
BUILT BY 1830 & STILL STANDING

Here are described the 509 structures that have been studied during the preparation of this book. A page reference or figure reference indicates that the building is discussed in the text.

For the meetinghouses and churches in the Puritan tradition—Congregational and Unitarian—four types are noted, corresponding to the types described in Chapters 3, 4, 5, and 6. (The buildings of other denominations do not usually conform to these types.)

The meetinghouse here identified as Type I is the more or less square structure of the latter half of the seventeenth century and the first few years of the eighteenth. Its four-sided hip roof rises to a central cupola.

Type II is the oblong, barnlike meetinghouse of the period 1710–1800, with its main entrance on one side, the pulpit opposite the entrance on the other side, and usually doors at the two ends. The steep roof rises to a ridgepole. The building may or may not have a tower and belfry projecting at one of its ends.

Type III is the church of the first quarter of the nineteenth century. Its main doors (sometimes there is only one) are at one end, the pulpit at the other. Over the front there is usually a porch or portico, provided with columns, pilasters, or other ornamentation. Over this, or partly set back on the roof, is a tower that carries a steeple or spire.

Type IV, built after 1825, is the Greek Revival church, with Doric columns, wide frieze, and the generally heavier ornament of the period.

Just before and after 1800, a few churches were built that were intermediate between Type II and Type III. They are like Type II in having a tower projecting from one end, but differ in having the main entrance also at this end instead of on the side, and the pulpit at the other end. These buildings differ from Type III in still having a plain tower rather than the more elaborate façade that came soon after. In this list, such structures are identified as Transitional.

CONNECTICUT

Abington (Pomfret). Cong. Ch., 1751. Type II, made III 1802, IV 1834. (Pp. 169–70, Fig. 178)

Avon. Cong. Ch., 1818. Type III. David Hoadley architect. Steeple, entrance bay of excellent proportion and design. Pews, pulpit replaced 1854, interior otherwise not greatly changed. Windows originally at pulpit end now closed. (Pp. 23, 103, Fig. 3)

Bethany. Christ Episc. Ch., 1809. David Hoadley architect. Little changed. Pews replaced by slips 1828. (P. 189, Fig. 195)

Bethlehem. Christ Episc. Ch., 1829. Brick. Tower partly projecting. Roof lowered about 2 ft. and side windows shortened, as shown in brickwork.

Bloomfield. St. Andrew's Episc. Ch., 1809. Moved 2 miles 1830, re-erected. Bell tower partly projecting, probably not orig. At base has recess with access to 2 doors. Windows round-topped. Palladian window behind pulpit. Pews made of panels from earlier ones.

Bridgewater. Cong. Ch., 1808. Type III. Unusual in having partly projecting tower, 1 door. Octagonal belfry, spire. Pews replaced 1842; interior much changed 1855. Ceiling at first vaulted, now level. Part of old pulpit preserved. (P. 126.)

Brooklyn. Old MH., 1771. Type II, with tower. (Pp. 50–51, Fig. 16)

Brooklyn. Trinity Episc. (Malbone Church), 1770. (Pp. 189–90, Fig. 196)

Burlington. Cong. Ch., 1804. Type III. Moved to green 1836 and re-erected as Type IV. Four Doric columns. Size reduced. Interior completely changed. (P. 137, Fig. 142)

Canterbury. First Cong. Ch., 1805. Type III. Thomas Gibbs builder. Behind portico of 4 square columns, recess for large central door and one at each end. Palladian window above. Old pews, pulpit replaced 1841. Gallery columns removed 1853, iron rods substituted. Unique in having gallery with level floors, used for social purposes. Octagonal belfry and upper stage; dome.

Canton Center. Cong. Ch., 1814. Type III. Interior made Gothic 1874. (P. 172, Fig. 182)

Centerbrook. Cong. Ch., 1790. Type II; turned and made IV 1839; then Victorian 1888. Tower, belfry modern. (P. 170, Fig. 179)

Chaplin. Cong. Ch., 1814. Type III. Deacon Benjamin Chaplin left bequest to build church if it was within 1½ miles of his house. Lifted, turned 1866, stone basement below. Main entrance now there. Three original doors above closed. Steeple remodeled.

Cheshire. Cong. Ch., 1826. Type III. Probably by David Hoadley. Pulpit at first next to entrance but moved to rear 1857. Large, shallow dome with orig. carved wooden ornament in center. Galleries, columns excellent and essentially unchanged. (P. 103, Fig. 92)

Derby. Cong. Ch., 1820. Type III. Building of David Hoadley type, but only 1 door. Richly carved, with Palladian window above and 4 columns in pairs. Pulpit at first next to entrance but moved to rear in 1848, when interior much changed. (P. 106).

East Canaan. Cong. Ch., 1822. Type III. Resembles Avon church but no balustrades. Interior much altered 1855. Gallery columns removed. (P. 105)

Eastford. Cong. Ch., 1829. Type III. Now 2 doors with long, round-topped window between. Square belfry, spire. Pulpit at entrance end.

East Granby. Cong. Ch., 1830. Type IV. Isaac Damon architect. Built of trap rock. (Pp. 109–10, Fig. 104)

East Haddam. Cong. Ch., 1794. One of first examples of Type III. (Pp. 91–92, Figs. 74, 75)

East Hartland. Cong. Ch., 1801. Transitional. Remodeled 1875 to mixture of Greek, Victorian styles. (P. 74, Fig. 49)

East Haven. Cong. Ch., 1772. Type II; changed to III 1850. (P. 171, Fig. 180)

East Plymouth. St. Matthew's Episc. Ch., 1792. Very plain. Small porch at door. Turned to face west, 1842. Ceiling now just above gallery level. Original pulpit, chandelier. Pews built 1830.

East Windsor. Cong. Ch., 1802. Transitional at first, but made Type IV 1842 by building forward around tower. Front now plain, 2 doors, 4 pilasters. Now 2 stories. Square, columned belfry, second stage.

Enfield. Old MH. and town hall, 1775. Type II with tower; made IV. Originally on site of present church across road. Here Capt. Thomas Abbey beat drum to notify congregation of Battle of Lexington. Portico of 4 Doric columns added. Made town hall 1876. Now 2 stories. Little used.

Farmington. Cong. Ch., 1771. Type II with tower. (Pp. 48–50, Fig. 15)

Guilford. Cong. Ch., 1829. Type III. Vestibule widened, gallery lowered, pulpit changed 1861. (P. 106, Fig. 96)

Hamden. Grace Episc. Ch., 1819. Probably by David Hoadley. Fully projecting tower, 1 door, gallery 3 sides, round-topped windows. Spire added, other alterations 1847. Spire blew off 1915. Present belfry, dome, built 1921. Much of interior original.

Hampton. Cong. Ch., 1754. Type II; made IV 1838. (P. 171, Fig. 181)

Hartford. Christ Church Cathedral, Episc., 1828. Ithiel Town probably drew plans. James Chamberlain builder. Gothic, of

stone. Tower projects slightly. Three doors, 1 row long windows. Top of tower finished 1839. Buttresses, pinnacles added 1902. Interior largely orig., and impressive.

Hartford. First Cong. Ch., 1806. Type III. Interior considerably altered 1851. (P. 128, Fig. 133)

Hartford. Second Cong. Ch., 1827. Type III. (P. 129, Fig. 134)

Hebron. St. Peter's Episc. Ch., 1825. Rose-colored brick, carefully laid. Tower, square wooden belfry. One row long Gothic windows. Exterior, interior much changed 1849.

Huntington. St. Paul's Episc. Ch., 1814. Shingled. Tower protrudes slightly. One door in it, Palladian window above. Windows now with colored glass, upper row round-topped. Original pews, gallery columns removed.

Kensington. Cong. Ch., 1774. Type II; changed to III 1837, but very simple. Front plain. Square belfry set back on roof. Scars of old front door, pulpit window in clapboards. Extensive alterations within, chiefly 1833.

Kent. St. Andrew's Episc. Ch., 1826. Stone; but upper part of tower, wood. Lower tower partly projects. One door. Windows Gothic. Galleries removed 1872. Other exterior and interior changes.

Killingworth. Cong. Ch., 1820. Type III. Ithiel Town probable architect. Well-designed and proportioned entrance bay, doors. Octagonal belfry, lantern, dome. Pews, pulpit changed 1853, 1868. Ceiling a flat dome, with elaborate ornament. Church of Titus Coan, missionary to Sandwich Islands.

Killingworth. Emmanuel Episc. Ch., 1810, but finish delayed. Very plain. One door, 1 window at front. One row side windows. Chancel added. Church of George Gilbert, the "Pastoral Parson."

Lebanon. Cong. Ch., 1807. Type III. Restored after almost complete destruction in 1938. (P. 123, Fig. 124)

Litchfield. Cong. Ch., 1829. Type III. Much like Cheshire and Southington; but much of steeple reconstructed. (P. 104, Fig. 93)

Lyme (Grassy Hill). Cong. Ch., 1812. Type III, made IV 1847. Simple. One door. Square belfry. Three long side windows. Withdrew from Hamburg ch. as a "separate" ch. 1755.

Lyme (Hamburg). Cong. Ch., 1814. Probably III at first; now IV. Portico with 4 columns. Square belfry on roof. Two stories. Ch. above, old town hall below. One door.

Marble Dale. St. Andrew's Episc. Ch., 1822. Brick. Gothic. Tower partly projects. One door. Square belfry with Gothic louvers. Short spire. Transepts, chancel added 1855.

Meriden. Center Cong. Ch., 1830. Body Type IV; steeple III. (P. 136, Fig. 140)

Middle Haddam. Christ Episc. Ch., 1787. Steep roof. Tower projects boldly. Square belfry added 1840. Pews, pulpit replaced 1856. Interior much changed.

Milford. Cong. Ch., 1823. Type III. Interior somewhat altered 1859. Pews, pulpit reversed 1918. Side galleries orig., with graceful columns, capitals. (P. 103, Fig. 91)

Milton. Cong. Ch., 1792. Early state unknown. Now very simple. Stood on green at first; moved across river 1828. Rear gallery added 1834, square belfry 1843. Remodeled to Type IV 1855. One door. Repaired 1881.

Milton. Trinity Episc. Ch., 1802. Oliver Dickinson builder. Simple. Plain front, 1 door. Belfry on roof. Pews, pulpit orig.

Mohegan (Montville). Cong. Ch., 1831. Built for the Indians, by subscription. (P. 206, Fig. 219)

Monroe. St. Peter's Episc. Ch., 1802. (P. 192, Fig. 199)

Monroe (East Village). Meth. Ch., 1811–1815. Type III. Small. Two rows windows. Tower partly projects. Belfry with pyramidal roof. Scars of 4 windows at rear. Galleries taken out some years ago, high pulpit lowered. Church once part of Stratford circuit.

New Hartford. North Cong. Ch., 1828. Type III. Brick, with wooden steeple. Three doors. Octagonal belfry, dome. Entrance bay with 3 doors. Doors, windows round-topped. Pulpit originally at front, moved to rear 1850. Side windows long; no side galleries. Interior much altered.

New Haven. Center Church (Cong.), 1814. Type III. (P. 130, Fig. 135)

New Haven. Trinity Episc. Ch., 1815. Stone. (Pp. 129, 138, 188, Fig. 194)

New Haven. United Ch. (Cong.), 1815. Type III. (P. 131, Fig. 136)

New Preston Hill. Old Cong. Ch., 1824. Type III. (P. 124, Fig. 127)

Newtown. Cong. Ch., 1808. Type III at first; changed to IV 1845–1852. Tower partly projects. Square belfry, octagonal spire. Pews, pulpit altered but gallery orig. Bullet holes in weathercock.

Norfolk. Cong. Ch., 1813. Type III. David Hoadley architect. (P. 102, Fig. 90)

North Branford. Zion Episc. Ch., 1819. Capt. Abraham Coan, builder. Interior unfinished until 1839. Enlarged 1863. Tower partly projects. Octagonal belfry, dome. Gothic windows. Interior largely orig. Side galleries do not reach front. Moved short distance recently.

North Cornwall. Second Cong. Ch., 1826. Type III. Hoadley-type ch. Exterior essentially unchanged. Much of interior original, including Ionic columns from floor to ceiling. Pulpit recess of 1926 originally part of auditorium. (P. 105)

North Guilford. Cong. Ch., 1813. Type III. (P. 124, Fig. 128)

North Guilford. St. John's Episc. Ch., 1814. Near Cong. ch. Simple square belfry replaced 3 earlier ones. Additions, changes 1869. Windows replaced, side galleries removed.

North Woodbury. North Cong. Ch., 1816. Type III. (P. 89, Fig. 70)

Norwichtown. Cong. Ch., 1801. Type III. Two upper stages of steeple square and in Greek Revival style. Interior entirely changed in 1845, 1877. (P. 91, Fig. 73)

Old Lyme. Cong. Ch., 1817. Type III. Burned 1907 but exactly restored. (P. 111, Fig. 106)

Orange. Cong. Ch., 1810. Suggests Transitional type. David Hoadley, architect. (P. 106, Fig. 97)

Oxford. Cong. Ch., 1795. History not clear. Probably Type II with tower, later removed. Now Type IV. Plain front, 1 door. Square belfry, short spire on roof. Completely remodeled 1836.

Plainfield. Cong. Ch., 1816. Type III. (P. 124, Fig. 129)

Preston. Bapt. Ch., 1812. Type III. In 1832, turned, steeple added, vestry built below. Renovated 1860, pulpit moved from front to rear. Plain front, 1 door. Handsome block trim on cornice. Square, open belfry, octagonal lantern, spire. Balustrades. Globe window in gable. Interior much altered.

Preston. Second Cong. Ch. ("Long Society"), 1817. Type II. (P. 69, Fig. 44)

Putnam Heights (formerly Killingly Hill). Cong. Ch., 1818. Type III. Elias Carter builder. Plain entrance bay. Three round-topped doors. Palladian window. Open, square belfry. Stage between belfry, spire removed. Made 2 stories, much changed, and moved to present site 1860.

Quaker Farms. Christ Episc. Ch., 1812. George Boult builder. One door. Upper windows Gothic. Octagonal belfry, lantern. Dome. Interior largely original. Side galleries do not extend to front. Good pulpit window.

Riverton. Union Ch. (St. Paul's Episc.), 1829. Stone with wooden steeple. First served 4 denominations. Named St. Paul's 1877. Tower projects slightly. Square belfry.

Rocky Hill. Cong. Ch., 1805. Type III; but old spire replaced by Type IV belfry 1843. (P. 126)

Salisbury. Cong., Ch., 1800. Type III. (P. 77, Fig. 51)

Salisbury. St. John's Episc. Ch., 1822. Brick. Extensive additions 1852. Chancel added at east end 1884. Extended at west end 1959.

Seymour. Trinity Episc. Ch., 1797. Finished 1816. Tower partly projects. Most details, without and within, altered to Victorian style 1857.

Sharon. Christ Episc. Ch., 1819. Brick. Gothic windows. Square tower on roof, with delicate open belfry, octagonal lantern, spire. Small porch added at door 1842, chancel 1880. Paint on brick removed 1920.

Sharon. Cong. Ch., 1824. Type III. Brick, with Hoadley-type steeple. (P. 105, Fig. 95)

Simsbury. Cong. Ch., 1830. Type III, with some details of IV. Isaac Damon architect. Interior altered 1865, 1883, 1896. (P. 109, Fig. 103)

South Britain (Southbury). Cong. Ch., 1825. Type III. Handsome Hoadley-type steeple, somewhat large for ch. Entrance bay, with pilasters. Doorways altered. Interior altered 1869. Little orig. work remains save large, circular dome. Pulpit at first next to entrance, now at other end. (P. 105)

South Canaan. Cong. Ch., 1804. Type III. Steeple changed 1843 to Type IV. Interior little altered. (P. 77, Fig. 52).

Southington. Cong. Ch., 1828. Type III. Closely resembles Cheshire ch. Pulpit first at entrance, moved to rear 1849. Interior altered 1866, 1923. Large elliptical dome with central ornament like that in Cheshire.

Sterling. Bapt. Ch., Sterling Hill, 1797. Built by MH. society. Taken over by Baptists 1812. Orig. state unknown. Now Type IV. One door, 3 side windows. Steeple top blown off and only partly restored.

Stonington. Cong. Ch. ("Road Church"), 1829. (P. 124, Fig. 126)

Stratfield. Bapt. Ch., 1813. Type III. Simple. Tower partly projects. Octagonal belfry, dome. Elliptical window high in tower.

Old pulpit, pews removed. Galleries now cut off by glass partitions.

Vernon. Cong. Ch., 1826. Type III; made IV 1851. Portico of 4 Ionic columns. High basement. Galleries orig. but rest of interior altered. Steeple replaced 1896. Now has octagonal belfry, tall spire.

Wapping. Community Ch. (Cong.), 1801. Orig. appearance not known. Now Type IV. Portico of 4 columns. Square belfry on roof. Now 2 stories. Built for several denominations. Congregationalists bought out others 1817. Interior altered 1829. Change to present style 1849.

Warehouse Point. St. John's Episc. Ch., 1809. Moved to present site 1844. Interior much changed 1856. Side galleries removed. Square belfry on tower replaced steeple. Palladian window in entrance bay.

Warren. Cong. Ch., 1818. Type III. Hoadley-type ch. Upper steeple replaced 1891 but restored to orig. design 1957. Well-designed entrance bay, with four pilasters, three doors. Horse block beside steps. Much of attractive interior orig., though pews, pulpit removed 1859. Orig. pulpit now restored. Columns from floor to ceiling. (P. 105)

Washington. Cong. Ch., 1801. Type III. (P. 78, Fig. 53)

West Avon. Cong. Ch., 1818. Type III. Plain entrance bay, 3 doors. Palladian windows 3 sides of tower. Octagonal belfry, but rest of steeple gone. Now 2 stories. Three box pews preserved.

Westminster (Canterbury). Cong. Ch., 1770. Type II changed to IV 1835–40. Turned to face road. Portico of 4 columns. Square, 2-stage steeple on roof. Interior much changed. Steep roof. Positions of old door, windows visible in clapboards. (Fig. 143)

Weston. Norfield Cong. Ch., 1830. Type III. Tower partly projects. One door. Octagonal belfry, lantern, short spire. Interior has much orig. work.

Westport. Saugatuck Cong. Ch., 1831. Type III steeple in David Hoadley manner, tall spire. Type IV portico. One door. Thirteen ft. added rear 1857. Much of interior orig. Church moved across road 1950.

Wethersfield. Cong. Ch., 1761. Type II. (P. 48, Fig. 14)

Wilton. Cong. Ch., 1790. At first probably Transitional; pulpit at entrance end. Changed to IV 1844. Front built out around tower to form vestibule and door recess. Octagonal belfry, spire. Roof steep. Interior largely remodeled. Large parish house.

Windsor. Cong. Ch., 1794. Transitional; changed to IV 1844. (Pp. 145–46, Figs. 145, 146)

Woodbury. First Cong. Ch., 1817. Type III. Pulpit removed 1881, restored 1928. Pulpit recess added. (Pp. 104–5, Fig. 94)

Woodbury. St. Paul's Episc. Ch., 1785. (Pp. 102, 191, Fig. 198)

Woodstock. Cong. Ch., 1821. Type III. Exterior like orig. state of Putnam Heights ch. Square belfry, octagonal stage, spire. Interior much changed 1887. Side galleries removed. Modern pulpit, curved slips installed. Spire blew off 1938; restored.

MAINE

Acton Corner. Cong. Ch., 1827. Type III, very plain. Two doors, square belfry on roof.

Alna. Old MH., 1789. Type II. (Pp. 59–60, Figs. 28, 31)

Belfast. First Ch. Fed., 1818. Type III. Exterior much like Asher Benjamin design. Revere bell, large clock. Pulpit, pews replaced by modern ones. Organized 1796, chiefly by Presbyterians. Became Unit. 1819 and Cong. group left. Two churches reunited 1921.

Belgrade. Old South Ch. (Rockwood's Corner), 1826. Samuel Tucker architect and builder. Type III. Small, simple, 2 doors, 1 row windows. Built for Baptists but has been used by others. Repaired 50 years ago, again recently. Steeple added 1925. Long inactive, now has summer services.

Benton Falls. Cong. Ch., 1828. Type III. Plain, 1 door, 3 side windows. Open octagonal belfry, lantern, spire. Interior modernized 1904. Has last bell made by Revere foundry. Scars of closed windows at rear.

Blue Hill. Bapt. Ch., 1817. Type III, changed to IV 1856 by Thomas Lord. Tower projects. Deep porch with 1 door, perhaps originally 3. Doric pilasters. No side galleries. Interior modernized. Long windows. Greek Revival belfry, spire.

Bridgton. Meth. Ch., 1811. Simple, 2 doors, 3 side windows. Open belfry on roof. Built at Brackett's Corner, moved here 1855. Repaired 1947. Now affiliated with both Cong. and Meth. denominations.

Bristol. Harrington MH., 1772. At first Type II like nearby Walpole, now much changed. Two doors at end, steep roof, gable-end to road. Old pulpit, originally at side, now lowered and at front. Interior greatly altered. Plans under way to restore building.

Bristol. Walpole MH., 1772. Type II. (P. 59, Figs. 26, 27)

Casco. Quaker Ridge Friends MH., 1814. One door, at side. Closed 1923, now has occasional summer meetings.

Castine. Cong. Ch. (Fed.), 1829. Probably Type III originally. Extensively remodeled 1848, 1867.

Castine. First Parish Ch. (Unit.), 1790. Type II, made III 1831. Plain front, 1 row windows. No services 1838–67. Town meetings, courts long held in this building. Oldest MH. eastern Maine. (P. 85, Fig. 66)

Dixfield. Cong. Ch. (union of three denominations), 1829. Type III. Small entrance portico. One door. Tower, square belfry, short spire. No galleries. Interior much changed.

East Harpswell. Bapt. Ch., 1817. Very simple. Two doors, 2 side windows. Repaired 1937. Exterior and interior essentially unchanged.

Eastport. Central Cong. Ch., 1829. Type III. Easternmost Congregational church in U.S. Plain front with pilasters but no porch. Octagonal belfry. Heavy spire with gabled base replaced one blown off 1869.

Eastport. North Bapt. Ch., 1819. Type III, now much altered. Tall, deep, 3-windowed porch rising above roof level, with large, square stage above. One door; 1 row side windows. Ch. originally of Christian denomination.

East Readfield. Meth. Ch., 1794. Dedicated 1795 by Jesse Lee. Type III. Moved and remodeled 1824. Roof raised, galleries added. Turned 1857, 2 galleries removed, steeple added. Two doors. Square belfry, spire. (P. 199)

East Winthrop. Bapt. Ch., 1823. Type III. Porch, 1 door. Square tower set well back, octagonal belfry and spire. Now 2 stories, auditorium above.

Fairfield Center. Meth. Ch., 1810. Type III. Two doors. Tower, square belfry on roof. Originally Union ch., became Meth. 1929. Renovated 1947.

Gardiner. Christ Episc. Ch., 1819. Gothic, of unhammered granite. Three doors. Tower partly projects. Belfry and spire. Battlements at eaves partly conceal roof. Gardiner family great benefactors of ch. Handsome interior.

Gorham. Cong. Ch., 1797. Type II, made III. Many alterations. Porch now on west, with door at its side. Square tower, belfry, clock stage, spire. Entrance first on south. Galleries removed, pews changed 1828. Pulpit moved to east 1848, windows lengthened, porch added. New gallery 1854. Present steeple modern.

Greene. Univ. Ch., 1827. Very simple. One door, 1 row windows. No ornament. Inside of pews blue. Completely remodeled 1880.

Harpswell Center. Town house (Old MH.), 1758. Type II. No tower. (P. 67, Fig. 41)

Holden. Cong. Ch., 1829. Type III. No porch. Two doors, 1 row windows. Well-designed belfry, dome. Interior not greatly changed. Attractive building.

Jefferson. Bapt. Ch., 1808. Type III. Tower projects, has small room on either side. Three long windows on sides. Square, open belfry, pyramidal roof. Remodeled 1904. Repaired, rededicated 1922.

Kennebunk. Christ Ch. (Cong.-Meth.) 1826. Type III, much altered. Tower projects. One door. Octagonal belfry, tall spire. Interior altered 1853; galleries removed. New spire, vestibule 1869. Assumed present appearance 1917. Auditorium reconstructed 1956, when union with Methodists took place.

Kennebunk. First Parish Ch., Unit., 1771. Type II, much changed. (Pp. 157–59, Fig. 160)

Kennebunkport. Second Cong. Ch., 1824. Type III. Three-door bay, as deep as fully projecting tower; portico of 4 Doric columns. Large clock, octagonal belfry, with delicate columns, cornice. Octagonal stage and dome. Now 2 stories.

Kittery Point. Cong. Ch., 1730. Type II, made III 1840. (P. 156, Fig. 158)

Leeds. Old MH., 1804. Now Bapt. Youth Center. Steep roof. Much altered 1839, 1891. Small porch at one end. Two large windows on side.

Lincolnville Center. United Christian Ch., 1819. Essentially unchanged. Perfectly plain. No belfry. One door. Galleries on sides, where servants sat. Two pulpits at entrance end, 1 at communion table and 1 above.

Livermore. Univ. Ch. (Norland MH., or "Devil's Roosting Place"), 1829. Type III. Orig. state not known. Modified 1839, 1850, 1873, then rededicated.

Machiasport. Cong. Ch., 1828. Type III. Very plain. Two doors, 1 row windows. Orig. belfry replaced by heavy spire. Group of men at store one evening decided to build this MH., began it next morning.

Newcastle (Damariscotta Mills). St. Patrick's Roman Catholic Ch., 1808. (Pp. 206–8, Fig. 220)

New Gloucester (Sabbathday Lake). Shaker MH., 1794. Plain, gambrel-roofed. Two front doors. Chapel on first floor, 5 rooms above.

North Buxton (Groveville). Cong. Ch., 1820. Type III. Plain front, 1 door. Gothic windows now on front and sides. Heavy belfry, spire added 1857. Pulpit at first next to entrance, now at rear.

North Manchester (Scribner Hill). Old Bapt. Ch., 1793. Small, 1 story. Plain front, 2 doors. Side windows round-topped. No belfry. Moved here 1833 from East Readfield. Unchanged.

Phippsburg. Cong. Ch., 1802. Type II, made IV 1846, strongly opposed by minority. Now 3 windows at sides, colored glass 1909. Tall Greek Revival steeple with square belfry, pinnacles, spire. Services in summer.

Poland. Com. Ch., 1825. Type III. Congregational until 1945. Plain, 1 story, 2 doors. Upper part of square belfry burned 1940. Large vestry added 1961.

Porter. Old Bullockite Ch., 1818. Built by Bapt. followers of Elder Jeremiah Bullock. Plain, pitched-roof structure with 2 doors on one side, pulpit opposite. Two rows windows. Unpainted square pews throughout. Town meetings long held here.

Portland. First Parish Ch., Unit., 1825. Type III. Stone. (P. 133, Fig. 139)

Readfield Corner. Union Meth. Ch., 1827. Type III. Built by 4 denominations. Brick. Wooden tower partly projecting. Large clock. Octagonal belfry with square, louvered openings. Octagonal stage. Dome. Long, round-topped, recessed windows. Interior much altered 1868.

Searsport. Second Cong. Ch. (Searsport Harbor), 1817. Type III. Closed when church at Village organized. Building then housed school under Elijah Kellogg, famous writer for boys. Repaired 1855, reorganized. Repaired 1904. Two doors, 3 Gothic windows. Simple belfry, spire.

South Acton. Bapt. Ch., 1828. Small, plain. Two doors. No belfry. Pulpit at front. A few box pews left. Inactive.

South Berwick. Fed. Ch., 1823. Type III but much changed. One door in small portico. Square open belfry. Dome. Two stories. Ch. of Sara Orne Jewett.

South Buxton. Cong. Ch., 1822. Type III. Called "Tory Hill" MH. because first pastor was loyalist, as were many members. High porch encloses base of tower. Large, square belfry, octagonal drum, spire. One row windows.

South Paris. Cong. Ch., 1818. Very plain Type III at first. Moved to present site 1835, when octagonal belfry, dome added. Pulpit, galleries later lowered and pews replaced by modern ones. Lengthened 1859 and made 2 stories, vestry below. More changes 1878.

Standish. Old MH., 1806. Type III. Originally Unit. church. Made 2 stories 1848. Ch. below, with old box pews; Standish Academy above until 1857, then high school. Two doors. Square tower on roof with open, columned belfry. Painted red. Closed since 1915 except for union services in summer.

Thomaston. "Old Church on the Hill," 1796. Type III, made IV in Greek Revival. Gen. Henry Knox built mansion here and helped found ch. Sounding board suspended by carved arm, hand. Now 2 stories. Plain front with 4 doors, 6 pilasters. Built for several denominations but long used by Baptists. Now inactive.

Waldoboro. German Lutheran MH., 1772. Much like Type II, but entrance is through a porch at end rather than side. (P. 200, Fig. 209)

Waterville. Bapt. Ch., 1826. Type III at first with shallow entrance bay, 3 doors, octagonal belfry, spire. Remodeled 1875 in Victorian style. S. F. Smith, author of poem "America," once pastor.

Webster Corner. Old Ch., 1827. Type III. Sampson Colby architect. Plain front, 2 doors. Good belfry with dome, spire. Repaired 1858. Univ. from then until 1899. Now inactive and in poor repair.

West Durham. Meth. Ch., 1804. Simple. Two doors. No belfry. Three long side windows. Much changed 1867.

Winslow. Cong. Ch., 1794. Type II, made III 1830, when steeple added. This removed 1884. Now entrance bay with 2 doors. Interior altered 1852, 1888, 1900, when building was made 2 stories and turned to face road. Other, more recent changes.

Woolwich. Nequasset MH., 1757. Type II, made IV in 1840s and greatly altered outside and in. Now very plain. One door, 2 side windows. No galleries. Repaired 1930. Cong. ch. till 1955 but now inactive. Oldest ch. east of Kennebec River.

Yarmouth. Old Bapt. MH., 1796. Type III, enlarged, remodeled 1837. Repaired 1949. Now maintained by Village Improvement Society and town.` (P. 159, Fig. 161)

York Village. Cong. Ch., 1747. Type II, changed to IV, then to Victorian style. (P. 157, Fig. 159)

MASSACHUSETTS

Adams. Friends MH., 1782. Weatherbeaten, plain, but well maintained. Large cemetery. Clara Barton brought up in this Meeting.

Agawam. Cong. Ch. Type III. Frame from old MH. in Suffield, brought here 1800. Sold by town to Congregationalists and Baptists 1830. Now much changed. Steeple added 1833. Belfry in tower. Upper stages without openings. Moved from common 1845. Galleries taken out 1875.

Amesbury. Cong. Ch., 1826. Type III. Doric portico added 1840. Built by Unitarians, taken over by Congregationalists. Square belfry, octagonal stage, spire. Seems never to have had side galleries. Lengthened 1849. Old pews removed 1873.

Amesbury. Rocky Hill MH., 1785. Type II. One of the best preserved of the old MHs. (Pp. 53–56, Figs. 18, 19, 20)

Amherst. Johnson Chapel, Amherst College, 1826. Type IV. Brick. (P. 137, Fig. 141)

Andover. West Parish Cong. Ch., 1826. Type III. Granite. In 1863, square tower replaced by octagonal belfry, tall spire; side galleries and 2 of 3 front doors removed, old pews, pulpit replaced. Now has shallow entrance bay, 1 door, 3 long windows on sides, 2 in front.

Annisquam. Village Ch., 1830. Type III. Plain front, 2 doors. One row windows; pointed tops with interlaced sash-bars. Square belfry, dome. Interior remodeled 1892. Pulpit, pews changed. Pulpit restored 1937. Cong. 1728–1811; Univ. 1811–1952. Now independent.

Ashby. Unit. Ch., 1809. Type III. Now 2 stories. Clock added 1846. (P. 86, Fig. 68)

Ashfield. St. John's Episc. Ch., 1827. Tower projects. Porch around its base. Half-window where porch meets body. Part of old horse block now door-stone. Since 1945 this church and Cong. Ch., retaining their organizations, have had same minister.

Ashfield. Town Hall (Old MH.), 1812. Type III. (P. 118, Fig. 117)

Assonet (Freetown). Cong. Ch., 1809. Type III. Large. Open cupola belfry, with dome, probably later than rest. Shallow entrance bay, 3 doors. Pleasing ornament on doors. Interior much changed. Rear fourth not now part of auditorium.

Athol. Old MH., 1827. Type III. Open belfry, second stage, dome. Shallow entrance bay, 3 doors. Two stories 1847, ch. above, town hall below. Became Unit. 1830. Club house for some time. Town took over 1922. Now to be used by Athol Historical Society.

Bedford. Unit. Ch., 1816. Type III. (P. 115, Fig. 115)

Belchertown. Cong. Ch., 1789. Type II, made III 1828. Thirty ft. inserted in middle. Quoins, cornice on orig. portion but not on new entrance bay. Two tiers of 9 windows reduced to 5 long ones 1871. Steeple rebuilt 1888. Interior altered.

Bellingham. Bapt. Ch., 1826. Type III. When Baptists left old MH. they built this under direction of militant pastor Abiel Fisher. Three round-topped doors, Palladian window above middle one. Square, open belfry, octagonal stage, spire.

Bellingham. Town Hall (Old MH.), 1802. Type II with tower. Once had cupola above. Door on long south side now closed. Two stories. At first used by 3 denominations, since 1853 only for town purposes.

Berlin. Fed. Ch., 1826. Type III. Deep entrance bay with 3 doors. Clock in tower. Square, open belfry, octagonal lantern, dome. Rear addition 1930. (P. 119, Fig. 120)

Beverly. Unit. Ch., 1770. Type II, made III 1835, IV 1867. (P. 167)

Billerica. Cong. Ch., 1829. Type III. No porch. One double door. Long windows on sides, originally round-topped. Vestry below. Steeple, on roof, has square belfry, octagonal stage above. Interior modernized.

Billerica. Unit. Ch., 1797. Type II, made IV 1844. (P. 167, Fig. 174)

Blandford. Cong. Ch., 1823. Type III. Galleries on sides only. At rear is scar of old door or porch, perhaps used when pulpit was at other end. (P. 108, Fig. 100)

Boston. Cathedral Ch. of St. Paul (Episc.), 1819. Alexander Parris, Solomon Willard architects. Stone. On Tremont St. facing Common. Daniel Webster on building committee. Said to be earliest Greek Revival building in Boston. Portico of 6 Ionic columns across front. Three doors. Interior simple, white, with high pews. Became Cathedral 1912.

Boston. Charles Street Ch., 1807. Type III. Built from designs by Asher Benjamin. Brick. Deep, 3-storied porch. Square belfry. Resembles West Church. Now a community center. (P. 115)

Boston. Christ Ch. (Episc.), 1723. Brick with square tower. (Pp. 181–82, Fig. 187)

Boston. King's Chapel (Unit.), 1749. Originally Episc. Stone. (Pp. 177–80, Figs. 184, 185)

Boston. Old South Ch., 1729. Type II with tower. (Pp. 19, 21, 44–46, Fig. 2)

Boston. Old West Ch., 1806. Type III. Built from designs by Asher Benjamin. Brick. Deep, 4-storied porch. (P. 115, Fig. 116)

Boston. Park Street Ch. (Cong.), 1809. Type III. Brick. (Pp. 127–28, Fig. 132)

Boston. St. Stephen's Roman Catholic Ch., 1802. Type III. Charles Bulfinch architect. Brick. Built for "New North" church. High-shouldered porch. Clock stage above. (P. 79)

Buckland. Cong. Ch., 1793. Type II, made IV. Now 2 doors. Six pilasters. Square belfry, spire set on roof. Three long windows on sides. Vestry below, long used as town hall. Rebuilt 1845, but changes not clear. Ch. of Mary Lyon, pioneer in higher education for women.

Burlington. Cong. Ch., 1732. Type II, made IV 1846. Further modified 1888. (Pp. 168–69. Fig. 176)

Cambridge. Christ Ch. (Episc.), 1761. (Pp. 182–84, Fig. 188)

Carlisle. Unit. Ch., 1811. Type III. Built by Templeton man, perhaps with aid from Elias Carter. Deep porch, 4 pilasters. Open belfry, octagonal stage, spire. Two stories 1852. Lower one used as town hall for a time.

Chicopee. Cong. Ch., 1826. Type III. Shallow entrance bay, 4 columns. Belfry in tower. Blind octagonal lantern. Dome. Suggests Isaac Damon influence. Vestry below. One row long windows. Pews, pulpit changed.

Cohasset. Cong. Ch., 1825. Type III, greatly altered by enlargement of porch in front, raising of bldg. for vestry below. Open, octagonal cupola, belfry, dome.

Cohasset. Unit. Ch., 1747. Type II with tower. (P. 47, Figs. 12–13)

Dartmouth (Russell's Mills). Apponegansett Friends MH., 1790. Large, dark-shingled, with back to road. Shuttered. Two chimneys. Cemetery. Meeting on last First Day of Seventh Month.

Dedham. Allin Cong. Ch., 1819. Type III. (Pp. 119–21, Fig. 121)

Dedham. First Ch. (Unit.), 1761. Type II, made III 1820. (P. 149, Fig. 148)

Deerfield. Unit. Ch., 1824. Type III. (P. 109, Fig. 102)

Dighton. Cong. Ch., 1826. Type III. Brick. Portico with 4 fluted columns, 2 doors.

Octagonal belfry, spire. No side galleries. Three long windows with false pointed tops.

Dighton. Elder Goff MH., now Cong., 1796. Very plain. One door. Belfry on roof. Enoch Goff, shoemaker, organized Bapt. church here 1772.

Dighton. Pedo-Baptist Ch. (Unit.), begun 1770, finished much later. Type II. Tower and steeple added 1827. Much changed 1861, restored 1930. Horse block. When British took Newport, 1776, Rev. Ezra Stiles served here as pastor for 2 years. Later used as barracks for American troops. Unit. after 1803.

Dorchester (Boston). St. Augustine's Chapel (Roman Catholic), 1819. Small brick chapel in walled cemetery with irregular, slate-tiled roof.

Dorchester (Boston). Second Cong. Ch., 1805. Type II. Oliver Warren builder. Design unique. Heavy square tower projects fully, built out to form porch below. Octagonal belfry, lantern. Dome. Interior somewhat changed after fire in 1908. Membership withdrew amicably from First Ch. and did not become Unit.

Dracut. Central Cong. Ch. ("Old Yellow Meetinghouse"), 1794. Type II made III. Used by 4 denominations 1834–47, then by Congregationalists. Radical changes 1897. Tower has square belfry, 2 octagonal stages, dome. Body of ch. built out on either side, at right angles to original axis, parallel to road. Still painted yellow.

East Blackstone. Friends MH., 1812. Essentially unchanged. Small porch, 1 door. Closed 1941 but recently repaired; monthly nondenominational services May to October.

East Bridgewater. Unit. Ch., 1794. Transitional, made III 1850. Galleries removed. Upper windows above arched ceiling do not open into auditorium. Steeple destroyed in 1938 hurricane.

East Haverhill. Second Bapt. Ch., 1822. Type III. Two-story porches in corners between tower and building. Doors in these. One row long, pointed windows. Top of orig. Asher Benjamin steeple now gone. History not clear.

East Longmeadow. Cong. Ch., 1828. Type III. Moved to present site 1859. Raised and much changed. Belfry in tower and blind steeple suggest Isaac Damon influence. New parish house.

East Sandwich. Friends MH., 1810. (P. 202, Fig. 211)

Edgartown. Federated Ch. (Cong. and Bapt.), 1828. Type III. Designed by son of Frederick Baylies, missionary to Indians. Tower, octagonal belfry, spire. Interior little changed. Square pews.

Essex. Cong. Ch., 1792. Type II, made III 1842. Plain front, 2 doors, 2 stories. Square steeple on roof. First minister, John Wise, resisted tyranny of Andros.

Falmouth. Cong. Ch., 1796. Transitional, made III. Built on common, moved across road 1857. Made 2 stories, new front added, with 1-doored porch. Steeple. Recently refurbished.

Falmouth (Hatchville). East End Cong. Ch., 1797. Probably Type II at first; scar of pulpit window on one long side. In 1842 turned to face road and belfry built on roof, with short spire. Scars of 6 upper windows at rear. No galleries. High auditorium, framing exposed.

Framingham Center. Bapt. Ch., 1825. Type III. (P. 99, Fig. 86)

Gill. Cong. Ch., 1798. Plain. No porch. Two doors. Square belfry, spire on roof. Greatly altered 1849. Brick basement added later.

Goshen. Cong. Ch., 1782. Type II, made III 1835 and moved to present site. Window-spacing and framing show changes made. Belfry in tower. Little ornament.

Granby. Cong. Ch., 1821. Type III. Built by Elias Carter. Externally like his Mendon church, except no entrance bay, and portico is attached directly to front of church. (P. 101)

Granville Center. Fed. Ch., 1802. Originally Transitional, as shown by sketch in vestibule. Tower removed 1890, when portico of 4 square columns and new steeple added. One door. Upper windows close under eaves. Monument to Granville jubilee of 1845 near door, with plaques added 1895, 1945.

Groton. Unit. Ch., 1755. Type II, made IV 1839. (Pp. 166–67, Figs. 171, 172)

Groveland. Cong. Ch., 1790. Type II, made IV 1849 and turned. Side galleries removed. Steeple now on roof. Doors in 2-columned recess. (P. 167)

Hadley. Cong. Ch., 1808. Type III. Moved here 1841. (P. 118, Fig. 118)

Hamilton. Cong. Ch., 1762. Type II made IV 1843 and turned. Front resembles Groveland and Groton. Now 2 stories. Second minister, Manasseh Cutler—congressman, physician, botanist, astronomer (P. 167)

Hancock. Shaker MH., 1798. Erected by Moses Johnson, builder of other Shaker houses. Gambrel roof, 2 front doors. Originally at Shirley but moved here as part of Shaker Village.

Harvard. Cong. Ch., 1821. Type III. Deep porch with low portico of 4 columns added 1860. Tower projects fully. Square belfry, dome. Remodeled 1882; 2 stories. One front door. Interior decorated 1821. Other changes 1957.

Haverhill. West Cong. Ch., 1820. Type III. Brick. Tower partly projects. One door. Belfry, spire of wood. Two windows on front were once doors. Church raised in 1870s and story added below. Interior remodeled. Gallery rear. Wing added recently.

Hingham. New North Ch., Unit., 1807. Type III. Interior unchanged except for pulpit. (P. 123, Fig. 122).

Hingham. Unit. Ch. ("Old Ship"), 1681. Type I; only example surviving. (Pp. 16, 32–35, Fig. 1)

Hinsdale. Cong. Ch., 1798. Type III. (P. 92, Fig. 76)

Holden. Cong. Ch., 1789. Type II made III 1827 and turned. In 1874 made 2 stories; other changes. Steeple removed after 1938 hurricane, replacement quite different.

Holliston. Cong. Ch., 1822. Type III. Entrance bay, steeple apparently copied from Mendon. Church has been raised about 4 feet. Doors rebuilt. Building now 2 stories. Clock in tower. (P. 101)

Hubbardston. Cong. Ch., 1827. Type III. At first 1 story and no galleries. Portico of 4 columns. Whole structure raised 1886, vestry built below. Entrance now at lower level. Simple belfry, dome.

Hubbardston. Unit. Ch., 1774. Type II at first. Belfry added west end and porch east, 1803. These removed 1842 and church became Type III. Remodeled 1869, brick story added below. Front door is through this. Plain front. One row long windows. Steeple on roof. Square belfry and upper stage. Spire, blown off 1938, restored.

Interlaken (Stockbridge). Cong. Ch., 1825. Type III. Brick. Entrance bay with 2 doors. Wooden steeple, with square belfry, lantern. Spire. One row windows.

Kingston. Cong. Ch., 1829. Type III, much changed. Plain front with pilasters. One door; 1 row pointed windows. Square open belfry, spire on roof.

Lancaster. Unit. Ch., 1816. Charles Bulfinch architect. (P. 79, Fig. 56)

Lanesboro. Com. Ch. of 3 denominations, 1828. Type III. Built by Baptists. Brick. Two doors. No side galleries. Cupola-belfry, dome. Monument in front to Jonathan Smith, active in state convention that voted to ratify U.S. Constitution.

Lenox. Com. Ch. ("Church on the Hill"), 1805. Type III. Interior twice altered. (P. 82, Fig. 61)

Longmeadow. Cong. Ch., 1767. Type II changed to III 1827, Victorian Gothic 1874, and recently back to III. (Pp. 161–62, Figs. 165, 166)

Ludlow Center. Grange Hall (Old MH.), 1784. Type II made III. Services discontinued 1839. Sold. Moved short distance and turned 90 deg. Town later bought it. Made 2 stories and used as town hall until 1893. Old pulpit window on long side, with handsome trim visible within, on second floor.

Manchester. Cong. Ch., 1809. Type III. (Pp. 85–86, Fig. 67)

Manomet. Second Cong. Ch. of Plymouth, 1826. Small and plain. Two doors at narrow end recently replaced by 1. Cupola belfry on roof 1865. Galleries on 3 sides. (P. 70, Fig. 46)

Marblehead. Cong. Ch., 1824. Type III. Stone, with plain front. (P. 123, Fig. 123)

Marblehead. St. Michael's Ch. (Episc.), 1714. (P. 180, Fig. 186)

Mashpee. Old Indian Ch., date uncertain. (Pp. 205–6, Fig. 218)

Mattapoisett. Friends MH., 1827. Entrance porch with 1 door. Original hip roof changed to pitched roof 1882. Part of old horse sheds made into Sunday school rooms 1890. Meeting every First Day.

Medfield. Unit. Ch., 1789. Type II with tower, cupola, dome. Made IV 1839, then turned to face south, portico of 6 columns erected, spire built, vestry added, and interior entirely changed. Spire blew off 1938. Became Unit. 1830.

Mendon. Unit. Ch., 1820. Type III. Elias Carter architect. Design influenced many other churches. (Pp. 99, 101, Figs. 87, 88)

Middleboro Green. First Cong. Ch., 1828. Type IV. Good example of Greek Revival. At original town site.

Milford. Cong. Ch., 1819. Type. Basement built and 30 ft. added to length 1859. Other changes 1868. Interior much altered. (P. 101)

Millbury (Bramanville). First Cong. Ch., 1804. Probably Transitional at first, made IV. Originally on town common, "re-erected" here and altered 1835. Portico of 4 Ionic columns across front.

Three doors. Square belfry. Octagon, lantern, spire.

Millbury. Second Cong. Ch. (Fed.), 1828. Type III. Shallow entrance bay with 4 columns across it. Long door. Windows round-topped, stained glass. Square belfry with arched openings. Spire has 3 "rings," suggesting Elias Carter's churches near Mendon.

Millville. Chestnut Hill MH., 1769. Type II. (P. 63, Figs. 33, 34)

Milton. Unit. Ch., 1788. Type II made III 1835 and turned. (P. 168, Fig. 175)

Nantucket. Center Street Meth. Ch., 1823. Plain. New roof built over old, portico of 6 columns added 1840. Interior retains early simplicity. In great fire of 1846 Maria Mitchell, famous scientist, stood on steps and defied firemen to blow it up. Building saved by wind change.

Nantucket. "Old North Vestry," 1711? Type II. (P. 43)

Nantucket. Unit. Ch., 1809. Type III. Plain 3-story porch rises above roof level. Octagonal belfry, windowed stage, dome. Orig. steeple replaced 1830. Extensive alterations 1844. Bell brought from Portugal by Capt. Charles Clasby.

Newburyport. First Presb. Ch. ("Old South Church"), 1756. Type II made Transitional, then IV. (Pp. 198–99, Fig. 207)

Newburyport. First Religious Society (Unit.), 1801. Type III. (Pp. 93, 95, Figs. 78, 79)

New Salem. Unit. Ch., 1794. Type II made IV 1837 and turned toward road. Scar of old porch in clapboards at rear. Gothic windows. Steeple set back on roof, with square belfry, spire, probably 1862. Small-columned portico removed that year.

North Amherst. Cong. Ch., 1826. Type III. (P. 119, Fig. 119)

North Attleboro (Old Town). Cong. Ch., 1828. Type III. Two doors in entrance bay, with long window between. Pulpit at entrance end. Good steeple, dome.

North Beverly. Second Cong. Ch., 1714. At first Type II. Tower, steeple added 1757. Made IV 1837, further altered 1867, and recently made part of a group of ch. buildings. Only frame of auditorium still orig.

North Brookfield. Cong. Ch., 1823. Type III. Much like Mendon. Pews, pulpit replaced 1842 and church lengthened 20 ft. at rear. New pews 1874. (P. 101, Fig. 89)

North Carver. Old MH., 1824. Very plain. Simple moldings on door. Round window in gable. Shingled. No services for over a century. Now used as cranberry barn.

North New Salem. Cong. Ch., 1807. Type III. Moved to present site 1835, and columns removed. Front plain, 2 doors. Pointed windows. Square belfry. Interior altered 1902.

North Orange. Com. Ch. (Universalist-Congregational), 1781. Type II, made III 1832, and turned to face road. Tower, belfry, dome probably added then. Now 2 stories, ch. below. (P. 160, Fig. 163)

North Pembroke. Friends MH., 1706. Gray shingles, clapboards. (P. 201, Fig. 210)

North Reading. Old MH., 1829. Type III, much altered. Built by Congregationalists, turned over to Universalists. Octagonal belfry. Dome. Two stories; upper was church, lower town hall. Now Grange hall above, American Legion below.

Oakham. Cong. Ch., 1814. Apparently Transitional, made Type IV 1845. Doors in recess. Square belfry, clock stage. Short spire blown off 1938, replaced by shorter one. Two stories, lower long used as town hall.

Orleans. Fed. Ch., 1829. Cong. and Univ. churches joined 1938. Much changed. Made 2 stories 1888, roof raised and dormers built on it. Victorian trim. Belfry, dome on roof.

Otis. Cong. Ch., 1813. Type III. (P. 78, Fig. 54)

Otis. St. Paul's Episc. Ch., 1828. One door. Square belfry. Long, pointed windows with interlacing sash-bars in delicate pattern. Old glass. Interior little changed; long inactive.

Oxford. Cong. Ch., 1829. Type III. Two doors. Pulpit at front. Moved to present site 1853, and basement built.

Oxford. Old Univ. Ch., 1792. Type II made III. "Oldest Univ. Ch. in the world." Long inactive. (Pp. 199–200, Fig. 208)

Paxton. Cong. Ch., 1767. Type II made III. Steep roof. Spacing of windows shows position of old entrance and pulpit window. Sides built out around base of old tower. Steeple not orig. Story added underneath.

Pelham. Town Hall (Old MH.), 1743. (Pp. 68–69, Fig. 43)

Phillipston. Cong. Ch., 1785. Type II, made IV. Steep roof. Doors in recess behind 2 columns. Steeple not orig. Church turned, raised, basement added. Pews, pulpit replaced. Wainscot made from sides of old pews. (P. 167, Fig. 173)

Plympton. Cong. Ch., 1830. Type III. Plain front. One door, with porte-cochère. One row windows. Square belfry, spire on roof.

Quincy. Unit. Ch. ("Stone Temple"), 1828. Type IV. (Pp. 26, 136, Fig. 4)

Rockport. Cong. Ch., 1804. Type III, made IV. Three doors, 4 pilasters. Greek Revival steeple. New galleries, pews, pulpit, steeple 1839, and exterior changed. Ch. cut across in 1871 and 20 ft. inserted. Other changes 1955.

Rockport. Univ. Ch., 1829. Type III. Tower projects. Two square stages, spire above, last added after 1878. One door. Ch. later elaborated in Victorian style. After losing contest with Congregationalists for the MH. of 1804, Universalists withdrew and built this one.

Roxbury (Boston). First Ch. (Unit.), 1803. Type III. (P. 95, Fig. 80)

Scituate. Cong. Ch., 1826. Type III. Plain front. One door, Palladian window above. Three round-headed windows on side. No side galleries. In 1853, orig. octagonal belfry, dome changed to present open belfry, square lantern, spire. Originally 2 front doors with window (where door now is) between. Old pews replaced in 1890s.

Scotland (Bridgewater). Cong. Ch., 1821. Type III. Small but charming. No side galleries. Open belfry. Dome. When old Bridgewater church became Unit., Trinitarians withdrew and built this.

Sheffield. Cong. Ch., 1760. Type II made III 1819. (Pp. 159–60, Fig. 162)

Shirley Center. Old MH., 1773. Type II made III. Tower and Asher Benjamin steeple added 1804. Small Victorian porch at front. Side porch preserved as part of broom shop. (Fig. 169)

Shrewsbury. Cong. Ch., 1766. Type II, made III 1834. (Pp. 164–65, Fig. 168)

Shutesbury. Fed. Ch., 1828. Type III, plus Greek Revival features. Belfry in tower; 2 blind octagonal stages above, dome. Suggests Isaac Damon influence. Four pilasters, 1 door. Now 2 stories. At first Bapt., now federated with Congregationalists. (P. 110, Fig. 105)

Somerset. Fed. Ch., 1803. Type III. At first Bapt. Building raised, story added below. Small portico, 1 door. Long side windows, but position of 2 orig. rows can be seen at rear. Roof blown off many years ago and rebuilt. Steeple damaged 1938, rebuilt without spire.

Southampton. Cong. Ch., 1788. Type II. Tower, belfry added 1822. Turned and made III 1840. Made 2 stories 1882. No entrance bay. Church built out around base of tower, but tower still projects slightly. One door. Steep roof.

South Dartmouth. Cong. Ch., 1817. Type III. White shingles. Pleasing cupola, belfry, dome. Three doors in entrance bay. Large addition rear.

South Dartmouth. Friends MH., 1819. Originally 2 doors. Turned 1880 and porch with 1 door added. Room at rear for

kitchen. Unusual in having organ. Worship every First Day.

South Deerfield. Cong. Ch., 1820. Type III. Shallow entrance bay with 4 columns close to front wall. Square tower with quoins. Square belfry, blind second stage, spire.

Southfield (New Marlboro). Cong. Ch., 1794. History not clear. Probably Transitional. Made IV in 1840s. Steep roof. Heavy entrance bay. One door. Octagonal belfry, second stage. Spire. Interior much changed.

South Hanson. Cong. Ch., 1826. Type III, much modified. Plain front. Three long windows at side and over 3 front doors. Steeple on roof. Square belfry. Heavy spire. No side galleries.

South Hingham. Second Parish, Unit., 1742. Type II made III 1829. (Pp. 144–45, Fig. 144)

South Natick. The Eliot Church (Cong.–Unit.), 1828. Type III. One door. Palladian window above. Deep entrance bay. Square, open belfry, square clock stage, octagonal lantern, dome. No side galleries, 1 row windows. Interior altered. On site of ch. of Eliot's "Praying Indians" of 1650.

South Uxbridge. Friends MH., 1776. (P. 202, Fig. 212)

Southwick. Cong. Ch., 1824. Type III. (P. 108, Fig. 101)

Southwick. College Highway Meth. Ch., 1826. Type III. Built by Methodists and Episcopalians. Entrance bay at first had 3 doors, now 1. Square belfry, set back on roof, removed. Made 2 stories 1923. Interior remodeled 1961.

South Yarmouth. Friends MH., 1809. Near village center. Meetings every First Day.

Springfield. First Cong. Ch., 1818. Isaac Damon, architect. Type III. (Pp. 107–8, Fig. 99)

Stockbridge. Cong. Ch., 1824. Type III. Ralph Bigelow builder. Brick with white wooden steeple. Founded by Jonathan Edwards. Interior little changed.

Stoughton. Univ. Ch., 1808. Type III. Cupola belfry, dome. Made 2 stories 1848. Enlarged 1870. Front looks rather blank because orig. 6 windows removed. Door also changed.

Sudbury. Unit. Ch., 1797. Transitional made Type III. (P. 164, Fig. 167)

Sutton. Cong. Ch., 1829. Type III with portico of 4 columns. Tall steeple, square belfry, 2 octagonal stages, spire. Interior much changed.

Taunton. Unit. Ch., 1830. Imposing stone structure. Gothic. Heavy tower, partly projecting, topped by tall pinnacles at its four corners.

Templeton. Fed. Ch. (Unit.–Cong.), 1811. Type III. (Pp. 95–96, Fig. 81)

Tisbury. Christiantown Chapel, 1829. Very simple. On site where Thomas Mayhew's "praying Indians" had MH. before 1680. Indian burying ground around it.

Townsend. Cong. Ch., 1830. Type III. Josiah Sawtelle architect. Brick. Wooden steeple, 4-columned portico. Two doors. Square, open belfry. Spire.

Townsend. Meth. Ch. (Old MH.), 1771. Type II, somewhat changed. (Pp. 165–66, Fig. 170)

Truro. Cong. Ch., 1827. Type III, perfectly plain. Repaired 1955. (P. 124, Fig. 125)

Wales. Town Hall (Old MH.), 1800. Now Type IV. Built by town and used at first by 3 denominations. Bought by Baptists 1846 and remodeled to present state, with portico of 4 Doric columns and Greek Revival belfry. Upper story, ch.; lower, town hall. Town bought and repaired building 1953.

Walpole. United Cong. Ch., 1783. Type II made IV. Moved 1839 and greatly altered, outside and in. Lengthened. Portico of 4 columns added. Three doors. Greek Revival steeple on roof. Top blown off 1938 but replaced. Church is union of Congregationalists, Unitarians, Methodists.

Ware Center. First Cong. Ch., 1799. Type II at first, with porch at each end and cupola on roof. Made IV 1843, and 2 stories. Plain front, 4 pilasters, 2 doors. Square belfry on roof.

Wayland. Unit. Ch., 1814. Type III. (P. 86, Fig. 69)

West Barnstable. Cong. Ch., 1717. Type II at first, later much changed. Now restored to Type II, state of 1723. (P. 42, Fig. 11)

West Bridgewater. Cong.–Unit. Ch., 1801. Type III. Shallow entrance bay. Three doors. Palladian window above. Quoins at corners. Excellent ornament. Clocktower, octagonal belfry. Steeple blew off 1938 and not restored. Remodeled, made 2 stories 1847. Town long used lower floor for town hall. Ch. now uses all. On site of original MH. for all the Bridgewater towns. One of the earliest buildings of ch. type.

Westford. First Parish Ch. United, 1794. Type II, made Transitional. (P. 68, Fig. 42)

West Granville. Cong. Ch., 1782. Type II, made III, later Victorian. (P. 160–61, Fig. 164)

Westhampton. Cong. Ch., 1829. Type III. Belfry in tower. Spire added 1860. Made 2 stories and remodeled. Old pulpit restored 1940.

West Medway. Second Church (Fed.), 1813. Type III. Malachi Bullard builder. Excellent entrance bay, doors. Greek Revival belfry, spire replaced orig. 1846. Blown off twice since. Interior altered.

Westport (Central Village). Friends MH., 1813. Many changes, 1872. Monument in yard to Capt. Paul Cuffe, son of freed Negro and Indian woman, who took 31 freed slaves back to Africa with help of this Meeting.

West Springfield. "Old White Church," 1800. Transitional. (Pp. 73–74, Fig.47)

West Springfield (Storrowtown). On grounds of Eastern States Exposition, 1790. Now

Type III. Originally at West Salisbury, N.H. Probably Type II. Re-erected here with addition of steeple, portico. Much altered.

West Taunton. Cong. Ch., 1824. Type III, Small, simple. Deep porch, 1 door. Tower, octagonal belfry, dome. One row windows, long and round-topped. Pulpit lowered, pews replaced 1899.

Westwood. First Bapt. Ch. (Clapboard Trees MH.), 1730. Type II, made III 1834. (P. 169, Fig. 177)

Westwood. United Ch. (Unit.–Cong.), 1808. Type III. Benjamin Robbins builder. Plain front, 3 doors. Square belfry, octagonal second stage. Spire. Pulpit, pews replaced 1855. Other changes since.

Whitman. Cong. Ch., 1807. Orig. Type III. Many changes to present Victorian style.

Acworth. Friends MH., 1820. Very simple, low. Two doors, the women's wider.

Acworth. United Ch., 1820. Type III. Like Templeton, Mass., but no columns or spire. (P. 98, Fig. 84)

Allenstown. Old Christian Ch., 1815. Low and very plain. Benches, square pews. On isolated road in Bear Brook State Park. Town meetings long held here but village now gone. No sign of old cemetery. D.A.R. owns building.

Amherst. Cong. Ch., 1771. Type II, made III 1836. (P. 153, Fig. 152)

Barnstead Parade. Community Ch. (Cong.), 1799. At old town center and drill ground. Type II made Transitional 1866. Belfry, bell added. Some window scars visible. Steep roof. Interior much altered. Windows memorials of early citizens. Bell given by George Peabody of London.

Bedford. Presb. Ch., 1832. Type III. Impressive building. Deep portico. One door. No side galleries. Large windows. Square open belfry, octagonal lantern. Orig. square pews. Long the most important ch. in town.

Boscawen. Cong. Ch., 1800. Type II, made IV 1839 and turned. New steeple added. Raised 1847 and room built below for town meetings. Turned again 1940, facing south. Interior much altered 1894. Only frame now orig.

Brentwood. Cong. Ch., 1815. Type III. Outside little changed. Deep 2-story porch around base of tower. Octagonal belfry, dome. Made 2 stories 1847, church below, town hall above.

Bridgewater Hill. Old Town House, 1806. (P. 205, Fig. 217)

Bristol. Fed. Ch., 1827. Orig. state not known; now Victorian. Altered 1844, 1870, 1886. Two doors. Long windows.

Canaan Street. Old MH. and Town Hall, 1793. Type II. Tower added 1829, with octagonal cupola belfry, dome above. Entrance on side remains. Small porch added at front. Modern stairway at rear. Made 2 stories 1841, and box pews removed. Church above, town hall below. Served all denominations at first. Now inactive.

Canterbury. Shaker MH., 1792. Plain structure with 2 doors, gambrel roof. (P. 204, Fig. 216)

Chester. Cong. Ch., 1773. Type II, turned and made IV 1839. Pulpit, pews replaced. Galleries removed. Roof lowered.

Cornish. Trinity Chapel (Episc.), 1793. Small and simple. Tower projects. No steeple. Orig. side galleries, upper row of windows removed. On site of original MH.

Cornish Flat. United Ch., 1803. Type III. At first Bapt., at Cornish Center. Re-erected here 1818. United with Cong. Ch. 1954. Two stories. No entrance bay. Modern steeple on roof.

Deering Center. Com. Ch. (Cong.), 1829. Type III. Entrance bay with 2 doors. Tower and square, open belfry. No spire. Pulpit at entrance end. Little ornament.

Dover. Cong. Ch., 1829. Type III. Brick. (P. 112, Fig. 108)

Dover. Friends MH., 1768. (P. 203, Fig. 214)

East Alstead. Cong. Ch., 1798. Type II, made III early in 19th century. Evidence of side entrance in clapboards. Tower, steeple not orig. Now 2 stories, with 2-door entrance bay. Steep roof.

East Andover. Cong. Ch., 1797. Orig. state unknown; made Type IV 1840. One door. Doric pilasters. Square tower set back. Open, square belfry; spire.

East Derry. Cong. Ch., 1769. Type II, now much changed. (Pp. 154–55, Fig. 156)

Effingham (Lord's Hill). Cong. Ch., 1798. Orig. appearance unknown. Now very simple: 1 story, 1 door. Square belfry and spire not orig. Remodeled 1845, 1898.

Exeter. Cong. Ch., 1798. Unlike any of the 4 main types. Ebenezer Clifford architect. (P. 111, Fig. 107)

Fitzwilliam. Town House, 1818. Type III. Almost exactly like Templeton, Mass. (P. 96, Fig. 82)

Francestown. Fed. Ch. (Unit.–Cong.), 1801. Type III, perhaps II at first. Plain front, 3 doors, pilasters. Open, square belfry, tall spire. Turned 1834 and "greatly improved." Long row of horse sheds.

Fremont. Old MH., 1800. Type II. (P. 60, Fig. 29)

Gilmanton Center. Cong. Ch., 1825. Type III. Deep entrance bay, 1 large door, 2 windows. Three round-topped windows on side. Tower projects fully. Square belfry, dome.

Gilmanton (Iron Works Village). Cong. Ch., 1826. Type III. Front wide and plain. Two doors. Square clock tower on flattened peak of gable. Square, open belfry, spire. One row side windows.

Gosport. Isles of Shoals Ch., 1800. Small stone building on Star Island, the third meetinghouse. Door on side. Square tower; square, open belfry, slender spire. Interior partly burned, restored 1822. Settlement gone but cemetery remains. Monument to Rev. John Tucke, for 40 years minister here before Revolution.

Grafton Center. Old MH., orig. Bapt. Ch., 1798. Type II made III. Position of door on side seen in clapboards. Moved from common across road 1857 and made 2 stories, town hall below. Short steeple on roof.

Greenfield. Union Cong. Ch., 1792. At first Type II. Tower and steeple added 1825; double octagon, dome. Made 2 stories 1848; church above, town hall below. Turned 1867 and changed to III by building out around tower. Plain front.

Greenland. Com. Cong. Ch., 1756. Type II, made III 1834, Victorian 1881.

Groton. Town House (Old MH.), 1793. Now much reduced in size and roof lowered. Formerly had galleries, pulpit. Town meetings still held here.

Hampstead. Town Hall (Old MH.), 1745. Type II. (Pp. 64–65, Fig. 37)

Hampton Falls. First Bapt. Ch., 1828. Type III. Plain front, 2 doors. Square belfry with "Memorial" clock face. Octagonal drum, spire. Building raised, room added below. Much altered.

Hancock. Cong. Ch. and Town Hall, 1820. Type III. Much like Templeton, Mass. (P. 98, Fig. 83)

Haverhill. Cong. Ch., 1827. Type III. Brick with wooden steeple. Plain front; 2 doors, round-topped. One row side windows. No side galleries. Square belfry, octagonal lantern, dome.

Henniker. Old MH., 1786. Doubtless Type II at first, entirely remodeled 1886. Sounding board remains. Long used as town hall. Now American Legion hall.

Henniker. Friends MH., 1799. Plain. One story. Two doors close together.

Holderness. Trinity Ch. (Episc.), 1797. Low plain building with one door, small porch. Square pews of unpainted pine. Samuel Livermore, distinguished statesman and judge, who helped found church, buried in well-kept churchyard.

Hopkinton. Cong. Ch., 1789. Type II, finally IV. (Pp. 153–54, Figs. 153, 154)

Hopkinton. St. Andrew's Episc. Ch., 1827. Simple church of native granite. Gothic windows. Short belfry. Orig. square pews. In 1920s interior enhanced, and Gothic bell-tower by Ralph Adams Cram added.

Jaffrey. Old MH., 1775. Type II. Tower, steeple added later. (P. 51, Fig. 17)

Keene. First Cong. Ch., 1786. Type II, made III 1826. (Pp. 155–56, Fig. 157)

Kingston. Cong. Ch., 1825. Orig. appearance unknown. Enlarged 1841, remodeled 1879. Victorian steeple on roof. New vestry 1955. On town common.

Lebanon. Cong. Ch., 1828. Type III, with narrow portico. Interior considerably altered. (P. 113, Fig. 109)

Lee. Friends MH., 1774. After Lee meeting discontinued, building used as school by Moses Cortland. Two doors. Section with 4 columns added at front. Two stories. Old podium remains in what was schoolroom. Building now property of Univ. of N.H.

Lempster. Old MH., 1794. Type II. (P. 66, Fig. 39)

Loudon. Cong. Ch., 1827. Type III. Plain front. Two doors. Tower on roof, with graceful, 8-columned belfry, dome. No side galleries. One row long windows. Interior little changed.

Lyme. Cong. Ch., 1810. Type III. Nearby store has frame of old MH. (P. 113, Fig. 110)

Middleton Corners. Old MH. About 1800. Type II. No tower or belfry. Two stories. Gospel chapel above, town hall below. Interesting frescoes on chapel wall.

Milford. Old MH., 1794. Type II with tower, made III. Plain front with pilasters. Formerly on "Oval" but moved across road. Tower, octagonal belfry, dome, with gilded eagle above. Two stories. Town took it over 1834. Turned 1847, and interior entirely changed. Now houses stores, fraternal organizations.

Milton. Town House, 1803. At first Type II, with porch at each end and portico in front. Now cut down to 1 story. Interior dismantled when town took over building. Home of first Cong. ch. here until 1835.

Mont Vernon. Old MH., 1781. Type II with 2 porches; made III 1837 and moved across road. Raised, story added below for town purposes. Town has used whole building since 1896.

Nashua. Bird MH. About 1746. Built by John Lovewell and others for Rev. Mr. Bird, follower of George Whitefield. Later sold and used as dwelling, then as factory. Retains some MH. features.

Nashua. Unit.–Univ. Ch., 1827. Type IV. Attributed to Asher Benjamin, then resident of Nashua. Portico of 6 Doric columns, 2 doors. Pulpit at first in front but moved to rear 1875. Old pews, pulpit replaced. Other changes 1924.

Newbury. Village Ch., 1821. Type III. Built by Free Will Baptists. Attractive little church. Shallow entrance bay, 2 doors. One row round-topped windows. Interior essentially unaltered. Pulpit at entrance end, on columns.

New Castle. Cong. Ch., 1828. Type III. Square pews apparently orig. Old pulpit preserved, but new one used. This building may be the preceding MH., extensively rebuilt in 1828.

New Hampton. Dana Hill MH., 1800. Old Free Will Bapt. church, remote from center. Much as at first though with some restoration. Low, 1-story, almost square, with doors on 3 sides. Square, spindle-top, unpainted pews. Long pulpit with deacons' seat. Church and hill named for Samuel Dana, who preached and practiced medicine here.

New Hampton. Town House (Old MH.), 1798. Probably Type II at first. Now cut down to half its former height, and very simple. Little of interior left but a few benches. Now used for town meetings.

Newington. Cong. Ch. and former MH., 1712. Type II, made III about 1830. Oldest Cong. ch. building in U.S. (P. 41, Fig. 10)

New London. First Bapt. Ch., 1826. Type III. Lengthened 1853 by inserting section. Entrance bay with 1 door. Wide, square, open-arched belfry with octagonal lantern, dome. Revere bell.

Newmarket. Com. Ch. (Cong.), 1828. Type III, much changed, especially in 1871. Small entry at door. One door, formerly 2. One row long, pointed windows; colored glass. Steeple on roof; square clock tower, square belfry, short spire. Building raised, story added below.

Newport. Second Cong. Ch., 1823. Type III. John Leach, builder. (Pp. 98–99, Fig. 85)

North Barnstead. Cong. Ch., 1820. Perfectly plain, 1 story, 1 row windows. Still active.

North Danville. Old M.H., 1760. Type II. (P. 56)

North Sandwich. Free Will Bapt. Ch. ("Old White Ch."), 1825. Almost square. One row side windows, 2 in front. One door. Only ornament here and in window above. Slip pews, Gothic pulpit furniture. Old pulpit in lobby. Gallery across front. Interior papered.

North Sutton. Old MH., now Bapt. ch., 1795. Type II. (P. 67, Fig. 40)

Ossipee. First Cong. Ch., 1827. Altered 3 times since erection. No sign of antiquity remains.

Ossipee. Second Cong. Ch., 1801. At the "Corners." Orig. Type II with tower. In 1880 made III and turned to face road. One door, in partly projecting tower. Two rows windows. Square belfry, spire. Was old MH., but town gave it up 1839. Cong. ch. took over 1894.

Peterborough. Unit. Ch., 1825. Type III. Brick. (Pp. 79–80, Fig. 57)

Portsmouth. St. John's Episc. Ch. Begun 1807, finished 1818. Brick. (Pp. 184–85, Fig. 189)

Portsmouth. Unit.–Univ. Ch. ("Old South Church"), 1826. Type IV. Built by Jonathan Folsom from design of Alexander Parris. Granite. Deep portico of 4 columns, not as wide as church. Three doors. Square belfry on roof. Interior renovated 1842. In 1858 17 ft. added at rear. Plain interior made more ornate. Renovated, improved 1925. Basement made vestry 1948. Became Unit. 1819. United with Univ. ch. 1947.

Richmond. Old Bapt. MH., 1781. Type II, no tower. Little outside change except main door at end. Interior much altered. Long used as town hall, and part as library since 1892. Ch. organization extinct.

Rindge. Cong. Ch., 1796. Type II, made III 1839. (P. 154, Fig. 155)

Rochester. Cong. Ch., 1780. Apparently Type II originally, now much changed. Base of tower enclosed in narrow porch, with smaller porches in corners. Modern belfry, spire. Interior has much Victorian ornament.

Salem. Town House (Old MH.), 1738. Type II, no tower. (P. 64, Fig. 36)

Salisbury. South Road Cong. Ch., 1788. Probably Type II, now anomalous Type III. Much material from old Searles Hill MH. used here. Entrance bay with 1 door. Three long windows on side. Tower, square belfry have pinnacles at corners. Building remodeled 1835: walls lowered, interior changed, new windows. Ch. at first shared with Baptists.

Salisbury (Heights). Old Bapt. Ch., 1794. Type II, made IV 1839. Remodeled by Deacon Parsons to present state. Entrance bay with 2 doors, tower, square belfry with pinnacles. Clock. No longer in use.

Sandown. Old MH., 1773. Type II. Fine example of its type. (P. 56, Figs. 21–25)

Sandwich. Center Sandwich Bapt. Ch., 1792. Probably Type II. Turned and altered 1847, now Transitional. Elder Joseph Quinby influenced change of church from Cong. to Free Will Bapt. faith 1799.

Seabrook. Village Ch. (One of Federated ch. group.) Probably Type II at first, turned and made III 1820. Two stories, lower long used as town hall. Presb., Bapt., Cong. churches have used it.

Somersworth. Cong. Ch., 1828. Orig. state unknown. Much altered 1876 in Victorian style. Raised, story added below.

One door, 1 row long windows. Short tower with octagonal belfry, dome.

South Barnstead. Cong. Ch. About 1816. History obscure. Tower probably not orig. Pulpit at entrance. One row windows. Square, open belfry. Short spire. Victorian furniture. Free Will Baptists and Adventists have used it. Congregationalists took over in 1890. Now unused.

Troy. Town House (Old MH.), 1814. Type III. Portico with 2 pairs of columns, 3 doors with common lintel, suggest Templeton, Mass. Eight-columned belfry. Rest of steeple lost 1938. Congregationalists withdrew from Unit. ch. 1833. Church body later became inactive, sold MH. to town. Moved to present site, made 2 stories 1855. Fire house put in lower floor 1864; 25 ft. added to length 1893.

Unity. Friends MH., 1820. Two doors, wider one for women. Now in poor repair. One yearly Meeting.

Unity. Town Hall. About 1810. Type III. Built by Bapt. ch., later turned over to town. Good design. Entrance bay with 2 doors. One row long windows. Square, open-arched belfry, dome. No side galleries.

Warner. United Ch., 1818. Type III. Now 2 stories, long windows in upper. Fifteen ft. added at rear. Square, open-arched belfry, octagonal lantern (with false, painted windows), dome, short spire. Balustrades on tower and belfry. Stone porte-cochère at front.

Washington. Old MH., now Town Hall, 1789. Type II. Asher Benjamin steeple added later. (Pp. 65–66, Fig. 38)

Webster. Cong. Ch., 1823. Type III. Plain front but much ornament on doors, windows. Tower on roof. Wide-arched, square, open belfry; square upper stage, dome. Interior little changed. Square pews around sides. Gallery on 3 sides.

Webster. Old MH., 1791. Type II. (Pp. 60–62, Fig. 30)

Wentworth. Com. Ch., 1828. Type III. (P. 113, Fig. 111)

West Claremont. St. Mary's Chapel, Roman Catholic, 1823. (P. 193.)

West Claremont. Union Episc. Ch., 1773. (Pp. 192–93, Figs. 200, 201)

Westmoreland. Park Hill Ch. (Cong.), 1767. Type II, made III 1824. (Pp. 147–49, Fig. 147)

RHODE ISLAND

Barrington. United Cong. Ch., 1806. Probably Transitional at first. (Pp. 172–74, Fig. 183)

Bristol. First Bapt. Ch., 1814. Type III. Stone. Wooden tower, octagonal belfry, portico. Two pairs Ionic columns. Spire blew off 1869. Interior renovated 1882. Now 2 stories.

Chepachet (Glocester). Free Will Bapt. Ch., 1821. Type III. Entrance bay with 3 round-topped doors. Square belfry with arched openings. Spire.

Coventry. Maple Root Ch. of Six Principle Baptists, 1797. Type II. (P. 198, Fig. 206)

Cumberland. Elder Ballou MH., 1740. Type II. (P. 197, Figs. 204, 205)

Foster Center. Old MH., 1796. Type II. Built for Calvinistic Baptists. Ch. founded by Elder John Hammond. In 1841 town paid to repair it. Since 1870, used for town meetings and other purposes. Very plain. No belfry. Simple benches. (Fig. 35)

Hopkinton. Union MH., now Second Seventh-Day Baptist Ch., 1789. Probably Type II, now very plain. One door; 1 row long windows. Square belfry. Seventh-Day, First-Day, and New-Light Baptists built it. Funds raised by lottery. Moved 1826 and remodeled with town's help. Used for town meetings until 1860, when church bought out town's rights.

Jamestown. Friends' MH., 1765. Small, simple; 1 story, no porch, 2 doors. Shingled. Meetings on First Days of Seventh and Eighth Months.

Kingston. Cong. Ch., 1820. Type III. Door in slightly projecting tower. Clock. Belfry. Octagonal windowed stage, flaring spire. (P. 126, Fig. 130)

Little Compton. Friends' MH., about 1700. Porch with 2 doors. Horse block. Windows, doors not orig. Now owned by Little Compton Historical Society.

Newport. Clarke Street Ch., 1733. Cong. at first, next Central Bapt. ch., now part of Roman Catholic School. Greatly altered. Two doors. Deep porch. Square belfry.

Newport. Friends' MH. One wing built about 1700, rest added 1808. Deep, 2-doored porch with 2 long windows. Now a recreation hall.

Newport. Knights of Columbus Hall, originally Dr. Hopkins MH. (Cong.), 1727. Apparently Type III at one time but not originally. Much altered. Three doors in recess. No steeple or belfry. Two rows of side windows.

Newport. St. Paul's Meth. Ch., 1806. Type III. Raised 1842 and story added below, with deep porch. Old box pews removed. Steeple has octagonal belfry, lantern, dome. Said to be oldest Meth. ch. in world with a steeple. Interior partly restored to early style 1946. New parish house 1960.

Newport. Seventh Day Bapt. Ch., 1729. Type II. Now incorporated in another building. (Pp. 193, 195, Fig. 202)

Newport. Touro Synagogue, Temple Jeshuat Israel, 1763. (Pp. 208–9, Fig. 221)

Newport. Trinity Episc. Ch., 1726. (Pp. 186–87, Fig. 192, 193)

North Kingston. Stony Lane Ch. of Six-Principle Baptists, 1709. Small, 1 story, very plain. One door front, 2 windows each side. Said to be essentially unchanged. Recently reactivated.

Portsmouth. Friends MH., 1700. (P. 203, Fig. 213)

Providence. Beneficent Cong. Ch., 1809. Like Type IV but much antedates Greek Revival. (P. 132, Fig. 137)

Providence. Episc. Cathedral of St. John, 1810. Stone. Designed by John Holden Greene. Clock tower, belfry. Deep porch; Gothic windows; domed ceiling. Transepts added 1868, new chancel early this century. Historic cemetery. Became Cathedral 1929.

Providence. First Bapt. Ch., 1775. (Pp. 195–97, Fig. 203)

Providence. First Unit. Ch., 1816. Type III. (P. 132, Fig. 138)

Rumford. Newman Cong. Ch., 1810. Transitional originally, but altered in Greek Revival. Square belfry as wide as tower. Small porch added 1890. Interior much changed. Samuel Newman, first minister, prepared first English concordance to Bible.

Saylesville (Lincoln). Friends MH. Small wing, now kitchen and social rooms, built 1703, main part 1745. Modern pews. Horse block.

Wickford. Bapt. Ch., 1816. Type III, made IV. Portico of 4 square columns. Square belfry above. Remodeled 1838; 15 ft. added north end. Old pews removed 1905.

Wickford. St. Paul's Episc. Ch. (Old Narragansett Ch.), 1707. Oldest Episc. ch. building in New England. (Pp. 185–86, Fig. 190, 191)

Wyoming (Richmond). Wood River Ch. of Six Principle Baptists, 1769. Orig. appearance unknown. Still very simple, but evidently changed during Greek Revival, as shown by cornices, frieze. Two doors; 3 long windows each side. Interior simple. Galleries on 3 sides.

VERMONT

Addison. Bapt. Ch., 1816. Type III, made IV. Door in recess. Heavy steeple. Now 2 stories. Scars of orig. windows at rear.

Arlington. St. James's Episc. Ch. (Orig. Bethel Ch.), 1829. Stone. Gothic. Tower partly projects.

Bethel. Christ Ch., Episc., 1823. Plain. Two doors, 5 side windows. Open belfry on roof. Interior orig.

Bethel. Fed. Ch., 1816. Type III. Brick. (P. 85, Fig. 64)

Brattleboro. Center Cong. Ch., 1815. Type III. Tower partly projects. Quoins on corners. Tall steeple with clock stage. Square belfry, octagonal lantern, spire. Moved to center of town, remodeled 1843.

Bristol. Bapt. Ch., 1819. Type III. Deep, narrow portico, 2 columns. Now 2 stories. Upper windows long. Octagonal belfry, spire. Remodeled 1925.

Burke Hollow. Old Union MH., 1825. Type III, but only 1 story. Built by 4 denominations. Barrel pulpit next to entrance. Square pews. All woodwork, originally unpainted, now white. Repaired 1896. Annual commemorative service.

Burlington. Unit. Ch., 1816. Type III. (P. 114, Fig. 112)

Calais (Kent's Corner). Old West Ch., 1824. Originally Transitional, now Type III. Plain front, 3 doors. Belfry in tower on roof. Two octagons, dome above. Painted false windows in upper stage, lower stage blind. Interior orig. Box pews, old pulpit. Endowed and well maintained. Some services.

Chelsea. United Ch. (Cong.–Meth.), 1811. Type III. Made 2 stories 1853, interior much altered. Entrance bay with 1 door. Steeple a double octagon and dome.

Chester. Cong. Ch., 1828. Type III. Built by 3 denominations. Steeple almost exact copy of that at Peterborough, N.H. Made 2 stories 1878. Other changes 1898, 1947. (Fig. 58)

Clarendon. Cong. Ch., 1824. Type III. Brick. Two doors, 1 row windows. Extensively remodeled 1859. Heavy spire atop fretwork belfry.

Corinth Center. Cong. Ch., 1800. Originally Transitional, made Type III 1845; galleries, tower removed. Plain front with 2 doors. Square belfry. Used as town hall 1805–45. Wood-burning stoves fed from outside.

Cornwall. Cong. Ch., 1803. Probably Type III, made IV 1846. High spire removed. Remodeled 1887, 1917. Damaged by hurricane 1950. Plain front, 1 door, 4 pilasters, wide frieze. One row long windows. Octagonal tower on roof, open belfry, dome.

Coventry. Cong. Ch., 1829. Type III. One door, 1 row windows. Square belfry, octagonal lantern, dome. Vestry below built 1868. Building remodeled, redecorated 1953.

Craftsbury Common. Cong. Ch., 1819. Type III. No entrance bay. Square belfry, spire. At first 1 door and 2 rows windows. Much changed 1848. Side galleries and 8 rear windows removed. Pulpit lowered, square pews taken out. Now 1 row long windows, and 2 doors with window between. Vestry below.

East Berkshire. Cong. Ch., 1822. Type III, much changed. Deep porch, 1 door. Now 2 stories. Square belfry with pyramidal top not orig.

East Montpelier. Center MH., 1822. Type III. Built by Methodists, now nondenominational. Entrance bay with 2 doors. Above tower are 2 octagonal stages, dome. One row windows on side. Interior unchanged. Old pews. Pulpit at entrance end, below single gallery. Church chained to ledge. Place was to have been center of Montpelier. Town meetings held here until 1847. Some services still.

East Poultney. Bapt. Ch., 1805. Type III. (P. 85, Fig. 63).

Franklin. Cong. Ch., now federated with Meth., 1827. Type III. Very plain, 1 door. Belfry on roof. Horse block. Meth. ch. and town hall nearby.

Greensboro. Cong.–Presb. Ch., 1827. Type III, large. Greatly altered 1905, old character lost. Two doors. Modern tower at side.

Hartford. Second Cong. Ch., 1828. Type III. (P. 115, Fig. 114)

Jamaica. Com. (Cong.) Ch. ("White Meetinghouse"), 1808. Type III but severely plain. One door. Made 2 stories 1833 and belfry added. Town meetings held below. Other changes 1883. Now belongs wholly to church.

Jericho. Second Cong. Ch., 1824. Type III. Brick. Orig. 2 rows windows and 3 doors, now 1 row and 1 door. Closed during litigation 1865–1876. Changes then made included steeple with latticed belfry, spire. Interior also altered. Annex at rear 1909.

Leicester Corners. Ch. of the Nazarene, 1826. Type III. Built by Leicester MH. society. Varicolored brick. Entrance bay with 1 door, Palladian window above. Long, round-topped windows at front and sides, in recesses. No steeple. A lovely little ch. Design adapted from one in St. Albans, Vt. Interior changed 1869. Meth., Cong., Pentacostal churches have used building.

Lyndon. Fed. Ch. (Cong.), 1829. Type III. Small, deep porch. One door, 1 row long windows at side. Steeple on roof. Open square belfry, spire. Interior much altered.

Middlebury. Cong. Ch., 1806. Type III. (P. 91, Fig. 72)

Middlebury. St. Stephen's Episc. Ch., 1827. Stone. Gothic. Many changes. Interior redesigned in 1860s.

Monkton. Old Bapt. Ch., 1794. Type III. Large. Entrance bay with 3 doors, 4 columns. Square belfry. Two stories, ch. above. Baptists used it 1794–1863, Methodists until 1945. Now Grange hall.

Norwich. Cong. Ch., 1817. Type III. (P. 114, Fig. 113)

Old Bennington. Cong. Ch., 1805. Type III. (P. 84, Fig. 62)

Peacham. Cong. Ch., 1806. Type III. First built on hill behind village. Probably Transitional, with belfry, lantern, dome on tower. Seven windows in 2 rows. Moved to village 1844. Remodeled in Victorian style 1871. Entrance bay with 1 door. Square, open belfry, heavy spire. Made 2 stories, lower for town meetings.

Post Mills (Thetford). Cong. Ch., 1818. Type III. Steeple suggests Asher Benjamin design. Galleries removed and pulpit, pews replaced 1855. Recently raised to make room below. Frieze under eaves made of old pew doors.

Richmond. "Round Church," 1812. Unique 16-sided structure. (P. 126, Fig. 131)

Rockingham. Old MH., 1787. Type II. (P. 62, Fig. 32)

St. Johnsbury Center. Cong. Ch., 1804. Orig. seems to have been Type II with 2 porches. Built across river. In 1845 re-erected here as Type III. Plain front. Belfry built on roof 1855. Now 2 stories.

Shrewsbury. Old MH., 1804. Type III. Plain front. Two doors. Tower on roof with square belfry, dome. Now 2 stories. Univ. ch. above, town hall below.

South Windham. Bapt. Ch., 1825. Plain. Brick on 3 sides, wood in front. Heavy framing in loft.

Strafford. Town Hall (Old MH.), 1799. Transitional. (P. 74, Fig. 48)

Sudbury. Cong. Ch., 1807. Type III. Entrance bay with 3 doors. Palladian window above, another at rear. Excellent workmanship in doors and windows. Front windows have orig. panes. Made 2 stories

1854. Ch. above, town hall below. Steeple replaced by minarets, gabled spire. Inside altered but some old pews left.

Swanton. Cong. Ch., 1823. Type III. Brick. Elisha Barney builder. Erected by 3 denominations, but 2 withdrew. One door, 1 row long side windows. No side galleries. Open octagonal belfry; spire.

Thetford Hill. Cong. Ch., 1787. Type II, made III. (Pp. 149–50, Fig. 149)

Townshend. Fed. Ch., 1790. Type II, made III. (Pp. 150–51, Fig. 150)

Wallingford. Cong. Ch., 1829. Type IV. Portico of 6 slender columns across front. Two doors. Square belfry on roof, with pointed openings. One row windows at sides. Stained glass 1902. One gallery, front. Addition at rear 1856. Interior much altered.

Washington. Union Gospel Ch., 1812. Cong. at first. Changed 1851. Raised and story added below. No entrance bay. One door. Tall tower on roof with belfry and spire. One row small side windows. Positions of original larger ones can be seen in clapboards on sides and rear.

Weathersfield Center. M.H., 1821. Type III. Brick. (P. 85, Fig. 65)

West Barnet. Reformed Presb. Ch. (Covenanters) ("Walter Harvey Meetinghouse), 1831. (P. 204, Fig. 215)

West Clarendon. Chippenhook MH., 1798. Simple. One door on side, another at end. Two rows windows, upper longer. Built by Baptists. Two stories, upper for church. Lower was long town hall. Building now little used.

West Townshend. Cong. Ch., 1817. Type III. Square belfry added 1839. Tower projects slightly. One door in it, with Palladian window above. Door on either side. Two rows windows, upper with false pointed tops, colored glass. Now 2 stories. Square belfry on tower, with pinnacles at corners. Shared by several denominations at first. Ch. of William Howard Taft's father, grandfather.

West Wardsboro. Bapt. Ch., 1795. Type II with square tower, open belfry. Door on broad side, and in tower. Steep roof. Now 2 stories, church above. Town hall for a time below. Built nearer Wardsboro, moved here 1834. Interior probably changed at that time. Services in summer.

Westminster West. Cong. Ch., 1829. Type III. Plain front. Tower. Belfry, dome added later. Steep roof. Remodeled, raised, story added below 1874. Front door now at this level. Side galleries removed, old pews, pulpit replaced. Renovated 1895.

Whiting. Com. Cong. Ch., 1811. Type III. Made 2 stories 1841 and changed toward Type IV. Town meetings held here until 50 years ago. Levi Walker of committee went to Boston to get advice on plans, perhaps from Bulfinch. Four denominations once used ch.

Wilmington. Masonic Hall (Old Meth. Ch.), 1825. Type III. Built at Upper Intervale, moved here 1834. Masons took over 1905, removed steeple, placed pews around sides of room. Building has been raised and room added below.

Windham. Cong. Ch., 1802. Probably Transitional at first, made III. (Pp. 151, 153, Fig. 151)

Windsor. Cong. Ch. ("Old South Church"), 1798. Type III at first, but many changes. (P. 89, Fig. 71)

Windsor. St. Paul's Episc. Ch., 1820. Brick. Door in recess, with columns. One row windows. Tower. Square belfry, dome rebuilt 1948.

Woodstock. Cong. Ch. ("Old White"), 1806. Type III. Originally much like Asher Benjamin design. Changed 1859 by deepening of entrance bay, erection of porte-cochère, remodeling of interior. Other changes 1890.

Woodstock. Old Christian Ch. (now Masonic Temple), 1826. Type III. Brick, with wooden clock tower, belfry, dome. Single column in auditorium once supported roof. Removed 1860 and walls pulled together by iron rods. Further changes 1876, 1895. Ch. inactive since 1949.

Index

NOTE: For page and figure references to meetinghouses and churches built by 1830 and still standing, consult the Check List, page 211.

Portsmouth, N.H., Queen's Chapel, 184
Pound, village, 56
Prayers, attitude during, 9
Praying Indians, 205
Presbyterian churches, 154, 198
Price, William (designer), 181
"Prime society," 23, 72
Prince, Thomas (minister), 45
Prutt, Zeb, 118
Pulpit, 19; at entrance end of church, 102, 124, 155
Pulpit window, 11
Puritan: character of, 8, 9, 10, 12, 13; objection to celebration of Christmas, 180; progress of, 15
Puritan tradition, 1, 209
Putnam, Daniel, 190
Putnam, Israel, 51

Quakers, 200, 201

Racial equality, absence of, 7
Religion, importance of, 6
Religious services, conduct of, 9
Religious toleration, increase of, 22
Restoration of meetinghouses: at Hingham, Mass., 35; at West Barnstable, Mass., 42; at Litchfield, Conn., 104
Revere, Paul, 182; bells by, 65, 132, 180
Rhode Island, Battle of, 203
Rhode Island, as haven for religious groups, 176
Rhodes, William (builder), 126
Ritz, Frederick Augustus Rodolphus (minister), 200
Roman Catholic Church, 206
Rudhall, Abel (bellmaker), 181

St. Martins-in-the-Fields, London, 131, 196
Salem, Mass., South Church, 94
Saybrook Platform, 18, 198
Scott, Elisha (builder), 85
Seabury, Bishop Samuel, 187, 191
Seating plan, 7, 33
Seats, 11
Separation of church and state, 71, 72, 73
Sewell, Judge Samuel, 30
Shakers, 204
Shays, Daniel, 22, 69, 165
Shays's Rebellion, 22
Sheffield Declaration, 160
Singing, in services, 18
Singing school, 19
Slave pew, Sandown, N.H., 56
Society for the Propagation of the Gospel, 177, 185, 193
Sounding board, pulpit, 19
Sprats, William (builder), 92

Steeple, double-octagon, 102
Stoddard, Anthony (minister), 105
Stoddard, Harman (designer), 105
Sumner, Joseph (minister), 165
Sunday school, 141

Taunton, Mass., church by Bulfinch, 78, 81
Taxation, as support for church, 22, 23
Theocracy, 175
Third Society of Boston, meetinghouse of, 30
Thursday Lecture, 6
Touro, Rabbi Isaac, 209
Tower, projecting, 126; separate from meeting-house, 21
Town, Ithiel (architect), 89, 124, 131, 188
Town halls, 73, 98
Town meetings, 23, 72; moderator for, 35
Trumbull, John (builder), 123

Unitarian Church, 72
Unitarianism, 180
Unitarians: unions with Trinitarians, 121; in Vermont, 114
Universalist Church, 199

Victorian Gothic architecture, 138, 139, 162

Wadsworth, David (designer), 128
Wanton, Edmund, 201
Ward, Gen. Artemus, 165
Warner, Nathan (builder), 92
War of 1812, 26
Warren, Joseph, 46
Washington, George, 184, 187
Weathercocks, 42, 65, 118, 157, 162
Wentworth, Benning, 193
Wesley, John, 132
West Springfield, Mass., meetinghouse of 1702, 31
White, Josiah, 63
Whitefield, George, 18, 198, 199
Whittier, John Greenleaf, 203
Wigglesworth, Michael (minister), 11
Willard, Solomon (architect), 99
Williams, John (minister), 162
Williams, Roger (minister), 176, 194, 197
Williams, Stephen (minister), 162
Wilson, James (minister), 132
Witchcraft delusion, 18
Woodruff, Judah (builder), 48
Woolsey, Theodore, 177
Wren, Christopher, 21, 25, 29, 75

Yale College, 22; commencements of, 131; defection of faculty, 177
Yankee, traits of, 209
Young, Ammi (architect), 113

About the Author
and His Photographic Collaborator

Edmund W. Sinnott, author of well-known McGraw-Hill texts in Botany, Genetics, and Plant Morphogenesis, and of several other books, was a professor at the Connecticut State College, Columbia University, and, until his retirement, at Yale University. New England meetinghouses have been his avocation for many years, in both library and field. He has "collected" them assiduously and gathered a wealth of material about them.

Jerauld A. Manter, a former colleague of Dr. Sinnott's, who took most of the pictures in *Meetinghouse and Church in Early New England,* is also a retired professor, having taught entomology and ornithology at the University of Connecticut during his academic career. Although photography was at first a hobby, he has made the illustrations for several publications prepared by the University of Connecticut that are concerned with the training of the physically handicapped.